IN THE LAST DAYS —
A PROPHECY

I0530060

by
LINCOLN P. MIRAFLOR

To my God, the Almighty Father, the God of Abraham, the God of Isaac, the God of Israel, the All-Loving, All-Powerful, All-Merciful Infinite God of all creation through our Lord Jesus Christ this humble work is wholeheartedly dedicated.

ACKNOWLEDGMENTS

The author hereby wholeheartedly acknowledges the indefatigable efforts of the production team lead by Jason Riggs and the members, namely Alex Nielson, John Nelson, Roy Harper, Steve Anderson, Natalia Adler, and Walter Krasniqi, in tirelessly helping shape the book to its wondrous appearance and perfection readable worldwide.

IN THE LAST DAYS —
A PROPHECY

Contents

PREFACE

In the last days, it would be known to the whole world all false teachings and doctrines taught by the Roman Catholic Church for many centuries. Such teachings are designed to waylay people toward eternal damnation — and not salvation. As a consequence, people who have acquired truthful knowledge would come to a critical realisation and subsequently decide for themselves to abandon such untruthful teachings into total oblivion and throw them away the same way a menstrual cloth (Isaiah 30:22) full of nasty blood is thrown away.

Some false teachings of Roman Catholic Church disputed in this book are: a) that Jesus Christ was born on December 25; b) that people would be saved by venerating patron saints; c) that it is right to pray to graven images and printed pictures of saints as these dead saints can help them obtain salvation and eternal life; d) that veneration to the Blessed Virgin Mary can save man from eternal damnation; e) that religious teachings must come from Vatican.

No. What is correct is religious teachings must come from Zion (Isaiah 2:3) and spread throughout the world. There are still many false Catholic teachings that a reader may find in this book and be enlightened of the real truth.

Likewise, the truth of the Second Coming of our Lord Jesus Christ is thoroughly discussed in this book. Nobody knows the final hour of the Second Coming. Only the Almighty Father knows it. Matthew 24:36 says: "But as for that Day and that Hour, no one knows when it will come, not even the angels of God nor the Son, but only the Father." Nevertheless, there is nothing that God Almighty will not tell people before it happens. The Almighty Father usually informs people in advance through His messengers or prophets. In Amos 3:7, it says: "Yet Yahweh does nothing without revealing his plan to his servants."

This book is a reliable guide and companion for people to walk straight along the path of life and eternal salvation. Read it!

INTRODUCTION

This book is primarily written so people of all walks of life, irrespective of their religion, race, or beliefs, who have faith in God Almighty and in our Lord Jesus Christ and believe in the Second Coming can be guided accordingly. For purposes of being informed of what will happen in the last days, those who have different faiths may likewise read this book so they may be forewarned of events to be ready and prepared. The revelations inscribed herein are solely designed to inform readers but not to frighten them nor entice them to join any other religion, as certainly there is no religion on Earth that can ever save mankind from eternal damnation. True religion can be found in James 1:27: "In the sight of God, our Father, pure and blameless religion lies in helping the orphans and widows in their need and keeping oneself from world's corruption."

Secondly, this book is written to help evangelise the Muslim world where Christ's teachings are strictly prohibited, as in Central Asia, more specifically Kazakhstan, Turkmenistan, Azerbaijan, Uzbekistan, Tajikistan, Kyrgyzstan, Afghanistan, Pakistan, and other Muslim countries. As revealed in Matthew 24:14, "The Good News of the Kingdom will be proclaimed throughout the world for all the nations to know, then the end will come." This does not follow that they will be converted to other faiths. It is sufficient that God's Gospel has reached them. Many preachers and missionaries impart

God's message and Gospel to nations that were already evangelised long ago, but they failed to spread them to our Muslim brothers. Romans 15:20-21 says: "I have been very careful, however, and I am proud of this, not to preach in places where Christ is already known, and not to build upon foundations laid by others."

Let it be as scripture says: Those not told about him will see, and those who have not heard will understand." It is for them to know and accept our Lord Jesus Christ as their personal saviour. In Muslim countries, the preaching about our Lord Jesus Christ is strictly prohibited. Mere possession of the Holy Bible in their land is already a crime with stern punishment attached to it. If they would finally decide to accept our Lord Jesus Christ in their life and hearts as their personal savior, they will surely be saved.

In 1st John 5:12, it states: "He who has the Son has life, he who does not have the Son of God does not have life." For in so doing, they will eventually become sons and daughters of God as anyone who receives our Lord Jesus Christ will become a real child of God. In John 1:12, it states: "...but all who have received him he empowers to become children of God for they believe in his Name."

Furthermore, this book is aimed at enabling mankind to know about the forthcoming destruction of primary cities on earth that will take place in the last days so people would be prepared and avoid untimely death. Truly, there will be 40 primary cities on earth that will be destroyed in the last days. Hebrew 13:14 states: "For we have here no lasting city, and we are looking for the one to come."

As revealed by God Almighty, the events described herein are exactly identical to events that will actually happen in the last days. Some of these events are already happening now in moderation, which serves as a reminder to mankind that a large scale proportion of these events will undoubtedly occur in the last days. Inscribed herein are some admonitions intended for people who are wicked and callous of hearts that are directed toward acceptance of sins and repentance.

In the last days, most people in this world will be doing things not in consonance with God's will. Shameless people would deliberately do what is evil before God's eyes. Selfishness, envy, jealousy, hatred, deceit, calumny, murders, and heinous crimes will be present all around. Many would pretend to do good acts in people's sight, but surreptitiously, they would do evil. Even church people and religious leaders, cloaked in righteousness, would intentionally commit evil acts for their selfish gain. With respect to priests and religious ministers, God Almighty advises us in Matthew 23:3-4, which states: "Listen and do all they say, but do not imitate what they do, for they themselves do not practice what they teach…"

On the contrary, no man acts and does things in accord with God's will. In prayer, they pray for their own cause. They do not include in their prayers people who are poor, marginalised, sick, widows, orphans, unborn children who are victims of wanton abortion, victims of calamities and terrorism, and homeless and abandoned children.

People pray, but their prayers are not heard by God. Why? Sinfulness obstructs their prayers. Before they come to God's presence, they should seek first atonement for their sins. Every prayer must be coursed through our Lord Jesus Christ. No prayer can be acknowledged and heard by God if it is not coursed through our Lord Jesus Christ. In Matthew 21:22, it says: "Whatever you ask for in prayer full of faith, you will receive."

Every prayer should be made private with God Almighty. Do not pray in public. Matthew 6:5-6 says, "When you pray, do not be like those who want to be seen. They love to stand and pray in the synagogues or on street corners to be seen by everyone. I assure you, they have already been paid in full. When you pray, go into your room, close the door and pray to your Father who is with you in secret; and your Father who sees what is secret will reward you." Some people no longer pray because they have no more time for that and instead devote their time mainly to their work so they can support their needs and their families.

In short, they are only looking for money all their life. If they will have money, they will wish to be rich and grow richer and richer. Psalm 49:17-20 states: "Fear not when a man grows rich, when his power becomes oppressively great, for nothing will he take when he dies; his wealth and pomp he will leave behind. Though in his lifetime he has been counted blessed, having done well for himself, he will join the generation of his forebears, who never again see the light."

They consider money as their god, apparently an erroneous way of life. Ephesians 5:5 says, "Know this: no depraved, impure, or covetous person who serves the god 'Money' shall have part in the kingdom of Christ and of God." Also, it says in 1st Timothy 6:10, "Indeed, the love of money is the root of every evil."

In Chapter 1, you will be informed of the impending destruction of Metropolitan Manila as revealed by God Almighty. Starting seventy years before this destruction, there will be minor calamities, like volcanic eruptions, earthquakes, tsunamis, storm surges, and pandemics claiming numerous lives and displacing people of their livelihood. Their inherent callousness and hard-headedness will be the usual reasons for their death. They will waste their lives by not heeding advanced warnings. Bible verses and events described in this chapter are not only addressed to the people of Metropolitan Manila but also to all people of other cities on Earth, as their sinfulness and wickedness are identical.

In chapter 2, you will be informed of forty cities on Earth to be destroyed in the last days. God Almighty has revealed only 35 of these cities. In God's infinite wisdom, He completely sealed the names of the last five cities to be destroyed so all other cities on earth would have time to reflect on their sinfulness. A city is included to be destroyed based on these indicators: a) if a city is rebellious to God Almighty in not obeying His will; b) if a city continues to commit sins and wickedness; c) if a city worships idols made of wood, stone, or any metal; d) if a city kills infants in abortion, then that city is doomed for total destruction.

If you want to be saved then depart from that city and settle elsewhere to a place where faithfulness to God is commonplace and religiously observed.

God specifically mentions cities to be destroyed because He does not want to destroy everyone owing to his promise in Genesis 8:21, which says: "Never again will I curse the earth because of man, even though his heart is set on evil from childhood; never again will I strike down every living creature as I have done." This is God's promise after the flood, where only Noah and seven of his household members were saved.

After these forty cities are destroyed, there will be a widespread famine where people wouldn't be able to buy or sell anything if they have no mark of the beast, which is 666. The real 666 will be explained in Chapter 7 of this book. Rapture will also be discussed with corresponding Biblical references.

Chapter 3 discusses Almighty God, His Infinity, His being the only God in the universe, His holiness, and His being jealous and just. This chapter will also discuss our obligation to Him, i.e., to love Him, serve Him, and worship Him in spirit and truth with all our heart, with all our mind, with all our soul, with all our spirit, and with all our strength. Also to be discussed in this chapter is our Lord Jesus Christ's divinity and the salient evidence leading to a conclusion without doubt that, indeed, our Lord Jesus Christ is a true Son of God, that He is the Lord of lords and God of gods.

In chapter 4, the definition of the true people of God is explained to erase the doubt that however sinful they are, they can still be considered the children of God if they repent, obey, and live the word of God, accept our Lord Jesus Christ as their personal saviour, do God's will, have faith in Him, and avoid sin. People of God in this chapter are instructed on what to do to prepare for the Second Coming of our Lord Jesus Christ. They are reminded in this chapter to observe strictly Sabbath day and the universal hymn as their marks and indications of being at God's side and as bases for the angel of God to have them marked as saved and redeemed.

Chapter 5 discusses the prime importance of correctly observing Sabbath day. People worldwide are encouraged to observe the Sabbath on Saturday and not on Sunday, as wrongly taught by the pagan Roman Catholic Church throughout centuries. In this chapter, employers and capitalists are also warned not to let their employees work on Saturday; otherwise, God's wrath will fall on them and on their families. You have to take note that arguments presented in discussing the Sabbath are solely coming from God.

Chapter 6 discusses churches in our country, which are also found worldwide. Criticisms of the activities of these churches can be read in this chapter, especially those that are not in accord with God's will.

In chapter 7, varied subject matters are discussed here, like 666, LGBT, death, resurrection, salvation, eternal life, the Second Coming, the First Nuclear World War, climate change, and viruses in the world.

At the end of chapter 7, there are synopses for readers to know the book's salient contents. There is also a chronology of events in the last days for readers to have a brief review. The autobiography of the author can also be found after the last chapter.

As this book contains truth from the infinite wisdom of the Almighty Father, readers are encouraged to share its contents with their neighbours, friends, enemies, relatives, in-laws, strangers, and acquaintances, irrespective of their beliefs, faith, religion, race, culture, and country so that their knowledge obtained here will be fruitful.

CHAPTER I
METROPOLITAN MANILA

On January 12, 2090, at 7:48 A.M., a Thursday, there will be a strong, violent earthquake never known before in human history that will strike Metropolitan Manila and neighbouring provinces of Bulacan, Rizal, Laguna, Cavite, and Batangas. However, this will not be the end of time. Matthew 24:6-8 says: "You will hear about war and threats of war, but do not be troubled, for these things must happen, but it is not yet the end. Nations will fight one another, and kingdom oppose kingdom there will be famines and earthquakes in several places, but all these are only the beginning: the first pains of childbirth."

This is almost 100 years — or to be exact 99 years, 5 months, and 26 days — after a strong earthquake struck Luzon, Philippines, on July 16, 1990, a Monday at 2:00 P.M. That earthquake, measuring an intensity of 8.2 on the Richter scale, destroyed Pines Hotel in Baguio City in a split of a second, killing instantly over a hundred guests and seriously injuring another one hundred people. It also caused the sudden collapse of the Cabanatuan Catholic College building, which horrendously killed dozens of students. The building comprising six storeys, whose foundation was only good for four storeys collapsed like cardboard. The forthcoming earthquake, with an intensity of 9.2 on the Richter scale, will be felt as well in provinces of Pampanga, Zambales, Nueva Ecija, Nueva Vizcaya, Tarlac, Pangasinan, Aurora, and Quezon Province with slight effect in these places. Though these places are far from the epicenter, many people will also die due to fear.

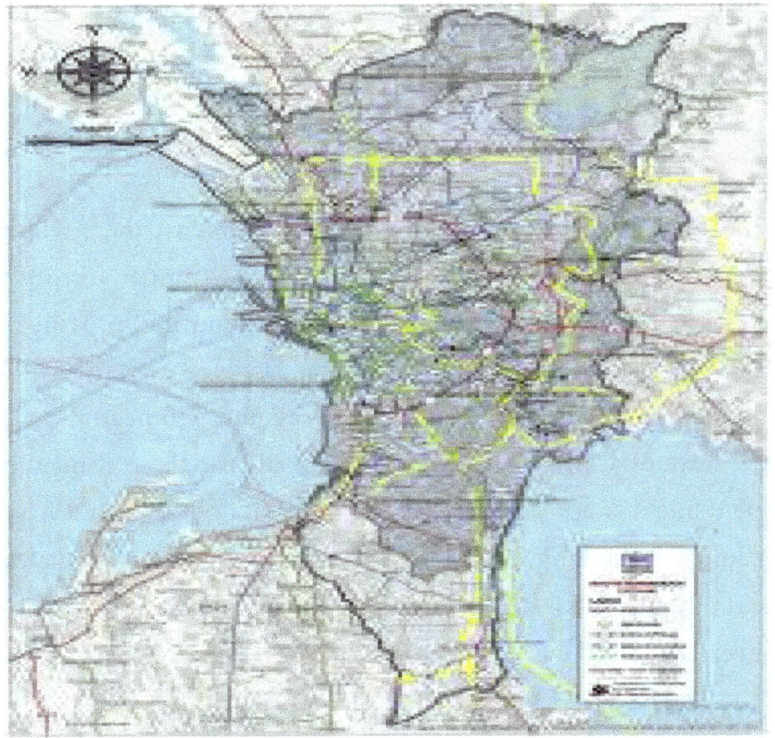

Map of Metro Manila

People in these places should pray constantly and turn away from their wicked ways so that they will not be affected. They should establish a seed of faith in God Almighty through our Lord Jesus Christ so that they will be delivered from fears and be saved and have true salvation. Unimaginable destructions will occur. How terrible it would be? In seconds, buildings will suddenly collapse. Infrastructures will be destroyed. Electric posts will sway and fall, emitting electrical charges that will char people to death. Thoroughfares, such as EDSA, NLEX, SLEX, skyway rails, and subway rails, will be totally destroyed beyond repair.

Subway project in Metropolitan Manila

High-rise buildings in Metropolitan Manila

Many people whose residential houses are built on faults will no longer be buried as they and their family members will be buried alive as their houses fall down under deep cracks. They could never be retrieved as the soil goes back to its original appearance. Many will die without recovering their remains. Rescuers will fail to rescue people as they themselves will need to be rescued. Matthew 24:22 tells us: "And if that time were not to be shortened, no one would survive. But God will shorten it for the sake of his chosen ones." These chosen ones will constantly pray long before these events and encourage others to pray also. They will repent of their sins and avoid wickedness in their lives. They will acquire faith in God Almighty through our Lord Jesus Christ, which ultimately leads to salvation and heavenly rewards. If God is convinced that people are truly repentant of their sins and will never again return to sin and begin to live a life in accord with God's will, he will make it very short that such destruction would only be minimal, or God may not proceed at all with such punishment as what he did in Nineveh.

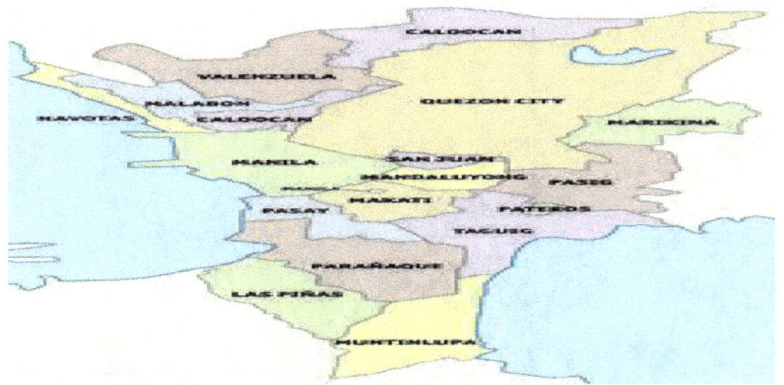

Map of Metropolitan Manila

In Jonah 3:10, Jonah was sent by God to Nineveh to give a warning to one hundred and twenty thousand people to repent, for if not, they would be destroyed. Upon hearing such a message, Nineveh began fasting and put on their sackcloths in order of the king and his nobles, who themselves took off their royal robes, put on sackcloths and sat in ashes. Jonah 3:10 states: "When God saw what they did and how they turned from their evil ways, he had compassion and did not carry out the destruction he had threatened upon them."

Location of Metropolitan Manila in the Philippines

They were saved because of their faith, accompanied by their action of repentance with humble hearts. Nineveh's population at that time was only 120,000 compared to the present population of 12,877,253 2 in Metropolitan Manila, which will eventually grow to 35 or 40 million, as revealed, in 2090. Nineveh was only given 40 days to repent, and they made it, while Metropolitan Manila and neighbouring provinces have been given 70 years, 3 months and 22 days to repent or 25,680 days or 2,218,752,000 seconds from today. Can you not make it? Will you take it as a joke? In Genesis 19:14, Lot, upon instructions from holy angels, announced to his would-be sons-in-law, who would marry his daughters, to leave Sodom immediately, for Yahweh would destroy it, but they took it as a joke. As a result, these Lot's would-be sons-in-law perished in Sodom's destruction because of their disbelief. Disbelief is a product of the absence of faith, which usually results in death.

Why did God destroy Sodom? What were their sins? If we compare what they had done before they were destroyed by God to what people now in Metropolitan Manila are doing, they are analogous. In Ezekiel 16:49-50, it says, "The sins of Sodom your sister were pride, over-indulgence in food, complacency and indifference to the poor and needy. They were arrogant and did detestable things in my sight. For that reason I destroyed them as you have seen."

Sodom and Gomorrah.

God will forgive people in Metropolitan Manila of their wickedness if there is resolute repentance in their lives and they start living a life in accord with his will. They will be saved from destruction if they nurture a true faith in God through our Lord Jesus Christ and display in their life complete humility in total obedience to His will. But if people will go on with their stubbornness and continue committing sins, God will surely destroy them. It says in Romans 2:5, "If your heart becomes hard and you refuse to change, then you are storing for yourself a great punishment on the day of judgment, when God will appear as just judge."

Mark it! If after this date, January 12, 2090, there will be no destruction as people had repented for a short while only to return to sin again, surely God will send destruction in the month of July of that year or, to be exact, **July 17, 2090, at 8:00 P.M., a Monday.** A strong, violent earthquake, never yet experienced by humanity since its existence, will strike Metropolitan Manila, leading to its complete destruction and would be followed by heavy rain of consuming fire and tsunami in coastal areas since such repentance was only superficial.

Psalm 21:10 says: "You will make them a blazing furnace, O Lord, when you appear. You will strike them down in your wrath, your fire will engulf and burn them up." People will be able to know this forthcoming catastrophe as it will be preceded first by rains of hailstones that can destroy vehicles. Starting seventy years before this event, God will test people due to their continued sinfulness by sending them several light earthquakes, volcanic eruptions, tidal waves, tsunamis, and pestilences to remind them in advance about this impending total destruction. Many people will help victims of calamities for various reasons. Some people offer their helping hand for humanitarian reasons, some for economic reasons, some for political reasons, and others pretend to help but secretly divest victims of their belongings. For this, God Almighty has this to say in Isaiah 44:26: "I confirm the word of my servant and carry out the plan announced by my messengers…" God Almighty further says this to you in Isaiah 45:22-24: "Turn to me and be saved, all you from the ends of the earth, for I am God and there is no other. By my own self I swear it, and what comes from my mouth is truth, a word that will not be revoked. Before me every knee will bend, by me every tongue will swear, saying, 'In Yahweh alone are righteousness and strength.'"

This date coincides with Noah's landing on Mount Ararat on the seventeenth day of Ethanim, the seventh month in Hebrew. It says in Genesis 8:4: "In the seventh month, in the seventeenth day of the month, the ark rested on Mount Ararat." Why 8:00 P.M.? This is symbolic because there will be eight cities in Metropolitan Manila that will be totally wiped out in a few seconds. There will be many cracks caused by this violent earthquake, measuring seventy-five feet wide, that could easily devour thousands of vehicles and hundreds of houses and infrastructures. The smaller cracks will measure forty-five feet wide. The total length of cracks in Metropolitan Manila and neighbouring provinces will be four hundred and fifty kilometres.

Earthquake

Shangrila you have allowed sinful people to come to your place. They make sinful acts while in your vicinity. They no longer think of doing good. They stayed in your place "persisting in their crooked ways, they plot mischief even in bed; committed to a life of sin, they know not how to reject evil" (Psalm 36:5). Because of this, your place becomes filthy already. Hosea 7:2 says: "They do not realise that I am mindful of their evil deeds. They are engulfed by their sins which are always before me." Hence, you will be completely destroyed. Many residential high rise condominiums will fall down instantly. Manila Cathedral will totally be destroyed, says God Almighty. No amount of retrofitting can save buildings from God's wrath. Buildings in Makati will fall down one after another like dominoes. Ayala Avenue will be totally destroyed, says God Almighty. Many buildings will be destroyed. Highways, bridges, subways, skyways and airports will be destroyed in an instant.

The longest fault ever seen on Earth

Satellite view of Metro- Manila doomed in last days

Jesus warned the paralytic whom he had just healed not to commit sin again lest something worse will happen. In John 5:14, Jesus said to a paralytic person whom he cured: "Now you are well; do not sin again, lest something worse will happen to you." This Christ's warning also applies to the people of Metropolitan Manila that after they are forgiven of their sins and that destruction is not carried out by God due to repentance of sin, they must refrain from committing sins again; otherwise, worse destruction will fall on them. Metropolitan Manila will be literally destroyed, says the Lord. Pasay City and Paranaque city will be completely wiped out, says God Almighty. North of Metropolitan Manila is Bulacan whose city of San Jose del Monte will be most affected.

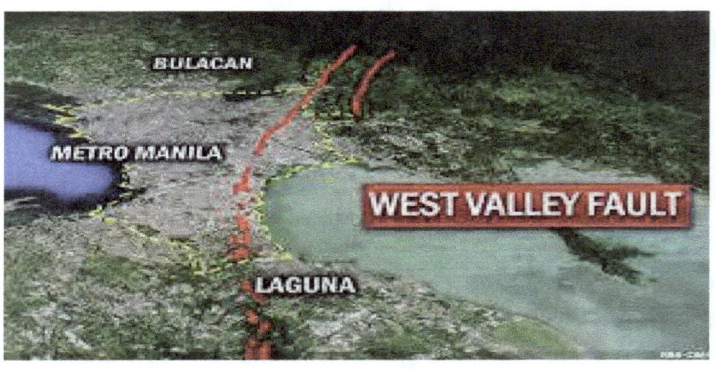

The eastern portion of Metropolitan Manila is Rizal province, where Cainta and Antipolo will be most affected. Teresa, your black magic and sorcery will be destroyed as your place will be devastated. It says in Micah 5:11: "I will do away with your witchcraft and rid you of soothsayers." No one can hide their secrets before the God of Truth and Spirit. All sorceries and black magic brought to Metropolitan Manila by people from their respective provinces and places will be targets of destruction. The places they stay in Metropolitan Manila will be completely destroyed, affecting other people. "Nothing that is covered that will not be uncovered, or hidden that will not be made known. Whatever you have said in darkness will be heard in daylight, and what you have whispered in hidden places will be proclaimed from the housetops." (Luke 12:2-3).

Likewise, Mark 4:22 says: "Whatever is hidden will be disclosed, and whatever is kept secret will be brought to light." Guadalupe bridges will be cut off. People cannot traverse through it. The southern parts of Metropolitan Manila are Laguna and Cavite provinces, where Binan, Cabuyao, Bacoor and Kawit will be most affected. Taal volcano erupted on January 12, 2020. This was exactly what God Almighty said to me on September 20, 2019. It is exactly 70 years before the initial date of the destruction of Metropolitan Manila. Batangas will experience another devastation when Taal will erupt again on August 10, 2065, which will kill many people and directly affect their livelihood, says the Lord. Their callousness and hard-headedness will cause their untimely death. Disastrous, violent volcanic eruptions will happen to Kanlaon Volcano on July 7, 2065; Mayon Volcano on July 8, 2065; Mt. Bulusan on September 7, 2068, and Mt. Apo on October 13, 2080, says God Almighty. More than eleven million people will die in Metropolitan Manila.

Metropolitan Manila

It says in Psalm 92:7-8: "The senseless will not know, nor will the stupid understand them. For though the wicked prosper and evildoers flourish like grass, they are doomed to eternal destruction." This number will increase if righteous people choose to remain in Metropolitan Manila as they will be the first to die. "For those who love him, the Lord has compassion; but the wicked, he will destroy." (Psalm 145:20). While wicked people will not depart as they have no fear of God. They do not even respect God. In Psalm 34:22-23, it says: "Evil will slay the wicked; the enemies of the just will be doomed." Those who regard themselves as righteous will be the first to die as they remain to see for themselves God's wrath.

"…For it shall be known that Yahweh's hand is with his servant, but his fury is upon his enemy." (Isaiah 66:14). But God first announces any destruction to give them time to repent before He punishes his rebellious people. In Numbers 16: 1-35, it says: "Korah, son of Izhar, son of Kohath, from the tribe of Levi- and also Dathan and Abiram, sons of Iliab, son of Peleth, from the tribe of Reuben- rebelled against Moses. Two hundred fifty Israelites followed him; all were well-known leaders in the community and members of the council.

"They came together and addressed Moses and Aaron, saying, 'It is enough! The whole community is consecrated to Yahweh, and he lives among them. Why, then, do you set yourselves over the community of Yahweh?'

"When Moses heard this, he threw himself face downward on the ground. Then he said to Korah and all his followers, 'Tomorrow morning Yahweh will make known who belongs to him and approach him, and who is consecrated to him may approach him. He himself will let the one he has chosen approach. You Korah with all your followers, take your censers tomorrow. Then you will fill them with burning coals and put incense in them before Yahweh, and Yahweh will indicate the one who is holy. Son of Levi, you have gone too far!'

"Moses said to Korah, 'Listen to me now, you sons of Levi. It is not enough for you that the God of Israel has set you apart from the rest of the community of Israel, and called you close to himself for the service in the Holy Tent of Yahweh, to stand before this community and perform the sacred service on their behalf? He has called you to be near him, you and your brother Levites with you, and now you want the office of priesthood as well! What is the misdeed of Aaron that you complain against him? It is against Yahweh himself that you and your followers have rebelled.'

"Moses sent messengers to summon Dathan and Abiram, the sons of Iliab, but they said, 'We will not come up. Is it not enough that you have brought us up out of a land flowing with milk and honey to die in the wilderness? Do you also want to lord it over us? You did not bring us into a land flowing with milk and honey, nor give us an inheritance of fields and vineyards. Do you suppose that all people are blind? We will not come.'

"Moses then became angry and said to Yahweh, 'Do not look favourably on their offering. I have not taken a single donkey, nor have I harmed any of them.'

"Moses said to Korah, 'You and all your company be present before Yahweh tomorrow, you and they together with Aaron. Each of you take his censer, put incense in it and present it before Yahweh- 250 censers – and Aaron will do the same.' So every man took his censer and put incense in it and they stood at the entrance of the Tent of Meeting with Moses and Aaron. Korah assembled all the community against them at the entrance to the Tent of Meeting and the Glory of Yahweh appeared to all the community.

"Then Yahweh spoke to Moses and Aaron, 'Stand aside from this community so that I may immediately destroy them.' They fell on their faces and said, 'God, God of the spirits of all mortals, for one's man sin will you become angry with the whole congregation?'

"Yahweh answered Moses, 'Speak to the community and say this: Move away from the tents of Korah, Dathan and Abiram.'

"Moses got up and went towards Dathan and Abiram, and the elders of Israel followed him. He spoke to the community saying, 'Move away from the tents of these wicked men and touch nothing that belongs to them lest you perish because of all their sins.' They withdrew from the area near the tents of Korah, Dathan and Abiram; they came out and were standing with their wives, their sons and little ones.

"Then Moses said, 'By this you shall know that Yahweh sent me to do all these deeds and that it is not my doing. If these men die a natural death, merely suffering the fate of all men, then Yahweh has not sent me. But if Yahweh works a miracle and the earth, opening its mouth, swallows them, together with all they possess, and they descend alive to Sheol, you will know that these men have rejected Yahweh.'

"As Moses finished saying all this, the earth under them split in two, opened its mouth and engulfed them with their household and all the men who belonged to Korah with their possessions. They descended alive to Sheol with all that belonged to them; the earth covered them and they perish from the midst of the assembly. On hearing their cries, all the Israelites who were around them fled, for they said, 'Let not the earth swallow us as well!'

"A fire then came forth from Yahweh and consumed the 250 men who were offering incense."

A similar thing will happen in the last days; first, a great earthquake, then a rain of consuming fire.

What are they doing now? They prepare for safety precautions and design ways for them to survive. They borrow money from the World Bank and other international banks for financial and technical assistance to ensure the resilience of critical structures and government buildings. They present to people impact scenarios and social, economic, and other aspects of risk assessment, tools, and methods that would be useful in planning program activities. They focus on the need to work together in dealing with earthquake risk and the importance of preparedness that could mean the difference between life and death, and between property damage and catastrophic loss. They created the Resiliency Program Management Office to address earthquake resiliency and preparedness. They are good in planning but not in doing.

Seemingly, most budget goes to the pockets of those who manage. Corruption prevails in their midst. The developer and builder of high-rise residential condominiums assure their unit buyers and tenants that their properties are strong and that they can resist an earthquake with an intensity of 7.2 as they used quenched-tempered steel bars with a grade of 40 and 60 in their construction. True, it can resist a 7.2-intensity earthquake. But what if the earthquake has an intensity of 9.2, as it will be in that strength? For sure, the building will easily collapse. Some propose that the most practical assurance that a high-rise residential condominium is reasonably safe is to make sure that the developer and builder of the building and their household reside on its top floor. But they will not do that for fear of death.

In 2014, the Philippine Institute of Volcanology and Seismology projected in a risk analysis that more than 41,000 people may get killed in Metropolitan Manila when the Big One strikes. Wrong. It is more than that number.

To be ready, they prepared things needed in abrupt evacuation and put them inside the bag. They also prepared kits for survival. They constantly perform earthquake drills, doing dock, cover, and hold procedures in schools, malls, hotels, offices, high-rise apartments, buildings, condominiums, and all workplaces. Their drills are not realistic as they are not serious in what they do. They failed to realise that their preparations are as weak as their sinfulness compared to the strength of God's wrath. How they should prepare is by strengthening their lives, having true repentance, and avoiding evil. So that by God's mercy, the earthquake may not be as destructive as foretold, or God himself, being all-forgiving, all-loving, and all-merciful, will forgive their sins and do away with the punishment. They should persistently establish unwavering faith in the Lord God Almighty through our Lord Jesus Christ to attain salvation and eternal life.

Engineers, architects, and contractors resort to retrofitting buildings, bridges, skyways, subways, railroads, airports, and other edifices, but these infrastructures cannot withstand the strength of the forthcoming earthquake. They can be destroyed in seconds. The aftershocks are as strong as its original intensity which will intermittently last for another 45 days. Many buildings not toppled by earthquakes will be officially condemned and declared unfit and unsafe for occupancy. These buildings will be demolished and replaced by new ones that can reasonably withstand the strength of intensity 9.2 as a similar earthquake as the Big One will recur after 591 years or in the year 2681 when the Earth will already be desolate. The Almighty Father says that the Big One will return after 591 years, but the brilliant geologists and other scientists in our country say that it will return after 400 years. Which will you believe?

Some buildings, despite apparently unfit for occupancy, will be declared fit for use by the government building inspector as bribe money is given to them to do it. Kobe, Japan, has prepared their buildings, skyways, subways, and other infrastructures for more than 50 years, ensuring them to be earthquake-proof, considering that the place is prone to such calamity. They used the latest state-of-the-art technology for their beams. Yet they were all destroyed in a matter of seconds. Take my advice: do not resist the will of God. Just repent, change your ways and live your life in accord with God's will. It says in 2ⁿᵈ Kings 17:13, "…Turn from your evil ways and keep my commandments and precepts according to the laws when I commanded your fathers and which I have sent to you by my servants, the prophets."

Talk to God in prayer with all your heart, with all your soul, and with all your spirit. Never use any carved or printed images in your prayer. Talk to God in spirit. Have faith in the Lord God Almighty through our Lord Jesus Christ so that you and your family household will be saved and have everlasting life. James 4:2-3 says: "...The fact is, you do not have what you want because you do not pray for it. You pray for something and you do not get it because you pray with the wrong motive of indulging your pleasures." Pray to God in spirit as He is Spirit. John 4:23-24 says: "But the hour is coming and is even now here, when the true worshipers will worship the Father in spirit and truth; for that is the kind of worship the Father wants. God is spirit and those who worship God must worship in spirit and truth." You will then be perfect as God wants you to be perfect as He is perfect. Anybody whose prayers are heard by God is a perfect person. Do not subscribe to the idea that there is no perfect person in this world. In Job 12:4, it says: "...The man who calls and whom God answers, the just and perfect man."

If you sincerely pray to God in spirit, without the aid of any carved or printed images or statues, and He answers you, it means that you are a just and perfect person. Try it alone inside your room and feel the immense love of God through our Lord Jesus Christ. Personally, I have tried it several times, and He answers me. Do not be afraid when you hear the soothing and beautiful voice of God. Be inspired and live justly.

Do not equate going to mass as a form of prayer. It is only a celebration for us to be reminded of what our Lord Jesus Christ had done before the crucifixion and sacrifice on the cross. Do not talk to graven idols, for they cannot respond to you. Psalm 115:4-8 says: "Not so the hand-made idols, crafted in silver and gold. They have mouths that cannot speak, eyes that cannot see, ears that cannot hear, noses that cannot smell. They have hands but cannot feel, feet but cannot walk; neither can they make sound in their throat. Their makers will be like them, so will all who trust in them."

God will get angry with you when you worship images. Psalm 97:"7 says: "Shame on worshipers of idols, on those proud of their worthless images…" Just talk to him in spirit with your heart and with your mind inside your room alone with him. In 1st Peter 4:7, it says: "The end of all things is near; live wisely and spend evening time praying." Pray that you can rightly change your ways.

Do not pray just to ask for material possessions or wealth, as many people usually do. Seek first the Kingdom of God and the rest shall be added unto you. In Luke 12:31, it says: "Seek rather the Kingdom and these things will be given to you as well." The wealth of this world cannot even suffice to ransom everlasting life for a single person (Psalm 49:8-9). But eternal life is freely given by our Lord in great abundance to a truly repentant sinner who has acquired contrite heart, meekness of being and faith in God through our Lord Jesus Christ by having a personal relationship with him. When you pray course through all you ask in the mighty name of our Lord Jesus Christ.

John 16:23 tells us: "Truly I say to you, whatever you ask the Father in my Name, he will give you…" In 1st John 5:14-15, it says: "Through him we are fully confident that whatever we ask, according to his will, he will grant us. If we know that he hears us whenever we ask, we know that we already have what we asked of him." Any prayer, even accompanied by tears and contrite of heart, if not coursed through our Lord Jesus Christ will just be blown by the wind as it will not be heard by God.

In the face of calamity or death, call upon the name of our Lord and be saved. For, in Romans 10:13, it says: "Truly, all who call upon the name of the Lord will be saved." For the upright of heart, if in your observation wickedness and sinfulness still prevail in Metropolitan Manila despite this warning, you should leave quickly the place and save yourself from destruction. You must depart from Metropolitan Manila and live safely in the province together with your family. In Revelation 18:4-5, it says: "...Depart from her, my people, lest you share in her evil and so share in her punishment; for her sins are piled up to heaven, and God keeps count of her crimes."

For the upright of heart shun what is evil. Do not imitate those who do evil nor envy what they do, for in Psalm 97:10-11, it says: "You who love the Lord, hate evil, for he preserves the lives of his faithful, he delivers them from their foes. He sheds light upon the upright, and gladness upon the just. Rejoice in the Lord, you who are blameless, and give praise to his holy name." To the upright, continue doing good, for in Romans 16:19, Paul tells us: "...I wish to warn you to do what is good and avoid what is evil." Likewise, we are advised in Colossians 3:5-8 in this way: "Therefore, put to death what is earthly in your life, that is immorality, impurity, inordinate passions, wicked desires and greed which is a way of worshiping idols. These are the things that arouse the wrath of God. For a time you followed this way and lived in such disorders. Well then, reject all that: anger, evil intentions, malice; and let no abusive words be heard from your lips." James 4:17 says: "Anyone who knows what is good and does not do it, sins."

How would you know that a person is upright or righteous? Any person can attest to himself that he is upright, but in the real sense, he might not. In Proverbs 14:12, it says: "To one, his way appears correct, but in the end it leads to death." God has a weighing scale to gauge whether a person is righteous or not. Ezekiel 18:5-9 says: "Imagine a man who is righteous and practices what is just and right. He does not eat in the mountain shrines, or look towards the filthy idols of Israel, does not defile his neighbour's wife, or have intercourse with a woman during her period; he molests no one, pays what he owes, does not steal, gives food to the hungry and clothes to the naked, demands no interest on a loan and doesn't lend for interest, refrains from injustice, practices true justice, man to man, follows my decrees and obeys my laws in acting loyally. Because such a man is truly righteous, he will live, word of the Lord Yahweh."

If you do not fall within the gauge of righteousness, you still have a chance to be saved because God gives you all possible opportunities to live. He does not want you to die because He truly loves you. What God wants from you, people of Metropolitan Manila, is that you turn away from your crooked ways. Have faith in God through our Lord Jesus Christ and certainly be saved. He reminds you from time to time that there will be an impending violent earthquake to be followed by the heavy rain of consuming fire that will come by sending you, at the moment, slight earthquakes, volcanic eruptions, tidal waves, storm surges, and pestilences caused by deadly viruses. He lets you feel that you are not fit to stay in Metropolitan Manila by giving you experiences of difficulties in life like unemployment, high prices of prime commodities, lack of food, lack of money, petty quarrelling, bickering between husbands and wives, low salaries, expensive house rentals, over-crowdedness, crimes, and pollution.

If your place of residence is situated on the fault or near the fault, then after reading this book, please pack your things and transfer to the province away from Metropolitan Manila. Here is the passageway of Big One: If you are not afraid of death, just stay put.

Villages traversed by West Valley Fault

But in Matthew 11:28-30, it says: "Come to me, all you who work hard and carry heavy burdens and I will refresh you. Take my yoke upon you and learn from me for I am gentle and humble of heart and you will find rest. For my yoke is good and my burden is light." God also says to you in Jeremiah 45:5: "Yet, though I am about to send disaster on everyone-word of Yahweh- you will be safe wherever you go." For this, God reminds you that you should go back to your respective provinces, live there peacefully, be content with whatever meagre resource you have, constantly pray to Him in spirit and truth, and have faith in him through our Lord Jesus Christ.

In Philippians 4:19, it says: "God himself will provide you with everything you need, according to his riches, and show you his generosity in Christ Jesus." Seek the Lord for your refuge and safety. For, in Zephaniah 2:3, it says: "Seek Yahweh, all you poor of the land who fulfil his commands, do justice and are meek, and perhaps you will find refuge on the day Yahweh comes to judge." In Hebrews 13:5, it says: "Do not depend on money. Be content with having enough for today because God has said: I will never forsake you or abandon you…" Do not aspire for great riches by working too hard. Just work to sustain your basic needs. It says in Proverbs 23:4: "Do not wear yourself out trying to be rich, do not dwell on it."

Also, Proverbs 127:2 says: "It is in vain that you rise early and stay up late, putting off your rest, toiling for your hard-earned bread, for he provides for his loved ones even when they are asleep." When you are consistently righteous before God's eyes, you are on the right path. But when you turn from being righteous and commit evil because you are influenced by wicked people around, punishment will surely fall on you. In Ezekiel 3:20-21, it says: "When the righteous man turns from what is good to do evil I shall put an obstacle in his path: he shall die. Since you did not warn him, he will die for his sin. His good deeds will not be remembered and I shall hold you responsible for his death. But when you have warned the righteous man to keep him from sinning and he has not sinned, he will live for sure for he was warned and you will have your life." In Joel 2:12, it says: "Yahweh says, 'Yet even now, return to me with your whole heart with fasting, weeping and mourning. Rend your heart, not your garment. Return to Yahweh, your God-gracious and compassionate.'"

Here are some places in Metro-Manila that will be destroyed in the last days:

Metropolitan Manila, the Lord says that of all cities in the world, you are the most corrupt. Your morality is in a state of decay. Shame on you! The Lord sternly warns you to repent and stop doing sinful acts. Do not test the Lord. Do not say to Him to strike you now with the painful calamity before the appointed time. Stop your beer houses, which pose as a front of prostitution and drug addiction. Stop your inns and motels that cater to sinful sexual acts and lusts. Most of your hotels are havens of high-class prostitution. Stop your DISCO

(Dancing in Satan's Company Overnight) parties where you play satanic music and Satan-inspired songs and chants. Stop your child pornography and child trafficking. Do not indulge in luxury. Refrain from getting angry and turn away from wrath. (Psalm 37:8). Refrain from sinful vices. Stop your prostitution, which is severely worsened by the presence of thousands of foreign nationals who have no fear of God. God will destroy you by sending you a dreadful sexual illness more fatal than AIDS (Acquired Immune Deficiency Syndrome) caused by the human immunodeficiency virus.

Financial districts of Metropolitan Manila

Aerial view of Metropolitan Manila

High-rise buildings in Metropolitan Manila

In Revelation 2:20-23, it states: "Nevertheless, I have a complaint against you: you tolerate your Jezebel, this woman who calls herself a prophetess and is deceiving my servants; she teaches them prostitution and the eating of food sacrificed to idols. I have given her time to repent but she is unwilling to leave her prostitution. So I am going to throw her onto a bed and inflict severe trials on her partners in adultery unless they repent of their evil. I will strike her followers dead and all the Churches will know that I am he who probes the heart and mind; I will give each of you what your conduct deserves." Stop going to the houses of the prostitutes. Proverbs 2:18-19 says: "For her house inclines towards death, her paths towards the grave. Those who go to her never return, they do not regain the paths of life."

Refrain from sinful sexual acts. Sex between man and man and sexual acts between woman and woman should be abhorred. In Leviticus 20:13, it says: "When a man lies with a man as one lies with a woman, both have committed a detestable act and they shall be put to death. They themselves shall account for their blood." Do not make Metropolitan Manila like Sodom and Gomorrah.

Your men, women, children, young and old: Psalm 5:10: "Not a word of their mouth can be trusted, for their heart is full of mischief. Their throat is an open grave; their tongue flatters with deceit." Stop your stupidity. The time is near. In 1st Corinthians 6: 6-10, Paul reminds us: "Do you not know that the wicked will not inherit the Kingdom of God? Make no mistake about it: those who lead immoral lives, or worship idols, or who are adulterers, homosexuals of any kind, or thieves, exploiters, drunkards, gossips or embezzlers will not inherit the kingdom of Heaven."

Continuance of evil deeds among the people can compel God to allow the enemy, Satan, to send destructive pestilences and deadly viruses that kill thousands. Only those who return to God's fold will be protected from these pestilences and viruses and be saved from death. The wicked, as his wickedness is deeply rooted in his heart, will merely be content with being destroyed as he has no desire to repent. Extremely proud of their wickedness and sinfulness, the wicked smile and enjoy his laughter while piling up more sins. In Psalm 10:4-7, it says: "In his pride the wicked says, 'There is no God to call me to account.' The wicked prosper in their ways, your laws are too far from their minds; haughtily they sneer at their rivals, each one saying to himself, 'Nothing will trouble me. I am secure, powerful and happy.' His mouth is full of curses, deceit and threats, spite and mischief are under his tongue."

But the righteous will persevere in changing their ways in accord with God's will and establish faith in God through our Lord Jesus Christ in order to be saved. In Psalm 32:10-11, it says: "The woes awaiting the wicked are beyond measure, but the Lord's mercy enfolds those who trust in him. Rejoice in the Lord, and be glad, you who are upright; sing and shout for joy, you who are clean of heart."

The other serious reason why Metropolitan Manila will be totally destroyed is its widespread idolatry. The majority of people worship the wooden black image of Nazarene. God is excessively infuriated with people who worship idols. He even destroyed his people, Israel, when they worshipped the golden calf in the desert in His presence. That was a big insult to Him when His people made a golden calf and said to the idol that it was the image that liberated Israel from Egypt's bondage. It was a just punishment to destroy them in the desert. Exodus 32:7-9 says: "Then Yahweh said to Moses, 'Go down at once, for your people, whom you brought up from the land of Egypt, have corrupted themselves. They have quickly turned from the way I commanded them and have made themselves a molten calf; they have bowed down before it and sacrificed to it and said: 'These are your gods, Israel, who brought you out of Egypt." And Yahweh said to Moses, 'I see that these people are a stiff-necked people. Now just leave me that my anger may blaze against them...'" The veneration of the wooden black image of Nazarene is a guarantee that Metropolitan Manila will be destroyed, as it has long been scheduled for total destruction before God's eyes. People in provinces follow same pattern of idol worship as they wish also to be destroyed. They also made replicas of black Nazarene and venerated it in their provinces.

Image Of Black Nazarene

Minor Basilica Of Black Nazarene In Quiapo, Manila

God is furious with those people who worship useless idols. In Habakkuk 2:18-19, it says: "What use is a statue? Why do the sculptors make them? Why these images and deceiving answers? Why do their makers trust them and produce mute idols? Woe to the one who says to a piece of wood, 'Wake up,' and to a dumb stone, Get up." Can it give any answer?

Devotees of The Black Nazarene In Quiapo, Manila

Devotees of Sto. Nino De Cebu

For this, God says to me: "Lincoln, my heart aches on these people who venerate idols made of wood. I swear, I will not destroy Cebu City, Cagayan de Oro City, and Tagum City, for they only adopted their idolatry from its source, which is Metropolitan Manila. They are only the veins of idolatry. But I sternly warn those people in Cebu City to stop their veneration of the graven image of the child. Also, I warn the people in Cagayan de Oro City and Tagum City to stop worshipping the replica of the graven image of Black Nazarene. If they will not stop their idolatry, I will set a date for their punishment."

Be reminded that there are faults in Cebu. God will only say one word, "DESTROY!" then, Cebu City, Cebu Province, Cagayan de Oro, and Tagum will be deleted from the Philippine Map. Here is the map of faults in Cebu City as it directly connects to the Pacific Ring of Fire:

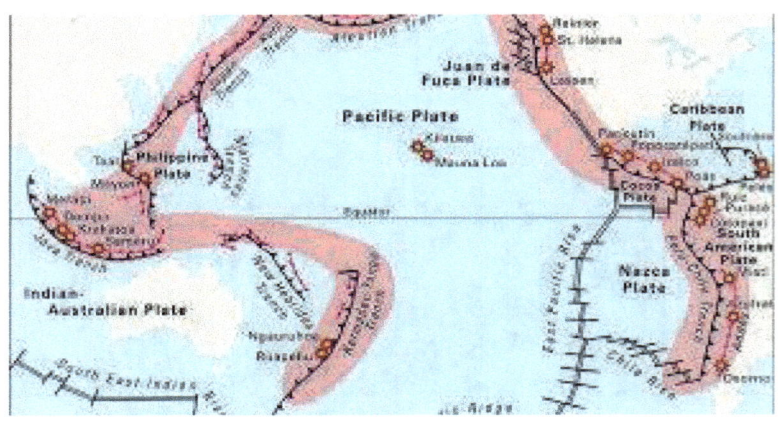

Image of Sto. Nino of Cebu

Cebu! God commands you to stop venerating this image now! Otherwise, you will be totally destroyed. Do not wait for God to do what he has done to his people in venerating the molten calf in the desert. There are also many places in the Philippines and in the world that venerate their patron saints made of wood adorned with silver and gold. They even proudly hold an annual procession in public without knowing that they continuously provoke the anger and wrath of God. That is one reason that 40 key cities of the world are already eyed by God to be destroyed unless they repent. They will be adversely judged in the last days.

Isaiah 24-25 says: "This is why the Lord speaks, Yahweh Sabaoth, the Mighty One of Israel: 'I will take vengeance on my foes and exact payment from my enemies. I will turn my hand against you, I will smelt away your dross and I will remove your impurities.'" You are considered an enemy of God if you worship graven or printed images. And you will be doomed for destruction. In Isaiah 30:22, it says: "You will see the uncleanliness of your idols and images overlaid with silver and gold. You will throw them out like menstrual cloth, 'Away with you then!' you will say to them." Jeremiah 10:8 also says: "They are all brutish and stupid; their idols are proof of their foolishness."

For the rich people in Metropolitan Manila and anywhere in the world, you are reprimanded on this: James 5:3: "Your silver and gold have rusted and their rust grows into a witness against you. It will consume your flesh like fire, for having piled up riches in these last days." Also, it says in Proverbs 16:25: "To one, his way seems honest, but ultimately it leads to death." The Lord admonishes you that you should not be arrogant to anyone. Do not put your confidence in your money, properties or connections. Do not boast of your wealth. It is not yours. You are only a steward over it. It says in 2nd Corinthians

8:9, "You know well the generosity of Christ Jesus, our Lord. Although he was rich, he made himself poor to make you rich through poverty."

It will only hinder your salvation in the last days. Do not spend your money on luxuries. Give to the poor and be rich in good deeds. Proverbs 28:27 says: "He who gives to the poor will not be in need; but he who turns a blind eye to them will have his fill of disgrace." When you fast, do not just fast for the sake of fasting. But fasting by giving some of your food to the hungry. It says in Isaiah 58:7-10: "Fast by sharing your food with the hungry, bring to your house the homeless, clothe the man you see naked and do not turn away from your own kin. Then will your light break forth as the morning and your healing will come speedily. Your righteousness will be your vanguard, the Glory of Yahweh will be your rear guard. Then you will call and Yahweh will answer, you will cry and he will say, I am here. If you remove from your midst the yoke, the clenched fist and the wicked word, if you share your food with the hungry and give relief to the oppressed, then your light will rise in the dark, your night will be like noon."

In Matthew 25:40, it says: "…Truly, I say to you: whenever you did this to one of the "least, of these my brothers, you did it to me." It says in 2nd Timothy 6:17-19: "Command the rich of this world not to be arrogant or put their trust in the uncertainty of wealth. Let them rather trust in God who generously gives us all we need for our happiness. Let them do good be rich in good deeds and be generous; let them share with others. In this way, they shall heap up a sound capital for the future and gain true life."

Here are the top ten rich people on Earth who have the responsibility of sharing their wealth with the poor:

For year: 2025

Rank	Name	Net Worth (USD)	Source of Wealth	Country
1	Elon Musk	$432.6 B	Tesla, SpaceX	US
2	Jeff Bezos	$243.8 B	Amazon	US
3	Larry Ellison	$216.9 B	Oracle	US
4	Mark Zuckerberg	$213 B	Facebook	US
5	Bernard Arnault & Family	$184.2 B	LVMH	France
6	Larry Page	$163 B	Google	US
7	Sergey Brin	$155.5 B	Google	US
8	Warren Buffett	$146.2 B	Berkshire Hathaway	US
9	Steve Ballmer	$125.9 B	Microsoft	US
10	Jensen Huang	$122.9 B	Semiconductors	US

It says in Psalm 112:9, "Since he has given generously to the poor, his virtue will last forever and his head will be raised in honour." The eternal salvation of the soul cannot be attained by having several churches say mass for the intention of the soul of departed loved ones. That is wrong! Instead of spending money for this purpose, you have to give money to poverty-stricken, poor people who cannot even afford to eat three meals a day. In Proverbs 11:24, it says: "Those who are generous increase their riches; others are misers and impoverish themselves." "Give alms from what you have to those who act justly and do good. Do not be grudging when you give alms. Do not turn away your face from anyone who is poor so that God may not turn away his face from you. Give alms in proportion to the amount you have; if you have a little, do not be afraid to give alms according to the little you have." (Tobit 4:7-8). Remember: he who sows meagrely will reap meagrely. There shall be generous harvests for him who sows generously. Let each one give what he decided upon personally and not reluctantly as if obliged. God loves a cheerful giver. And God is able to fill you with good things, so that you have enough of everything at all times, and may give abundantly for any good work." (2nd Corinthians 9:6-8). "In this way you are storing up treasure against the day of tribulation, because almsgiving frees us from death and keeps us from wandering in the darkness. For, in fact, almsgiving is, for the man who practices it, a precious treasure in the eyes of God." (Tobit 4:9-11). In Luke 12:15, it says: "Be on your guard and avoid every kind of greed, for even though you have many possessions, it is not that which gives you life." Your money, even how great it is, cannot save your soul. In Matthew 6:19-21, it says: "Do not store up treasure for yourself here on earth where moth and rust destroy it and where thieves can steal it. Store up treasure for yourself with God, where no moth or rust can destroy nor thief come and steal it. For where your treasure is, there also your heart will be."

While millions of people in the world today, especially in Asia, Africa, and South America, are experiencing extreme poverty that they can hardly afford to have three meals a day, the latest study conducted by Credit Suisse in Zurich, Switzerland, shows that there are additional 46.8 million people who became millionaires collectively possessing $158.3 trillion in net assets. In the same study, it showed that there are 100 million Chinese people who ranked in the global top 10 percent, together with 99 million Americans. The annual wealth survey forecast the wealth of this world to increase by 27% in the next five years or to a tune of $459 trillion by 2024. In the Philippines, the present national wealth of P26.8 trillion or $536.14 billion will increase to P34.13 trillion or $680.89 billion in the next five years. It means that the number of millionaires will also increase by 63 million throughout the world. Ninety percent of the people in the world today own only 18% of global wealth, while ten percent of the people own 82% of global wealth. The wealth of this world, as forecasted for the year 2024, will be $459 trillion. If we multiply that figure by 7 and the product is multiplied again by 77, the product of it cannot even suffice to ransom salvation for even one soul. In Psalm 49:8-12, it says: "For no one may redeem himself or pay God the ransom for his life. For redeeming one's life demands too high a price, and no ransom will ever suffice for him to remain forever alive and never see the grave. For he can see that even wise men die, the fool and the stupid alike pass away leaving to others their fortune and wealth. Their graves are their eternal homes, from generation to generation, no matter how big the tracts of land they own." Also, Psalm 89:49 says: "What mortal can live and never see death? Who can evade the netherworld?" Choose your while.

Cemetery in China

Cemetery in Kavala, Greece

Cemetery Cernavodă, Romania

Soviet cemetery Saaremaa, Estonia.

Remember that, you millionaires! In Proverbs 11:28, it says: "He who trusts in riches will stumble; while the upright will flourish like leaves." Likewise, it says in Zephaniah 1:18, "Neither their gold nor their silver will rescue them when the anger of God burns against them." In Proverbs 11:4, it says: "On the day of vengeance riches will prove useless but honest living will save from death." Revelation 4:17-19 says: "You think you are rich and have piled up so much that you need nothing, but you do not realise that you are wretched and to be pitied, poor, blind and naked. I advise you to buy from me gold that has been tested by fire, so that you may be rich, and white clothes to wear so that your nakedness may not shame you, and ointment for your eyes that you may see. I reprimand and correct those I love. Be earnest and change your ways." The poor and the rich are the same. In 2nd Corinthians 8:15, it says: "...what Scripture says shall come true: To him who had much, nothing was in excess; to him who had little, nothing was lacking."

In fact, there is nothing wrong if you become rich as long as your riches come from honest living and you do not wear yourself out trying to amass wealth, put others down, or oppress anyone. In 2nd Corinthians 9:11, it says: "Become rich in every way, and live abundantly. What you give will become, through us, a thanksgiving to God." In Matthew 5:42, it says: "Give when asked and do not turn back on anyone who wants to borrow from you."

By God's grace, these revelations were given to me by God on the night of September 20, 2019, and henceforth, which is the 35th anniversary of the Escalante Massacre in Escalante City, Philippines, that claimed the lives of more or less 150 poor peasants, marginalised fishermen, farm labourers and student activists. That day also marked the 1st anniversary of horrendous landslides in Naga City, Cebu,

Philippines, that buried alive dozens of sleeping people. God always gives warning before he destroys a place. When I received the message from God after my night prayer, I was terribly frightened. My heart began to pound harder and harder. I was not able to sleep that whole night thinking about the message that had reached me. I was utterly shocked. You will feel the same thing or worse than what I felt when you read all these. God said to me: *"Don't be disturbed Lincoln. Just do what I say. Write all these things and tell the people on this that they can prepare for the place is already filthy. It needs to be destroyed. Use only simple words for the people to know clearly."*

I said to God: Father, I have my wholehearted obedience to you. I will do what you say. I said this to the Lord in reference to 2nd Peter, 1:10-11, which states: "Therefore, brothers and sisters strive more and more to respond to the call of God who chose you. If you do so, you will never stumble. Moreover you will be generously granted entry to the eternal kingdom of our Lord and Saviour Jesus Christ…" I am grateful to God through our Lord Jesus Christ for choosing me to be his messenger to tell you what may happen in the coming days. Out of eight billion people on earth in 2019, I was chosen by God to spread the message to all.

As time gradually comes near, the economy will be adversely affected. Investors will flee the country and transfer elsewhere. The Philippine Stock Exchange and the Manila Stock Exchange will come to very low levels. Work will be affected as people will experience difficulty in finding a stable one. Graduates wouldn't be able to find work in line with their courses. Underemployment will be prevalent among job seekers. It will be hard for the family to make both ends meet, which will cause constant bickering between husbands and wives. Many couples will resort to divorce, it being the only solution seen to solve economic difficulty.

In 2nd Timothy 3:1-5, Paul reminds us this: "Be quite sure that there will be difficult times in the last days. People will become selfish, lovers of money, boastful, conceited, gossips, disobedient to their parents, ungrateful, unholy. They will be unable to love and to forgive; they will be slanderers, without self-control, cruel, enemies of good, traitors, shameless, full of pride, more in love with pleasure than with God. They will keep an appearance of piety, while rejecting its demands…" People who were alive when this book was written will no longer be around when this event happens. They will be in their eternal rest. But their descendants will still be here who comprise a perverse and crooked generation whose morality is excessively twisted. They will have no regard for life. They will kill unborn children in the womb as allowed by law. They have no fear of God. They will not respect their parents and elders.

In Psalm 75:5-6, it says: "To the proud I say, 'Be proud no more.' And to the wicked, 'Raise not your head. Do not lift yourself so high, do not insult God.'" They do things on their own will to be notoriously known. "Woe to the rebellious children, says the Lord; they make plans which are not mine, they form alliances I did not inspire, and thus add sin upon sin." (Isaiah 30:1). "They exchanged God's truth for a lie, they honoured and worshiped created beings instead of the Creator, to whom be praise forever, Amen! Because of that, God gave them up to shameful passions: their women exchanged natural sexual relations for unnatural one. Similarly, the men, giving up natural sexual relations with women, were lustful of each other, they did, men and men, shameful things, bringing upon themselves the punishment they deserve for their wickedness. And since they did not think that God was worth knowing, he gave them up to their senseless minds so that they committed all kinds of obscenities." (Romans 1:25-28). Marriage will no longer be sacred to them. They will marry not to live for a lifetime but to have a divorce due to constant marital bickering caused by infidelity mutually committed by both parties and, thereafter, look for another partner. Grievously, a deplorable marital life. They will marry not because of love but for material or monetary reasons and for the flesh. In their boastful language, there will be no such thing as "forever" in marriage, as they can have a divorce anytime they want.

In Isaiah 4:1, it says: "On that day, seven women will fight over a single man…" There will be laws strengthening marriage between man and man, between woman and woman. Marriage between man and woman will already be a past thing. It says in Hosea 4:1-2: "… There is neither truth nor goodness nor knowledge of God in the country; only perjury, lies, murder, theft and adultery, with continual bloodshed."

Many couples will cohabit without the benefit of marriage. In the guise of favouring women, lawmakers will pass laws intended to benefit them but ultimately destroy family and society as these laws will push husbands and wives to separate ways. Young people will become narcissists as they always view on mirror most of the time to check on their looks. They will become pleasure seekers- hedonists. What will be important to them would be their gadgets that they always carry around wherever they go. Their songs and music would be inspired by the devil, which they will play at high volumes that disturb others. They will play computer games designed by Satan, thereby destroying their life and family as they devote all their time to games. They will have no more time for their family as they are addicted to their vices, thus spending their resource other than for their household needs. They will play games on cell phones even while driving vehicles, which usually ends in fatal accidents resulting in untimely deaths. In short, they will clearly become hypocrites.

In Job 36:13, it says: "These hypocrites harbour resentment: they do not pray for help in their bonds, therefore they die in their youth and perish among the reprobate." Infidelity is widespread all around. Drugs worsen the destruction of society. Everywhere, dishonesty is widespread. Everyone is dishonest and a sinner, including the one who is holding and reading this book right now. In Romans 3:10-17, it states: "...*Nobody is good, not even one, no one understands, no one looks for God. All have gone astray and have become base. There is no one doing what is good, not even one. Their throats are open tombs, their words deceit. Their lips hide poison of vipers, from their mouth come bitter curses. They run to where they can shed blood, leaving behind ruin and misery. They do not know the way of peace, they have no respect for God.*"

Also, in Psalm, 53:2-4, it states: "The fool says in his heart, 'There is no God.' They are corrupt, their ways are wicked; not one of them does good. From heaven God looks down upon the sons of men, to see if there is anyone who seeks God and understands. None! They have all fallen away. Depraved-they are all alike. There is no one who does good, no, not even one." In 2nd Samuel 23:6-7, it says: "But godless men are like thorns that are thrown away. They cannot be held with one's hand but are uprooted with iron and the shaft of a spear, and they are burned in fire." Psalm 12:8-9 says: "Hold us, O Lord, in your keeping; protect us always from this generation, where the wicked prowl on all sides, and the basest are exalted."

Woe to them who curse their father and mother as their lamps will be extinguished in the midst of darkness (Proverbs 20:20). In

Matthew 15:4, it says: For God commanded: Do your duty to your father and your mother, and whoever curses his father or his mother is to be put to death." Also in Leviticus 20:9, it says: "The man who curses his father or mother shall be put death." "Woe to them who abandon their fathers as they would be like a blasphemer and woe to them who annoy their mothers for they are cursed by the Lord" (Sirach 3:16).

Micah 7:6 says: "For son treats father like a fool, daughter rebels against mother, daughter-in-law against mother-in-law. The enemies of each one are those of his household." Woe to you, priests, because you did not glorify the Name of the Lord. You and your blessings will be cursed (Malachi 2:1); Woe to you lawmakers for passing immoral laws, legalising abortion, same sex marriage, divorce and other wicked laws unknown to humankind and "Woe to those who enact unjust laws and issue oppressive decrees!" (Isaiah 10:1); "Woe to him who amasses what is not his and fills himself with extorted pledges." (Habakkuk 2:6); Woe to you political leaders, presidents of states and nations for you decide without consulting God who is the author of your authority (Colossians 1:15-16); "You rulers, are your decrees just, and are your judgments upright? No, you wilfully commit crimes; you deal in violence and corruption." (Psalm 58:2-3). "…Woe to the wicked; the evil that their hands have done shall be done to them" (Isaiah 3:11). "Woe to you, wicked people who have forsaken the law of the Most High! At birth you are born to be cursed and you will be cursed at death." (Sirach 41:8-9). Woe to him who raises his house on unjust profits and fixes his nest so high that he thinks he can thereby escape misfortune!" (Habakkuk 2:9). Woe to those who rise early in the morning to run after strong drink, and tarry late in the evening till they are inflamed with wine; Woe to those who draw iniquity with cords of deceit, to those who draw sin with cart ropes, to those who say, 'Let God hurry, let him speed up his work, so that we may see it; Let the plans of the Holy One of Israel draw near and come true so that we may know what they are.' Woe to those who call evil good, good evil, who put darkness for light and light for darkness, who put bitter for sweet and sweet for bitter; Woe to those who are wise in their own eyes and cunning in their own sight; Woe to those who are valiant in mixing drinks and heroes at drinking bouts but acquit the guilty for a bribe and deprive the innocent of his right (Isaiah 5:11,18-23); Woe to you doctors who do not attend to medical needs of patients by reason of poverty. In Psalm 14:6, it says: "You may confound the hope of the poor, but you will get nowhere, for the Lord is their refuge." Psalm 72:13 states: "His mercy is upon the weak and the poor, he will be his protector."

Also in Psalm 34:7, it says: "When the poor cry out, the Lord hears and saves them from distress." It says in Jeremiah 9:1-8 this: "...For they are all adulterers, a band of traitors. They bend their tongue like a bow. It is deceit and not truth that prevails in the land. They go from crime to crime and do not know me. Each one is wary of his friend and no one trusts his brother and every friend is a slanderer. They deceive each other; no one speaks the truth. Their tongue has become used to lying; they are perverse and too hardened to repent. They live in the midst of deceit they refuse to know me. That is why-word of Yahweh God of hosts- I will refine and test them, for what else can I do for my people? Their tongue is a deadly arrow, uttering deceitful words. With their friend they speak of peace but in their heart they set a trap for him. Because of this shall I not punish them? Shall I not avenge myself on such a nation?"

Many people will get angry with me while reading this book because they cannot accept the truth in themselves, as their hearts are full of deceit and filth. These people have no reason at all to be angry with me as I am only inscribing words given to me by God. In John 13:20, it says: "Truly, I say to you, whoever welcomes the one I send, welcomes me, and whoever welcomes me, welcomes the One who sent me." I am sent to let people of every race know of what may happen to them. Blessed by God in truth and spirit, I, in my absolute humility, the meekness of being, contrite heart, and unwavering faith in God through our Lord Jesus Christ, surrendered everything to Him by living a life away from sin and indulging in constant prayer to God through our Lord Jesus Christ.

Many would hurl accusations that I am a false prophet. But can you distinguish between a true prophet and a false prophet? First, I, a true prophet of God in the last days, am inspired by the Holy Spirit coming from Him, and my authority is from God through our Lord Jesus Christ, who is the Way, the Truth and the Life. Romans 8:30 says: "And so, those whom God predestined he called, and those whom he called he makes righteous, and those whom he makes righteous he will give his Glory," while a false prophet has no authority from God. Second, I, a true prophet of God in the last days, tell people of truth, giving them spiritual strength, encouragement, and consolation (1st Corinthians 14:3), while a false prophet never gives strength to people, never encourages them, and never consoles them. Third, I, a true prophet of God in the last days, act and prophesy in order to build the church (1st Corinthians 14:4) by warning church authorities of their teachings which are not in accord with God's will and by warning people in advance of impending catastrophe; while a false prophet never builds the Church, instead destroys it. Fourth, I, a true prophet of God in the last days, do not prophesy to make myself famous but to magnify the Glory of God (1st Corinthians 1:31.

For, it says in John 7:18, "He who speaks on his own authority wishes to gain honour for himself. But he who wants to give glory to him who sent him is truthful and there is no reason to doubt him," while a false prophet prophesy to be popular for himself alone and for his master, Satan. Fifth, a false prophet prophesy to gain material things in this world as his reward for his work; while I, a true prophet of God in the last days, give you a true and verifiable prophecy without any material reward in this world but my reward is an assurance from God to have everlasting life. My reward is not, therefore, in this world but in God through our Lord Jesus Christ. Sixth, a false prophet will attempt to heal illnesses of people but with monetary consideration but cannot heal sickness; while I, a true prophet of God in the last days whose authority comes from God through our Lord Jesus Christ, our Redeemer, can lay my hands on the sick and have them be healed without any monetary consideration and without pharmaceutical interventions. In Mark 16:18, it says: "They will lay their hands on the sick and they will be healed."

Please take note that I can, by God's power through our Lord Jesus Christ, only heal righteous people but not the wicked ones. I usually do this in utmost secrecy as God has told me to do it in secret. Seventh, a false prophet does not pray to God as his prayers will not be heard because he has no faith in God; while I, a true prophet of God in the last days, who has unwavering faith in Him through our Lord Jesus Christ, can talk to Him in prayer, talk to Him as a friend talks to a friend, and He truthfully instructs me on everything that I have given to you.

In 2nd Peter 1:19-21, it says: "Therefore, we believe most firmly in the message of the prophets which you should consider rightly as a lamp shining in a dark place, until the break of day, when the Morning Star shines in your hearts. Know this well: no prophecy of Scripture can be handed over to private interpretation, since no prophecy comes from human decision, for it was men of God, moved by the Holy Spirit, who spoke."

The ultimate truths contained in this book come from the infinite wisdom of God Almighty. Those who read, let them read. Those who listen, let them listen. Those who will not listen, let them not listen. For, it says in Ezekiel 3:27, "But when I speak to you I shall open your lips and you shall say to them: This is the word of the Lord Yahweh! He who listens, let him listen and he who refuses to listen, let him refuse for they are a rebellious people." In Habakkuk 2:4, it says: "The proud will never possess my favour, the upright, on the other hand, will live by his faithfulness."

Those who will judge me, judge the One who caused me to write all things written herein. They will be adversely judged in the last days by the Supreme Judge of the Universe, the Almighty Father. Those who believe in me and the things written in this book believe in God, who caused me to write the truth contained in this book. In John 12:44, it says: "…He who believes in me, believes not in me but in him who sent me." They will have an unwavering faith in God through our Lord Jesus Christ, bearing fruit of redemption and everlasting life. Hence, believe so you may be saved because prophecy is a sign for those who believe, not for those who refuse to believe. (1st Corinthians 14:22).

CHAPTER II
THE DESTRUCTION OF 40 PRIMARY CITIES

As revealed by God of Truth and Spirit, the time left for the world is only less than ONE DAY. In fact, this is now the last hour. One day for the Lord is 1,000 years to mankind. In Psalm 90: 4-6, it says: "A thousand years in your sight are like a day that has passed, or like a watch in the night. You cast them off like a dream. They are like grass in the morning, springing up at dawn, but fading and withering in the evening." Then, the judgment day. When will that be? Nobody knows. Only God knows when will the Last Judgment be.

Mark 13:32 says: "But, regarding that Day and that Hour, no one knows when it will come, not even the angels or the Son, but only the Father." In Luke 21:25-27, it says: "Then there will be signs in sun and moon and stars, and on earth anguish of perplexed nations when they hear the roaring of the sea and its waves. People will faint with fear at the mere thought of what is to come upon the world, for the forces of the universe will be shaken. And at this time they will see the Son of Man coming in a cloud with power and great glory." Also Mark 13:24-27 says: "Later on, in those days after that disastrous time, the sun will grow dark, the moon will not give its light, the stars will fall out of the sky and the whole universe will be shaken. Then the people will see the Son of Man coming in the clouds with great power and glory. And he will send the angels to gather his chosen people from the four winds, from the ends of the earth to the ends of the sky."

In Matthew 24:37-39, it says: "At the coming of the Son of Man it will be just as it was in the time of Noah. In those days before the Flood, people were eating and drinking, and marrying, until the day when Noah went into the ark. Yet they did not know what would happen until the flood came and swept them away. So will it be at the coming of the Son of Man."

These events will be first preceded by the destruction of many world's cities, killing millions of people. God will send hailstones, tsunamis, rains of consuming fire, and violent, strong earthquakes to the target, destroying cities in an instant. In Zephaniah 3:8, it says: "Therefore, wait for me, says Yahweh, for the day when I come to accuse, when I have the nations gathered and the kingdoms assembled to vent my wrath on you with all the fury of my anger. Then the fire of my jealous wrath will burn the whole land." People may ask where they should go in order to save their lives. In Jeremiah 15:2, it says: "And if they say 'Where shall we go?' tell them: Yahweh says this: Those destined for the plague, to the plague; for the sword, to the sword; for starvation, to starvation; those for captivity to captivity."

This destruction of cities had been foretold long ago by Isaiah. In Isaiah 26:5-6, it states: "He brought down those who dwell on high, he laid low the lofty cities, he razed it to the ground, levelled it to the dust, and there it is trampled underfoot by the destitute, by the footsteps of the oppressed."

As revealed by God, there will be 40 primary cities to be destroyed in the last days. God revealed to me one city at a time daily. Sometimes, He revealed to me three cities in a day. The number one being the first to be revealed, and the 40th being the last. Why 40 cities? Why not more than 40 cities or less than 40 cities? In the Bible, forty signifies penalty and sacrifice. It rained for forty days and forty nights to flood the earth (Genesis 7:4). The people of God were punished for forty years wandering in the desert before God gave them the promised land because they sinned by being stiff-necked people, worshipping molten calf made of gold. This is an abhorrent idolatry most detestable before God's eyes. Also, our Lord Jesus Christ fasted for forty days before He began His ministry. Believe it and be ready.

Again, Isaiah 13:3-11 confirms the destruction of 40 cities, and it says: 'I have commanded them to carry out my wrath. Listen, a rumbling on the mountains as of a great multitude! Listen, a tumultuous uproar as of kingdoms massing together! Yes, Yahweh Sabaoth is mustering an army for war. From faraway lands, from the ends of the heavens they come — Yahweh and the instruments of his wrath — to destroy the whole earth. Wail, for the day of Yahweh is near; it will come as destruction from the Almighty. Every man's arm will go limp, every man's heart will fail him. Everyone will be gripped with terror. Pain and sorrow taking hold of them, men will be in anguish like women in travail. They will look aghast at each other, their faces aflame as with fever. See how the day of Yahweh comes: it is a cruel day coming with wrath and fierce anger. It will make the earth desolate; it will destroy sinners within it. The stars and constellations at night will send forth no light, the moon will not shine; in the morning the sun will be dark as it rises. I punish the world for the evil it does, and the wicked for their sins. I make the arrogance of the proud cease; I end the haughtiness of the ruthless."

In Joel 2:10-11, it says: "Before them the earth shakes and the heavens tremble, the sun and moon grow dark and the stars lose their twinkle. Yahweh thunders before his army, his vast and mighty forces. The day of Yahweh is exceedingly great, terrible and dreadful – who can endure it?" Also, Isaiah 42:14-15 says: "For a long time I have held my peace; I have kept still and restrained myself. But now I cry out like a woman in labour; I will destroy and devour! I will lay waste mountains and hills and wither all their vegetation; I will turn rivers into waste land and dry up the pools."

There are questions in Nahum 1:6-8, which says: "Who can stand before his fury? Who can face his blazing anger? His wrath is poured out like fire, and the rocks are rent asunder. Yahweh is good for those who hope; in the day of trouble he shelters them. He remembers those who trust in him when the flood engulfs them. He remembers those who trust in him when the flood engulfs them. He utterly destroys his adversaries and pursues his foes into darkness."

In Psalm 2:4-5, it says: "The One enthroned in heaven laughs; the Lord looks at them in derision. Then in anger he speaks to them, terrifying them in the fury of his wrath." Also, Psalm 7:12 says: "A righteous judge is God, his anger ever awaiting those who refuse to repent." In Psalm 21:10, it says: "You will make of them a blazing furnace, O Lord, when you appear. You will strike them down in your wrath, your fire will engulf and burn them up."

Here are the forty cities doomed to be destroyed in the last days.

Metropolitan Manila, Philippines

The details of the destruction of Metropolitan Manila are discussed in Chapter I.

I asked God if Tacloban City and Ormoc City were included. The answer is no. What happened in Tacloban was only a trial for people to repent. The storm surge that destroyed Tacloban and Ormoc caused by typhoon Yolanda, with the international name Haiyan, on November 8, 2013, was announced in advance to the people, but they never believed the warning. In Job 33:14, it says: "See God gives a warning but does not repeat it a second time." The same thing happened in Sodom, where they took it as a joke. In 2nd Chronicles 36:15-16, it says: Yahweh the God of their ancestors, continued to send prophets to warn his people, since he had compassion on them and on his dwelling place. But they mocked the messengers of God, ignored his words, and laughed at his prophets, until at last the anger of Yahweh rose so high against his people that there was no further remedy."

People were warned beforehand but they never believed. As a result of their disbelief, more than seven thousand people were washed away to death. In Hebrews 13:1-2, it says: "Preserve brotherly love. Do not neglect to offer hospitality; you know that some people have entertained angels without knowing it." In Psalm 110:6, it says: "He will judge the nations, heaping up corpses, crushing the rulers of the earth."

This event is a true fact. Believe it. Those who died in Tacloban may not have died if they had faith in God through our Lord Jesus Christ. It is simple. Just cling to where there is life. Do not be detached from life. And that life is on your faith in God through our

Lord Jesus Christ. Again, in the case of Metropolitan Manila, I am bringing them God's message clearly. I surmise many of them will laugh at God's words, whose character is innate to being intrinsically wicked. Such an attitude paves toward disgrace and death. Proverbs 1:24-27 says: "Indeed if I cry out and you refuse to listen, if I offer my hand and no one cares, if you ignore my advice and reject my warning, I, in turn, will laugh at your disaster, I will sneer when terror grips you; when terror comes down on you like a hurricane, and distress and anxiety befall you."

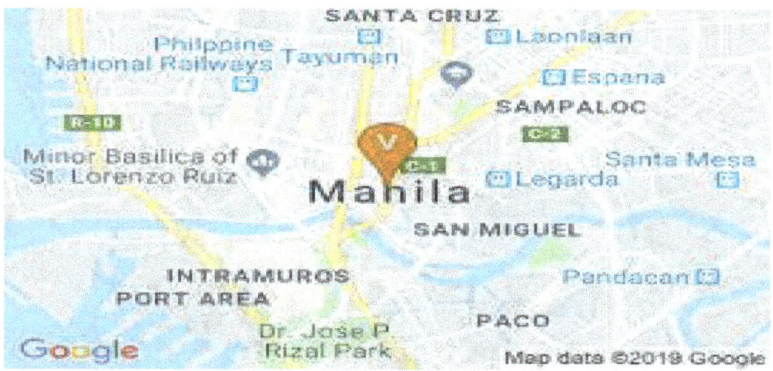

There will be more than 11 million people who will die in Metropolitan Manila, says the Lord. But before that time comes, people will experience, from time to time, calamities, like earthquakes of minor intensity, volcanic eruptions, storm surges, pestilences caused by deadly viruses that will constantly mutate into more deadly viruses, and tsunamis that will destroy life and property. God advises people in Ecclesiastes 7:17, saying:" Do not be too wicked or stupid, lest you die before your time."

Taal volcano erupted on January 12, 2020, or seventy years before the initial date of destruction of Metropolitan Manila, as revealed by God to me on the night of September 20, 2019. On August 10, 2065,

Taal Volcano will erupt again. This time, it will be a major eruption that will claim many lives and dislocate people. In Proverbs 1:32, it says: "For the error of the ignorant leads to death, the idleness of fools brings about their ruin."

The other major destructive volcanic eruptions are Kanla-on Volcano on July 7, 2065; Mayon Volcano on July 8, 2065; Mt. Bulusan on September 7, 2086; and Mt. Apo on October 13, 2080, says the Lord. Mindanao will experience slight earthquakes from time to time to remind people that the last days are at the brim and the end is near. People must repent and place their faith in God through our Lord Jesus Christ. In 1st Thessalonians 5:20, it says: "Do not despise the prophet's warnings."

Metropolitan Manila

Being a true-blooded Filipino myself, I fervently begged God for his grace and mercy to spare Metropolitan Manila from destruction. He answered me right away that because of sin, the place would be totally destroyed. The other serious reason for its destruction is widespread idolatry in worshiping the wooden black statue of Nazarene. Millions of Filipinos become devotees of this worthless idol. They are blinded by their ignorance and invite God to destroy them. In 2nd Kings 17:14-15, it says: "But they did not listen and refused as did their fathers who did not believe in Yahweh, their God. They despised his statutes and the covenant he had made with their fathers, and the warnings he had given them. They went after worthless idols and they themselves became worthless, following the nations which surrounded them. In spite of what Yahweh had said, 'Do not do as they do.'"

Also, in 2nd Kings 17:29-31, it says: "Yet each of these nations made its own gods, and placed them in the sanctuaries on the hills which the Samaritans had built. Each of these nations put their god in the city where they settled: the Babylonians set up the idol Succoth, the inhabitants of Cuth made Negal, the inhabitants of Hamath made Ashima, those of Avva made Nibjaz and Tartak. Those of Sepharvim burned their children in the fire in honour of Adrammelech and Anammelech, their gods."

Whereas, in the Philippines, they proudly have their statue of black Nazarene made of hard wood and blindly venerated by millions of Filipinos. This is a worthless idol with eyes that cannot see, ears that cannot hear, a nose that cannot breathe, a mouth that cannot talk, and feet that cannot walk. Yet millions of Filipinos proudly say to this lifeless statue that it is their god who saves them. They are stiff-necked people who mockingly insult God by this idolatry. Thus inviting God to strike them in the last days. God is extremely furious with those people who worship idols. Destroying these disobedient people is the last appropriate thing to appease God. There will be no mercy for these people. They will be uprooted from the face of the earth. Let the vengeance of God fall on them. God advises me on this: Jeremiah 11:14, "For your part, do not intercede for this people, nor offer a plea or petition because I will not listen when they cry to me in the time of their distress."

Also, Proverbs 1:28-30 says: "Then people will cry to me but I will not respond. They will seek me but will not find me, because they despised knowledge and did not choose the fear of Yahweh, they would not listen to any advice and they rejected all my warnings."

I know that God is just, and his decision is always fair and right. He is all-knowing. He knows the righteousness of divine plan since the penalty of sin is death. If there are people in Metropolitan Manila with the same qualities and faith as Noah, Job, and Daniel, destruction may not come upon it. Wicked people in that place increase more and more each day and God perceives that there is no more chance for them to repent. Hence, the place is doomed for destruction. Those righteous people may go to a safer place before the day of destruction to be saved. God wants you to be saved as he truly loves you. The love that he gives you is true and perfect.

It says in Deuteronomy 30:19-20, "Therefore, choose life that you and your descendants may live, loving Yahweh, listening to his voice, and being one with him..." As God truly loves you, compensate also his love for you by obeying all his commands and by avoiding evil in your life. Reject worthless graven images. Do not use them in your prayer. Sustain your personal relationship with God by praying to him in spirit and truth. God gives you this message in Isaiah 45:22-24, saying: "Turn to me and be saved, all you from the ends of the earth, for I am God and there is no other. By my own self I swear it, and what comes from my mouth is truth, a word that will not be revoked. Before me every knee will bend, by me every tongue will swear, saying, 'In Yahweh alone are righteousness and strength.'"

Tashkent, Uzbekistan

Tashkent is the capital city of Uzbekistan, near the border of Kazakhstan. It is the largest city in Uzbekistan, which is historically known as Chach, Shash, and Binkat. It has a population of 3,000,000 in the capital city and 6,986,6024 in Metro Tashkent.

Tashkent was largely influenced by Sogdian and Turkic cultures before it was influenced by Islam in the 8th century A.D. In 1219 A.D., it was conquered and destroyed by Genghis Khan. Subsequently, it was rebuilt due to the economic activity of silk trading as it passed through Tashkent going to Europe. It acquired independence as a city-state in the 18th and 19th centuries before it was conquered again by the Khanate of Kokand. Again, Tashkent, being a vulnerable place in Central Asia having no high natural boundaries, was conquered by the Russian Empire in 1865. From then on, it became the capital of Russian Turkestan. Due to forced deportation throughout the Soviet Union, it experiences major growth and demographic changes. After it was rebuilt after its destruction caused by a strong tectonic earthquake in 1966, it became the fourth largest city of the Soviet Union after Moscow, Leningrad, and Kyiv in Ukraine.

Location of Tashkent in Uzbekistan

Tashkent celebrated its 2200 years in written history in 2009 as the capital of Uzbekistan, retaining its multi-ethnic population. Because it had a history of earthquakes in 1966, Tashkent has a great possibility of being hit again by a very strong earthquake in the last days. As revealed, Tashkent will be totally destroyed in the last days. It sits at the confluence of the Chirchiq River and is built on deep alluvial deposits. The city itself is dangerously situated in an active tectonic area, which is why there are frequent earthquakes. The Lord says: "*Tashkent will perish from the face of the Earth.*"

Here are some structures and places in Tashkent that might be destroyed in the last of the days:

Zangi-Ata shrine

Barak Khan Madrasa, Shaybanids

Alisher Navoiy Park

Japanese Gardens in Tashkent

Residential Towers in Tashkent

Amir Timur

Taras Shevchenko Hotel

Kukeldash Madrasa

Tashkent, your day will be on August 19, 2091, a Sunday at 11:30 P.M.

Earthquakes and heavy rains of consuming fire will fall on you. You can escape this destruction if you will repent of your sin. In the absence of sincere repentance, your neighbouring cities will also be destroyed, like Samarkand, Urgench, Nukus, and Bukhara. In Psalm 21:10, it says: "You will make of them a blazing furnace, O Lord, when you appear. You will strike them down in your wrath, your fire will engulf and burn them up." For this, God has this to say in Isaiah 44:26: "I confirm the word of my servant and carry out the plan announced by my messengers…"

In Isaiah 45:22-24, the Almighty Father says this to you: "Turn to me and be saved, all you from the ends of the earth, for I am God and there is no other. By my own self I swear it, and what comes from my mouth is truth, a word that will not be revoked. Before me every knee will bend, by me every tongue will swear, saying, 'In Yahweh alone are righteousness and strength.'"

Guatemala City, Guatemala

Map of Guatemala

The Mayan city of Kalinaljuyu, which was founded in 1500 B.C., turned out to be the site where the present city of Guatemala stood. It was founded as a city following an earthquake in La Antigua in 1776 and became the capital of the Captaincy General of Guatemala. It was the place where the declaration of independence of Central America from Spain took place in 1821. A little while later, it became the capital city of the newly established United Provinces of Central America, which was named later as the Federal Republic of Central America. Guatemala City became the capital city of Guatemala after the latter obtained its independence in 1847.

The entire city of Guatemala

Guatemala City is known to have active volcanoes, the most destructive of which is the Pacaya volcano, which has been doomed for total destruction in the last days. Numerous infrastructures will turn into rubbles when her time comes on **July 5, 2090, at 7:50 P.M**. A strong, violent earthquake will strike you and will be followed by a rain of consuming fire. Its neighbouring cities, such as Coban, Puerto Barrios, and Quetzaltenango, will also be totally destroyed if they do not sincerely repent. According to divine revelation, this date will not be changed anymore unless the populace of Guatemala seriously repents of their sins. Their religion, Roman Catholicism, drags them into worshipping idols, which infuriates God. In fact, that is the primary reason for God to include Guatemala as one of the targets for total destruction in the last days.

Some infrastructures that will be pulled down in the last days:

Zone 10 Skyline in Guatemala

Ciudad Cayala, a city within Guatemala

Guatemala National Palace of Culture

University of San Carlos Central Campus

Museo nacional de Arqueología, Etnologia

Paseo Cayala

There are indicators that the soil in Guatemala is somewhat fragile and that it can easily create sinkholes. These sinkholes are classified by geologists as either a "piping feature" or "piping pseudokarst," estimated to be 100 metres deep, caused by fluid from sewer eroding the loose volcanic ash, limestone and other pyroclastic deposits. It means that in the last days there will be more sinkholes bigger than the previous ones that can claim numerous lives and destroy properties and livelihoods.

These are the sinkholes:

2007 Sinkhole in Northeastern Guatemala City

The 2010 Sinkhole in Zone 2

This impending destruction of Guatemala will never be postponed unless Guatemalans repent of detesting worship of idols and return to worship only God through our Lord Jesus Christ. On July 5, 2090, at 7:50 P.M. violent earthquake will strike you and will be followed by rains of consuming fire that will totally destroy your place. **In Psalm 21:10, it says: "You will make of them a blazing furnace, O Lord, when you appear. You will strike them down in your wrath, your fire will engulf and burn them up." For this, God has this to say in Isaiah 44:26: "I confirm the word of my servant and carry out the plan announced by my messengers…"**

In Isaiah 45:22-24, the Almighty Father says this to you: "Turn to me and be saved, all you from the ends of the earth, for I am God and there is no other. By my own self I swear it, and what comes from my mouth is truth, a word that will not be revoked. Before me every knee will bend, by me every tongue will swear, saying, 'In Yahweh alone are righteousness and strength.'"

Lima, Peru

Map of Lima, Peru

Lima, as seen from the International Space Station

The modern history of Lima began upon its Spanish foundation in 1535. Its territory is formed by valleys of rivers Rimac, Chillon, and Lurin, which were also the settlements occupied by people during the pre-Inca period. The rise of civilisation in that part of the Meso-American region began to improve from one occupant-conqueror to another. The area of Lima faces some degree of problems in terms of its security and stability. To facilitate its sustainable growth in politics and economy, it was finally decided by those who manage the seat of government in Lima to erect a high wall around the city for protection against pirates and other invaders.

There were many occasions in the past when it was destroyed due to a strong earthquake. Memorable to the lives of the populace are two strong earthquakes that tremendously destroyed the city. The first strong earthquake happened in the year 1687, which marked a turning point in Lima's history as it coincided with a recession in trade due to economic competition with neighboring cities. The second strong earthquake occurred in 1746 which severely damaged the city. It also destroyed the adjacent city of Callao, which forced the viceroy to undergo massive reconstruction.

Considering the fact that Lima City had already experienced devastation due to a strong earthquake, there will be a great probability that such an earthquake will recur as it is eyed by God to be destroyed on **July 14, 2092, at 9:10 P.M. a Monday. A strong, violent earthquake will strike you, followed by a rain of consuming fire.** This city will be destroyed because of its sin. If its neighbouring cities, such as Arequipa, Callao, Cuzco, and Trujillo, do not repent, they will also be destroyed. People in this city venerate carved images of saints as their religion requires such kind of worship, which is abhorrent to God. The ones who can save the city are the residents themselves. If they will stop their idolatry and return to God through our Lord Jesus Christ by praying in truth and spirit and avoiding sin, they can stop this impending destruction as what had happened in Nineveh.

Here are the places targeted by God to be destroyed in the last days:

Overview of Costa Verde and the Pacific Ocean, Miraflores District

Financial Center of San Isidro

Basilica of Sto. Domingo

Rocc Casa de Osambela

Lima Stock Exchange Building

Casona and Chapel of National University

Lima Golf Club

Estadio Monumental "U"

Plaza de Toros de Acho

In Psalm 21:10, it says: "You will make of them a blazing furnace, O Lord, when you appear. You will strike them down in your wrath, your fire will engulf and burn them up." For this, God has this to say in Isaiah 44:26: "I confirm the word of my servant and carry out the plan announced by my messengers..."

In Isaiah 45:22-24, the Almighty Father says this to you: "Turn to me and be saved, all you from the ends of the earth, for I am God and there is no other. By my own self I swear it, and what comes from my mouth is truth, a word that will not be revoked. Before me every knee will bend, by me every tongue will swear, saying, 'In Yahweh alone are righteousness and strength.'"

Tegucigalpa, Honduras

Map of Tegucigalpa, Honduras

As the capital city of Honduras, Tegucigalpa was founded and initially developed by Spanish settlers as *Rea de Minas de San Miguel de Tegucigalpa* on September 29, 1578, on the site of the native settlement of *Lenca and Tlupans*.7 Tegucigalpa became the official capital of Honduras on October 30, 1880, when President Marco Aurelio Soto transferred the seat of government from Comayagua, 8, which was the capital of Honduras since its independence in 1841.

These two cities, Tegucigalpa and Comayagua, alternately served as the capital city of Honduras. Until such time, during the enactment of the Honduran Constitution, Tegucigalpa was permanently named the national capital.9

Tegucigalpa City

Honduras and Tegucigalpa are places that have been visited by calamities, such as hurricanes and earthquakes. On October 30, 1998, hurricane Mitch destroyed the capital, including several portions of Honduras, creating havoc such as landslides and floods that claimed the lives of thousands. Earthquakes occur from time to time, considering that there are geological faults as identified in the district's high regions around the capital. 10.

With an apparent manifestation of the fragility of the place, Tegucigalpa is set to be destroyed by God in the last days. **Your day, Tegucigalpa, will be on November 15, 2093, a Sunday at 7:18 P.M.** You can only alter this divine declaration if you repent of your sins. Refrain from worshiping images as it is abhorred by God. Your religion teaches you to venerate images, and it will cause your fall. Earthquakes and rains of consuming fire will strike you, leading toward your total destruction.

In Psalm 21:10, it says: "You will make of them a blazing furnace, O Lord, when you appear. You will strike them down in your wrath, your fire will engulf and burn them up." For this, God has this to say in Isaiah 44:26: "I confirm the word of my servant and carry out the plan announced by my messengers…"

In Isaiah 45:22-24, the Almighty Father says this to you: "Turn to me and be saved, all you from the ends of the earth, for I am God and there is no other. By my own self I swear it, and what comes from my mouth is truth, a word that will not be revoked. Before me every knee will bend, by me every tongue will swear, saying, 'In Yahweh alone are righteousness and strength.'"

Here are some of the places and structures that will turn into rubbles:

Tegucigalpa City

Basilica of Our Lady of Suyapa

Metropolis Tower

Chelato Ucles Football Stadium

Chochi Sosa Baseball Stadium

North of the city

Civic Center of Tegucigalpa

New Delhi, India

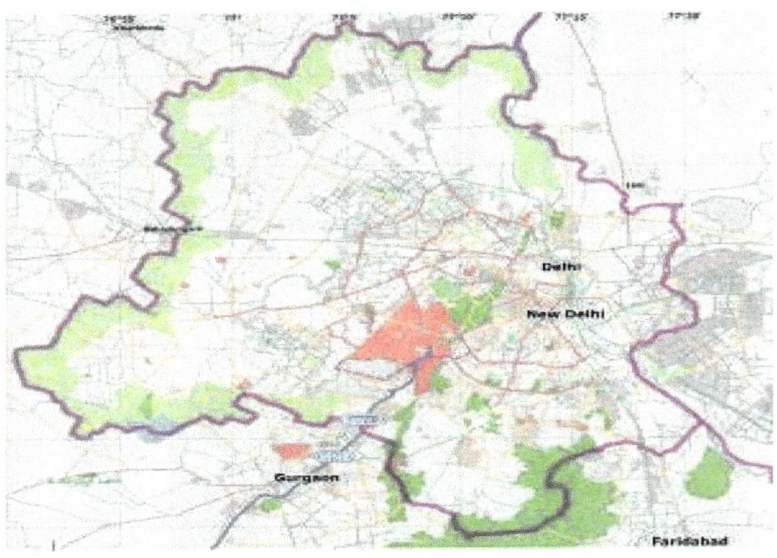

New Delhi is the national capital of India. Being a colony of Britain for many years, India's capital was placed in Calcutta. It was only in 1911 that New Delhi was made the capital upon the declaration of George V, Emperor of India. There were several reasons for its transfer. First, as the capital of India for many years until 1911, Calcutta became the centre of nationalistic movements since the late nineteenth century, which led to the division of Bengal by Viceroy Lord Curzon. This division resulted in political and religious upsurge, including political assassinations of British government officials in Calcutta. For this, the British rule in India spawned anti-colonial sentiments among the Indians, which led to a complete boycott of British goods. Likewise, it forced the colonial government to unify Bengal and shift the capital to New Delhi. Second, the government of British India felt that it was logical to transfer the capital to New Delhi since it was easier to administer India from Delhi because it

was the centre of Northern India.11

New Delhi

New Delhi is notably vulnerable to violent earthquakes since it falls under the seismic zone-IV. It experiences frequent earthquakes, though mild at this stage of geologic development because it lies on several fault lines. Between 2011 and 2015, there was a spike in the number of earthquakes, mostly with magnitudes ranging from 4.7 to 5.4, with the epicentre in Nepal. A swarm of 12 earthquakes struck the place in November 2013.

With New Delhi's geologic predicament, we can, therefore, conclude that the prediction about New Delhi is true. This prediction says that New Delhi will be destroyed in the last days. Its neighbouring cities of Bangalore, Bombay, Calcutta, Delhi, Hyderabad, and Madras will likewise be destroyed if they do not repent of their sinfulness and wickedness and avoid committing sins.

The Lord says, New Delhi, your day will be on November 22, 2091, a Thursday at 7:45 P.M. A Violent earthquake will strike you and will be followed by a rain of consuming fire. In Psalm 21:10, it says: "You will make of them a blazing furnace, O Lord, when you appear. You will strike them down in your wrath, your fire will engulf and burn them up." For this, God has this to say in Isaiah 44:26: "I confirm the word of my servant and carry out the plan announced by my messengers…"

In Isaiah 45:22-24, the Almighty Father says this to you: "Turn to me and be saved, all you from the ends of the earth, for I am God and there is no other. By my own self I swear it, and what comes from my mouth is truth, a word that will not be revoked. Before me every knee will bend, by me every tongue will swear, saying, 'In Yahweh alone are righteousness and strength.'"

Here are some places and structures that will be reduced to rubbles:

Rashtrapati Bhawan

New Parliament House

Bharat Mandapam

L.I.C. Connaught Place

National War Memorial

India Gate

Laxminarayan Temple, a Hindu Mandir

Sacred Heart Catedral

Gurudwara Bangla Sahib, a Sikh Gurdwara

Qila-i-Kuhna Mosque, inside Old Fort

Connaught Place in Delhi is an important economic hub of the
National Capital Region.

New York, United States Of America

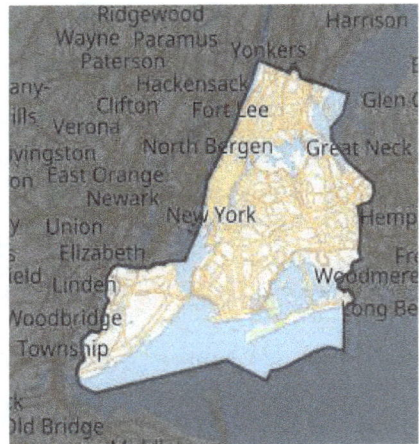

Map of New York City

Satellite view of New York City

The area of present-day New York City was formerly resided by natives comprising the tribes of Algonquians and Lenape. Their homeland, called Lenapehoking, is the place of present-day Staten

Island, Manhattan, the Bronx, the western portion of Long Island, which includes Brooklyn and Queens, and the Lower Valley.12

Today, New York City is the most densely populated area in the United States of America, situated in the southern portion of New York State on one of the world's largest natural harbours. It comprises five boroughs, namely Manhattan, the Bronx, Queens, Brooklyn, and Staten Island, each of which is coextensive with a respective county. It is the centre of the world's culture, finance, technology, entertainment, media, commerce, healthcare, scientific output, life sciences, research education, politics, tourism, dining, art, fashion, and sports. It is an important centre of international diplomacy as it is home to the United Nations Headquarters.

Midtown Manhattan, the world's largest central district13

With all the developments, improvements, affluence, and everything in New York City, residents have been experiencing prosperity and abundance without thinking about themselves and their spiritual needs. Most people indulge in sinfulness and wickedness. This is one reason that God of Host has been eyeing this city to be destroyed in the last days. This city cannot escape God's wrath. It will be levelled to the ground. The only solution for people to be saved is to repent and refrain from committing sins. Those upright people should depart from this place and settle elsewhere to avoid sharing the punishment.

Unless you repent, New York, your day will be December 15, 2090, a Friday at 9:30 P.M. A great, violent earthquake will strike you and will be followed by a rain of consuming fire. In Psalm 21:10, it says: "You will make of them a blazing furnace, O Lord, when you appear. You will strike them down in your wrath, your fire will engulf and burn them up." For this, God has this to say in Isaiah 44:26: "I confirm the word of my servant and carry out the plan announced by my messengers…"

In Isaiah 45:22-24, God says this to you: "Turn to me and be saved, all you from the ends of the earth, for I am God and there is no other. By my own self I swear it, and what comes from my mouth is truth, a word that will not be revoked. Before me every knee will bend, by me every tongue will swear, saying, 'In Yahweh alone are righteousness and strength.'"

Here are some of your places and structures that will be destroyed:

Statue of Liberty

The Pond and Midtown Manhattan

New York-Presbyterian Hospital

Lower Manhattan

Flatiron District

The headquarters of the New York Times Company

Flushing Meadows-Corona Park in Queens

New York County Courthouse

Yankee Stadium in the Bronx

The George Washington Bridge

Metropolitan Museum of Art

New York Panoramic

Solomon R. Guggenheim Museum

The Manhattan Bridge and Brooklyn Bridge

Honolulu, United States Of America

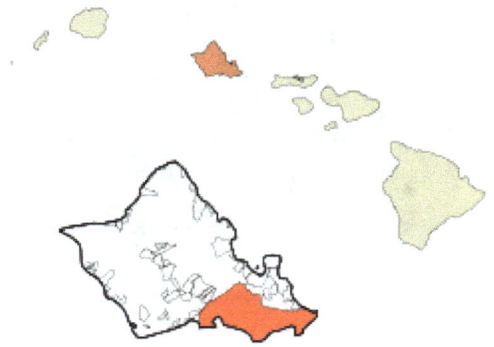

Map of Honolulu, U.S.A.

Satellite view of Honolulu

Oral history, as supported by unearthed artefacts, points to the fact that the first people who settled in Honolulu and in the archipelago of Hawaii were Polynesian migrants. It indicates that as early as the 11th century, there was already a settlement where Honolulu presently stands.14

As recorded, in 1804, a certain chieftain from neighbouring

island, named Kamehameha I, attacked and conquered O'ahu in the Battle of Nu'uanu at Nu'uanu Pali and, thereafter, transferred his royal court from the Island of Hawaii to Waikiki. In 1809, he transferred his court to what is now downtown Honolulu. In 1812, for some undisclosed reasons, the capital was moved back to Kailua-Kuna.

The first foreigner who sailed the seas and docked at Honolulu Harbor was Captain William Brown of Great Britain in November 1794.15 But the first one who dropped by Hawaii's archipelago and Honolulu in March 1521 to circumnavigate the world was Ferdinand Magellan.16 From then on, more foreign ships visited and docked at the port of Honolulu, making the place a converging zone of ships sailing between North America and Asia. From a handful of homes in the area, it grew into a big city after Kamehameha I chose it as his permanent residence at Waikiki in 1810.17

In 1850, seeing prosperity in the place, Kamehameha III made Honolulu the permanent capital of the Hawaiian Kingdom from Lahaina on Maui.17 He and his successors gradually transformed Honolulu into a progressive modern capital, constructing commercial buildings and infrastructures. As a consequence, commerce became more and more progressive, which propelled traders, merchants and American missionaries to settle and establish major businesses in the capital. Honolulu until now remains Hawaiian Island's capital notwithstanding the turbulence it experienced in the late 19th century and early 20th century, like the overthrow of the Hawaiian monarchy in 1893, annexation of Hawaii as the 50th State of the U.S.A. in 1898, conflagration in 1900, and kamikaze attack on Pearl Harbor in 1941.18

Underneath the ground of Honolulu lie the veins of the Pacific

Ring of Fire as the city itself partially stood on a volcanic field.19 Such geologic predicament concretely supports the prediction that Honolulu city will be destroyed in the last days. God says Honolulu, including Maui, Oahu, and Hawaii Islands, will be destroyed in the last days. As the city economically progresses, the people become sinful and wicked, which infuriates God. Unless you repent and avoid committing sins and worship God with all your heart, with all your mind and with all your soul, **your day will be on April 6, 2091, a Friday at 6:58 P.M. Violent earthquake** tsunami **and rain of consuming fire will fall on you. In Psalm 21:10, it says: "You will make of them a blazing furnace, O Lord, when you appear. You will strike them down in your wrath, your fire will engulf and burn them up." For this, God has this to say in Isaiah 44:26: "I confirm the word of my servant and carry out the plan announced by my messengers..."**

In Isaiah 45:22-24, God says this to you: "Turn to me and be saved, all you from the ends of the earth, for I am God and there is no other. By my own self I swear it, and what comes from my mouth is truth, a word that will not be revoked. Before me every knee will bend, by me every tongue will swear, saying, 'In Yahweh alone are righteousness and strength.'"

Here are some of your places and structures that will be destroyed:

Downtown Honolulu

Pearl Harbor

Honolulu Hale

Statue of King Kamehameha I

Waikiki Beach

Bishop & King Streets

First Hawaiian Center

Honolulu viewed from Diamond Head crater

Queen Liliuokalani Building

Hawaii State Library

Pacific Forum

Hawaii State Capitol

Honolulu's Waterfront

Phnom Penh, Cambodia

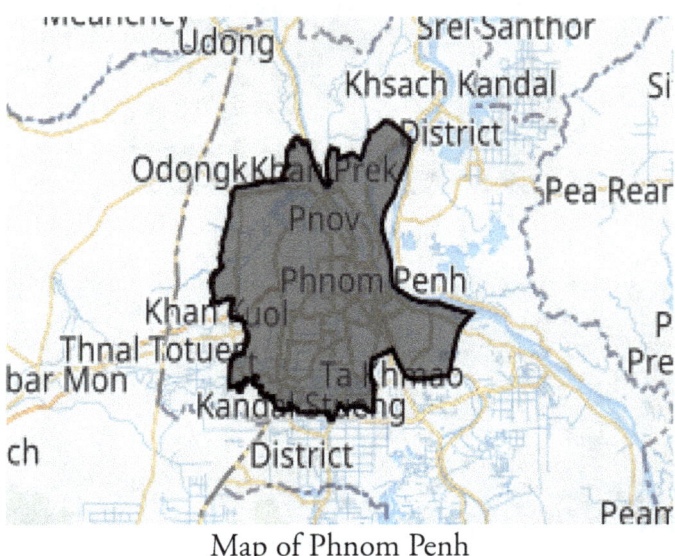

Map of Phnom Penh

Phnom Penh was the national capital of Cambodia even before it became a protectorate of France. Prior to it becoming a capital, Oudong was first recognised as the capital of Cambodia. It replaced Angkor Thom as the capital of Khmer, but several times, it was abandoned, only to be reestablished again by King Norodom in 1865. The city became progressive as it became the centre of trade and industry. It produced textiles, pharmaceuticals, and machines. As a staple food of the country, rice was also milled in the city. The progress continued until several structures were built, such as schools and commercial establishments.

The settlement in Phnom Penh is believed to have begun in the 5th century A.D. based on the discovery of an ancient kiln site in Choeng Ek commune of Dangkao district which is situated in the southern portion of Phnom Penh in 2000. It was believed that

Choeung Ek archaeological site was the largest kiln pottery centre in Cambodia and the earliest recorded kiln site in Southeast Asia to produce ceremonial vessels called kendi from the 5th to the 13th century. There are also remnants of other ancient village structures, irrigation systems, inscriptions, brick temple foundations, and ornate remains that date back to the Funan period. (20, 21)

Phnom Penh became the permanent seat of government and capital of Cambodia during the reign of King Norodom I in 1866 when he built the Royal Palace thereat. Starting in 1870, French colonial authorities began improving the city by constructing hotels, schools, prisons, banks, offices, and other infrastructures. Progress began to pour in as Phnom Penh experienced rapid growth, thereby dubbing the place as the "Pearl of Asia." In short, Phnom Penh became relatively well-developed in terms of economy despite several trials that besieged Cambodia, especially during the Vietnam War as it was used as the base for military troops and during the reign of Pol Pot when Cambodia became Choeung Ek or Killing Fields.

With the sad experiences of Cambodia, the populace has no knowledge at all that Phnom Penh is already being targeted by God to be destroyed in the last days because of sin.

Their religion of Buddhism hinders them from knowing the truth of salvation as they do not believe in our Lord Jesus Christ. Unless you change your behaviour and stop committing sins, your day, Phnom Penh, will be on September 4, 2091, a Tuesday at 11:08 P.M. The only salvation left for this place is to turn to God, ask for forgiveness and repent. Other than that, there will be no more salvation. Other places in Cambodia, like Kampong Cham and Battambang, will also be destroyed if they do not repent of their sins. Earthquakes and rains of consuming fire will fall on you.

In Psalm 21:10, it says: "You will make of them a blazing furnace, O Lord, when you appear. You will strike them down in your wrath, your fire will engulf and burn them up." For this, God has this to say in Isaiah 44:26: "I confirm the word of my servant and carry out the plan announced by my messengers…"

In Isaiah 45:22-24, God says this to you: "Turn to me and be saved, all you from the ends of the earth, for I am God and there is no other. By my own self I swear it, and what comes from my mouth is truth, a word that will not be revoked. Before me every knee will bend, by me every tongue will swear, saying, 'In Yahweh alone are righteousness and strength.'"

Here are some of your places and structures that will be destroyed:

The National Assembly Building

Supreme Court Building

The Central Post Office Building

The Hong Kong Center

Royal University of Phnom Penh Campus

Institut de Technologie du Cambodge

Ministry of Land Management

National Museum

The Capital City of Phnom Penh

Phnom Penh at Night Time

Moskva, Russian Federation

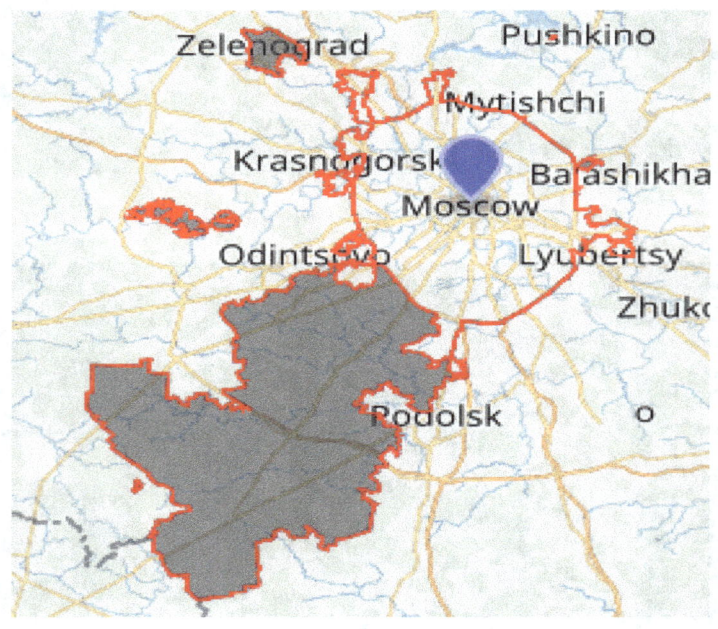

Moskva, or Moscow, the largest city in Russia, is the capital city of the Russian Federation, situated on the Moskva River in Central Russia. Within city limits, its population is more or less 13 million residents,22 in the urban portion of the city, its residents numbered more than 18.8 million 23, and in the metropolitan area, it has more or less 21.5 million residents.24 It comprises an area of 2,511 square kilometres (970 square miles),23 the urban area comprises 5,891 square kilometres (2,275 square miles)24, and the metropolitan area covers more or less 26,000 square kilometres (10,000 square miles).24 As the capital of the largest country on earth with over one-ninth of the world's land area, Moscow is the political, industrial, and cultural centre of Russia.

The country itself, being the largest area on earth, extends from

Eastern Europe through the Ural Mountains east of the Pacific Ocean. The Caucasus Range forms its natural boundary with Georgia and Azerbaijan. It is here that the highest peak in Europe, Mt. Elbrus, can be seen. In the East, Siberia is drained toward the Arctic Ocean by great rivers Ob, Yenisey, and Lena and their tributaries. To the south of the Central Siberian Plateau lies Lake Baikal, the world's deepest freshwater lake. The Ural Mountains form the boundary between Asia and Europe.

Moscow has resided since time immemorial by Neolithic Slavic hunters of Vyatichi and Krivichi tribes, which formed Moscow's core of indigenous residents.25 The earliest archaeological finds support the belief that Moscow's first pre-historic settlers, based on the relics of Lyalovo culture, came between the Neolithic period and the last phase of the Stone Age era.[26]

Moscow's written history began in A.D. 1147. From then on, it gradually became a prosperous and powerful city and was made the capital of the Grand Duchy of Moscow. It remained Russia's centre of politics and economy until the coming of Tsardom. In 1712, its influence decreased when Peter the Great came to power in Russia as the capital was transferred to Saint Petersburg. After the Bolshevik Revolution's victory and the formation of Soviet Federal Socialist Republics, the capital was transferred back to Moscow in 1918, converting the place into a political centre of the Soviet Union. 27 Even after the dissolution of the Soviet Union, Moscow preserved its status as the capital of the Russian Federation.

As revealed, Moscow will be destroyed by God in the last days due to the sinfulness and wickedness of its inhabitants, as they have no desire to repent. Other cities in Russia, like its neighbouring cities of St. Petersburg, Nizhniy, Novgorod and Novosibirsk, will also be destroyed if they do not repent.

Moscow, your day will be on September 8, 2090, a Friday at 8:30 P.M. Hailstones, strong, violent earthquakes and rains of consuming fire will fall on you for your total destruction. Isaiah 29:6 says: "For suddenly, Yahweh Sabaoth will come with thunder, earthquake and great noise, with whirlwind and thunderstorm and flames of consuming fire." Long ago, you had been prophesied in Ezekiel 38:2-4 which states: "Son of man, turn towards Gog of the country of Magog, the chief prince of Meschech and Tubal and prophesy against him. Say to him: Hear the word of Yahweh: I come to strike you, Gog, chief prince of Meschech and Tubal. I will turn you round, fix hooks in your jaws and bring you out, you and your entire army, horses and riders all perfectly equipped, a great army, all with shields and bucklers and brandishing swords."

Also, in Ezekiel 38:20-23, you are being told this: "Mountains will fall, cliffs crumble and walls collapse. I will summon the sword against Gog on all my mountains- word of Yahweh. Each one's sword will turn against his brother. I will punish Gog with plague and bloodshed. I will send torrential rain, hailstones and burning sulphur on him, and on his battalions and on the many nations with him. I will manifest myself as the Mighty and Holy One in the sight of these people, and they will know that I am Yahweh."

In Psalm 21:10, it says: "You will make of them a blazing furnace, O Lord, when you appear. You will strike them down in your wrath, your fire will engulf and burn them up." For this, God has this to say in Isaiah 44:26: "I confirm the word of my servant and carry out the plan announced by my messengers..."

In Isaiah 45:22-24, God says this to you: "Turn to me and be saved, all you from the ends of the earth, for I am God and there is no other. By my own self I swear it, and what comes from my mouth is truth, a word that will not be revoked. Before me every knee will bend, by me every tongue will swear, saying, 'In Yahweh alone are righteousness and strength.'"

Here are some of your places and structures that will be destroyed:

Moscow International Business Center

Moscow Exchange

Microdistrict in Mitino

Nikolskaya Street

Tretyakovsky Proyezd

Moscow State University

Pirogov Russian National Research Medical

Bauman Moscow State Technical University

Moscow Conservatory Building

Russian State Institute of Cinematography

Russian Academy of Sciences

Mayakovskaya Station

Sheremetyevo International Airport

Floating Bridge in Zaryadye Park

Red Square with the Spasskaya Tower, Saint Basil's Cathedral and
Ostankino Tower

Cathedral of Christ the Savior

Bolshoi Theatre

Moscow City and Third Ring Road

The State Historical Museum

Ho Chi Minh, Vietnam

Ho Chi Minh City was previously Saigon, a capital city of former South Vietnam. As the capital of the entire country of Vietnam, Ho Chi Minh is densely populated, with residents numbering more or less 9.3 million in 2023.28 Seen in the Southeast portion of Vietnam, the city surrounds the Saigon River with a land area of more or less 2,006 square kilometres (796 square miles).

It became the capital of French Indochina from 1887 to 1902, and also in 1945, up to its cessation in 1954. Upon the partition of French Indochina, it became the capital of South Vietnam until 1975, after Saigon's defeat. When the communist government took control of Vietnam, Saigon was changed into Ho Chi Minh in honour of their communist leader. Under communist rule, Ho Chi Minh started its modernisation efforts in 1990, speeding up post-war economic recovery.29

With the fast recovery of its economy, the city is now economically progressive. Accompanying this progress, people have already forgotten to worship God and indulged in a sinful way of life, which God of Truth and Spirit dislikes most. Because of this, Ho Chi

Minh becomes already a target for destruction in the last days.

As prophesied, your day, Ho Chi Minh, will be on January 4, 2091, a Thursday at 7:50 P.M. You will experience a violent earthquake and rains of consuming fire, leading to your total destruction. Its neighbouring cities, Hanoi, Haipong, Hue, and Da Nang, will also be destroyed if they do not repent. The only solution to this forthcoming destruction is for you to stop committing sins and live a life acceptable to God.

In Psalm 21:10, it says: "You will make of them a blazing furnace, O Lord, when you appear. You will strike them down in your wrath, your fire will engulf and burn them up." For this, God has this to say in Isaiah 44:26: "I confirm the word of my servant and carry out the plan announced by my messengers…"

In Isaiah 45:22-24, God says this to you: "Turn to me and be saved, all you from the ends of the earth, for I am God and there is no other. By my own self I swear it, and what comes from my mouth is truth, a word that will not be revoked. Before me every knee will bend, by me every tongue will swear, saying, 'In Yahweh alone are righteousness and strength.'"

Here are some of your places and structures that will be destroyed:

Ho Chi Minh City Hall

Landmark 81, the tallest building in Vietnam

Headquarters of Stan Vac

Nguyen Hue Boulevard

Ho Chi Minh City Museum of History

Tan Son Nhat International Airport

Saigon Opera House

Independence Palace

Street View of Saigon

Vietnam National University

District 1 Skyline

H.T.V., Television Network in Vietnam

Bui Vien Walking Street

Vaduz, Liechtenstein

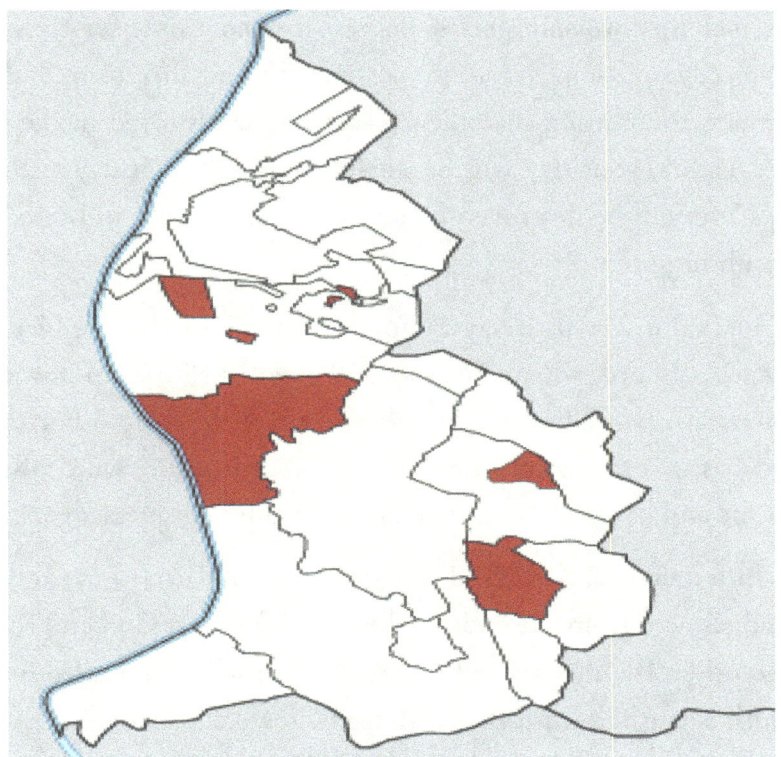

Vaduz and its exclaves in Liechtenstein

Vaduz is the capital city of Liechtenstein, a tiny central European state located on the east bank of the Rhine River. It is bounded by Austria to the east and Switzerland to the west. To the east and south lie the foothills of the Austrian Alps. The highest peak is Grauspitz on the border with Switzerland. The city is a residence to a population of 5,696.30

Despite it being a small city, God has seen something sinful in this place and decided that the place be totally destroyed in the last days. The city residents should examine themselves on why God wants them to be destroyed. I surmise that their worship of graven images, being devotees of Roman Catholicism, infuriates God. If it is true that they worship graven images, it is now time for them to completely stop doing it for the sake only of saving their place. If they continue committing sins, their place will be destroyed in the last days. **Vaduz, your day will be on July 7, 2090, a Friday at 9:46 P.M. You will be destroyed by a violent earthquake and rains of consuming fire.**

In Psalm 21:10, it says: "You will make of them a blazing furnace, O Lord, when you appear. You will strike them down in your wrath, your fire will engulf and burn them up." For this, God has this to say in Isaiah 44:26: "I confirm the word of my servant and carry out the plan announced by my messengers…"

In Isaiah 45:22-24, God says this to you: "Turn to me and be saved, all you from the ends of the earth, for I am God and there is no other. By my own self I swear it, and what comes from my mouth is truth, a word that will not be revoked. Before me every knee will bend, by me every tongue will swear, saying, 'In Yahweh alone are righteousness and strength.'"

Here are some of your places and structures that will be destroyed:

Panoramic view of Vaduz

Castle of Vaduz

Government Building

Museum of Fine Arts

Rotes Haus (Red House)

House of Parliament

Cathedral of St. Florin

Tre Cavalli (Three)

Gardens in Central Vaduz

Monrovia, Liberia

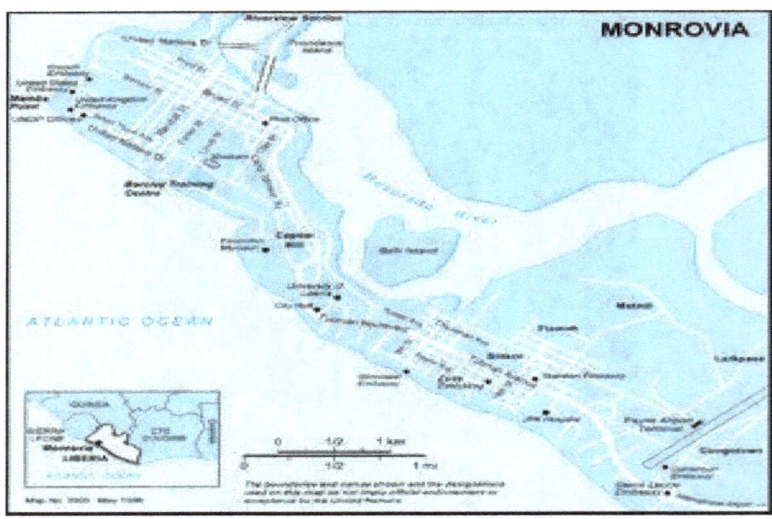

Monrovia is the capital city of Liberia, West Africa. Situated on Cape Mesurado on the Atlantic coast, Monrovia was founded in 1822 and named after the United States President James Monroe, a popular supporter of colonisation in Liberia. Based on the 2008 census, the residents of Monrovia are 1,010,970, comprising 29% of the total population of Liberia.31 As Liberia's primary city, Monrovia is the centre of economy, finance, and culture. Its economy is bolstered by its important harbour called the Freeport of Monrovia. It is the seat of Liberia's government.

The area where Monrovia presently stood was called Ducor prior to the year 1816. It is an area around Cape Mesurado and the mouth of the Mesurado River. The place was the converging zone of fishermen, traders and farmers of various ethnicities and cultures, such as Dey, Kru, Bassa, Gola, and Vai. This is where slave traders got black people and sold them to other lands.

For purposes of putting up a self-sufficient colony of freed American slaves, as what had been accomplished in Freetown, the first batch of African-American settlers arrived in West Africa from the United States as a program of the U.S. government. They landed at Sherbro Island, now called Sierra Leone. Later, they were transferred to Dazoe Island, presently called Providence Island, which is part of the Mesurado River. These African-American people established a settlement in that place, which they called Christopolis.32, 33 The city was renamed Monrovia after James Monroe, who was president of the U.S.A. at that time. As a solution and an alternative to abolishing the institution of slavery in America, President James Monroe became a strong supporter of developing the city as a place to relocate previously enslaved black people from the United States of America and the Caribbean islands. A constitutional convention was called in Monrovia in 1845 to draft a document that would be adopted two years later, declaring the nation as an independent and sovereign Republic of Liberia.

At the beginning of the 20th century, there were already 4,000 residents in Monrovia, 2500 of which comprised Americo-Liberian. So, the city was divided into two: Monrovia proper, where Americo-Liberians resided and Krutown, where ethnic Krus, Bassas and Grebos resided.34 Due to economic progress in Monrovia, proper ethnic groups from Liberia's interior began looking for jobs beginning in 1926, which caused the increase of population of Monrovia to 10,000 residents in 1937.35

The Organisation of African Unity, chaired by William Tolbert, then president of Liberia, conducted their conference near Monrovia in 1979. Despite Tolbert's fruitful rule in Liberia, establishing public housing and decreasing college tuition by 50%, his government was overthrown by a military coup in 1980 led by Samuel Doe. From then on, Liberia was beleaguered by civil wars. The first civil war occurred between 1989 and 1997, and the second civil war between 1999 and 2003, which resulted in the destruction of numerous buildings in Monrovia. The conflicts came to a halt when, in 2002, a certain woman, Leymah Gbowee, organised Women of Liberia Mass Action for Peace, where they gathered in the marketplace to pray and sing peace songs.36

Monrovia, a prophecy is hurled upon you that you will be destroyed in the last days. God has destined you for your total destruction in the last days. **Your day, Monrovia, will be on August 14, 2090, a Monday at 9:08 P.M. Strong, violent earthquakes and a tsunami will strike you and will be followed by a rain of consuming fire.** The only thing that can save you is for you to repent of the sin you have committed and never commit sin again. Return to God through the Lord Jesus Christ, and pray always. **It says in Psalm 21:10 "You will make of them a blazing furnace, O Lord, when you appear. You will strike them down in your wrath, your fire will engulf and burn them up." For this, God has this to say in Isaiah 44:26: "I confirm the word of my servant and carry out the plan announced by my messengers…"**

In Isaiah 45:22-24, God says this to you: "Turn to me and be saved, all you from the ends of the earth, for I am God and there is no other. By my own self I swear it, and what comes from my mouth is truth, a word that will not be revoked. Before me every knee will bend, by me every tongue will swear, saying, 'In Yahweh alone are righteousness and strength.'"

Here are some of your places and structures that will be destroyed:

Monrovia Skyline

Liberian Capitol Building

Broad Street, Monrovia, at night

Dwellings along the Mesurado River

Aerial view of the University of Liberia

Roberts International Airport Terminal

Ankara, Turkey

Ankara is the capital city of Turkey. Historical records show that its ancient name was **Ancyra** and ANGORA.37 Situated in the central portion of Anatolia, the city is residence to 5.1 million in urban area and 5.7 million in Ankara Province 38,39, thus making it Turkey's second largest city after Istanbul.

The city already existed in antiquity, considering the fact that it became the capital city of the ancient Celtic state of Galatia (dated 280 – 64 B.C.) and later the capital city of the Roman province (25 BC-7th century). As evidence, there are numerous archaeological sites left by those empires that occupied the place, such as the Hattian, Hittite, Lydian, Phrygian, Galatian, Greek, Persian, Roman, Byzantine, and Ottoman. The Ottoman Empire first made it the capital of Anatolia Eyalet (1393-late 15th century), then the capital of Angora Eyalet (1827-1864) and the capital of Angora Vilayet (1867-1922). The historical centre of Ankara is a rocky hill rising 150 meters over the left bank of the Ankara River, a tributary of the Sakarya River. By length of time, only a few of Ankara's historical relics have survived. There are others that are well-preserved, such as Roman and

Ottoman architecture. Remarkable of which is the Temple of Augustus of Rome, dated 20 B.C.

Turkey, where Ankara lies, partly occupies the continent of Europe and partly the continent of Asia. It is a bridge between these two continents. It guards sea passage between the Mediterranean Sea and the Black Sea. It occupies an area in which seismic activity frequently occurs, and the country regularly experiences devastating earthquakes. Thrace is a place in Turkey where 5 % of its land belongs to Europe, and 95% belongs to Asia. Asiatic Turkey is bordered to the north by the Pontine Mountains and to the south by the Taurus Mountains.

As prophesied, Ankara will be destroyed by God in the last days. A strong, violent earthquake will strike it, then it will be followed by heavy rains of consuming fire. Its neighbouring cities, like Istanbul, Izmir, Adana and Bursa, will also be destroyed if they do not repent. Ankara, your day will be on August 9, 2091, a Thursday at 2:00 A.M. The only solution to this is for you to change your ways. Stop committing sin. Refrain from venerating graven images. Turn to God and ask for His forgiveness through our Lord Jesus Christ, and you will be saved. Other than that no more solution.

It says in Psalm 21:10 "You will make of them a blazing furnace, O Lord, when you appear. You will strike them down in your wrath, your fire will engulf and burn them up." For this, God has this to say in Isaiah 44:26: "I confirm the word of my servant and carry out the plan announced by my messengers..."

In Isaiah 45:22-24, God says this to you: "Turn to me and be saved, all you from the ends of the earth, for I am God and there is no other. By my own self I swear it, and what comes from my mouth is truth, a word that will not be revoked. Before me every knee will bend, by me every tongue will swear, saying, "In Yahweh alone are righteousness and strength.'"

Here are some of your places and structures that will be destroyed:

Ahmet Hamdi Akseki Mosque

Kocatepe Mosque

Armada Shopping Mall

Hittite Sun Course Monument

Victory Monument

Ankara railway station

Cengelhan Rahmi M. Koc Museum

A.T.G. Terminal, High-speed Rail

Kizilay Square, Emek Business Center

Anitkabir

Presidential Complex

Presidential Library

Esenboga International Airport

Ankara Opera House

YDA Center in Sogutozu, Ankara

Ankara Arena

Mausoleum of Mustafa Kemal Ataturk, Founder of Turkey

Ethnography Museum of Ankara

C.S.O. Ada Ankara

Nation's Garden in Ankara

State Art and Sculpture Museum

Ottoman houses in the Hamamonu District

Ankara Castle and citadel

Goksu Park

Atakule Shopping Mall

Rome, Italy

Map of Rome, Italy

Rome is the capital city of Italy. It is also the capital city of the Lazio region, the centre of the Metropolitan City of Rome Capital, and a special commune called Commune di Roma Capitale. Comprising 2,860,009 residents, Rome, with a land area of 1,285 square kilometres, is the most populated commune in Italy and the third most populous city in the European Union.[40] With a population of 4,355,725 people, the Metropolitan City of Rome is the most populous metropolitan city in the country.[41] Its metropolitan area is the third most populous in Italy.[42] Vatican City, the smallest country in the world, is an independent country within the boundaries of Rome.[43] Due to its geographic location, Rome is referred to as the City of Seven Hills and also as the "Eternal City."[44] Rome is generally considered the cradle of Western civilisation and Western Christian culture and the centre of the Roman Catholic Church.[45,46,47]

Rome Skyline

It is believed that Rome has been in existence for a period of 28 centuries, making it a major human settlement for a longer period of time, and it is one of the oldest continuously occupied cities in Europe.48 The population of Rome originated from a mixture of Latins, Etruscans, and Sabines. Successively, the city became the capital of the Roman Kingdom, Roman Republic, and Roman Empire.49

The country where Rome can be found is Italy. It is a country in southern Europe that comprises a large peninsula and the two islands of Sicily and Sardinia. The Alps form a natural boundary with its northern and western European neighbours. The Adriatic Sea to the east separates it from countries of former Yugoslavia. The Apennine Mountains form the backbone of Italy and extend the full length of the peninsula. Po Valley lies between the Alps and the Apennines. Sicily and Sardinia are largely mountainous. A large portion of Italy is geologically unstable due to its numerous active volcanoes, such as Etna, Vesuvius, and Stromboli. Rome and the Vatican, a country within a city, will be totally destroyed in the last days by God, for it is a place where the blood of martyrs, saints, and apostles are found.

All other places near Rome, such as the cities of Milan, Naples, Turin, Genoa, and Palermo, will also be destroyed if their inhabitants do not repent. The focal point of destruction is the city within the city — that is, the Vatican City. It will be totally destroyed by God because that is the place where many Christians were killed in many ways. The early Christians were forced to worship Roman Emperors. Those who did not worship the emperors were summarily killed in cold blood. Emperors Nero, Domitian, Titus, and Diocletian reduced early Christians to living torches and others were fed to hungry lions in Roman amphitheatres. They killed thousands upon thousands of early Christians and established their church called the Roman Catholic Church, making Peter the first Pope of Rome, whom they themselves tortured and then inhumanly killed.

It says in Hebrews 11:36-38: "Others suffered chains and prison. They were stoned, sawn in two. Killed by the sword. They fled from place to place with no other clothing than the skins of sheep and goats, lacking everything, afflicted, ill-treated. These men of whom the world was not worthy had to wander through wastelands and mountains, and take refuge in the dens of land." There being no more true Christians in the empire to oppose them, they claimed that their newly established Roman Catholic Church was a true church. This falsehood presented as truth and spread throughout the whole world was embraced and believed by people. They continued worshiping their highest pagan god, Jupiter, every December 25 and successfully fooled the whole world that our Lord Jesus Christ was born on December 25. That is a false doctrine and a wanton distortion of history.

In the last days, it would be known that the birthday of our Lord Jesus Christ is April 14, 12 B.C. Before our Lord Jesus Christ comes back, all those who sincerely follow him will no longer celebrate December 25 as His birthday. Only those who remain in Satan's fold will celebrate December 25 not as a Christmas day but as Jupitermas Day. Roman Catholics, or those who follow the doctrines of the Roman Catholic Church, are not Christians. They are Jupiterians because they celebrate the feast day of the highest pagan god, Jupiter, every December 25. In fact, the Roman Catholic Church was mainly established so that people would be forced to worship Roman Emperors at that time. Those true believers of our Lord Jesus Christ during the time of Imperial Rome, who refused to worship the emperors, were just killed right away.

Rome, the Eternal City and the city of Seven Hills (the Aventine Hill, the Caelian Hill, the Capitoline Hill, the Esquiline Hill, the Palatine Hill, the Quirinal Hill, and the Viminal Hill) and Vatican City, your last day in this world will be on January 15, 2091, a Monday at 7:49 P.M., says the Lord. A strong, violent earthquake will strike you and will be followed by a rain of consuming fire.

It says in Psalm 21:10, **"You will make of them a blazing furnace, O Lord, when you appear. You will strike them down in your wrath, your fire will engulf and burn them up."** For this, God has this to say in Isaiah 44:26: **"I confirm the word of my servant and carry out the plan announced by my messengers…"**

In Isaiah 45:22-24, God says this to you: **"Turn to me and be saved, all you from the ends of the earth, for I am God and there is no other. By my own self I swear it, and what comes from my mouth is truth, a word that will not be revoked. Before me every knee will bend, by me every tongue will swear, saying, 'In Yahweh alone are righteousness and strength.'"**

Here are some of your places and structures that will be destroyed:

Temple of Portunus

Ruins of the Roman Forum

Ancient-Imperial-Roman Palaces

The Imperial Fora

Colosseum

Fontana della Barcaccia

The Esquilino rione

Archbasilica of Saint John Lateran

Santa Maria Maggiore

153

Palazzo Senatorio on Capitoline Hill

St. Peter's Square in Vatican City

Palazzo del Quirinale

F.A.O. Headquarters in Rome

Palazzo Eni

Orizzonte Europa, B.N.L. Headquarters

Enel's Headquarters in Rome

Trnita del Monti

Piazza Navona

Sapienza University of Rome

Biblioteca Casanatense

Palazzo della Civilta Italiana

Trevi Fountain

Flaminio Obelisk, Piazza del Popolo

Ponte Vittorio Emanuele II

Teatro dell' Opera di Roma

Via Condotti

Cinecitta Studios

Stadio Olimpico

Stadio dei Marmi

Rome-Fiumicino Airport

Port of Civitavecchia

Victor Emmanuel II Monument

Colosseum

Saint Peter's Basilica

Castel Sant' Angelo

Dhaka (Dacca), Bangladesh

Map of Dhaka, Bangladesh

Dhaka, formerly spelled as Dacca, is the largest city in Bangladesh and the seventh most densely populated city on earth. With a population of 10.2 million people in 2022, it is considered as megacity. In the metropolitan area, the population is over 22.4 million people.50,51,52 It is categorically considered the most densely populated built-up urban area in the world.53,54 As a major Muslim–majority city, Dhaka, displays its importance in Eastern South Asia in the field of culture, economy, and sciences. Situated in the Ganges Delta, it is bounded by Buriganga, Turag, Dhaleshwari, and Shitalakshya rivers.

Since the first millenium, Dhaka has been inhabited by Muslim Bengalese-speaking people. Being developed in the 17th century and made the capital of the province with a commercial center during the

Mughal Empire, Dhaka was developed as a modern city. For seventy-five years, Dhaka became the capital of proto-industrialised Mughal-Bengal between 1608-1639 and 1660-1704. It became the center of Muslin trade in Bengal, which enriched its economy for quite some time. It improved its economy and infrastructure during the British rule. In 1962, it was officially declared as the legislative capital of Pakistan. After the Liberation War in 1971, it became the capital city of independent Bangladesh. In 2008, Dhaka celebrated its 400 years as a municipal city.55,56,57

The city of Dhaka became sinful and wicked as its economy improved. Their wickedness reached the sky, so God has decided that the city will be totally destroyed. **Dhaka, your day will be on September 8, 2090, a Friday at 7:42 P.M. An earthquake and rains of consuming fire will destroy you completely.** In the absence of sincere repentance, its neighbouring cities, Chittagong and Khulna, will also be destroyed.

It says in Psalm 21:10, "You will make of them a blazing furnace, O Lord, when you appear. You will strike them down in your wrath, your fire will engulf and burn them up." For this, God has this to say in Isaiah 44:26: "I confirm the word of my servant and carry out the plan announced by my messengers..."

In Isaiah 45:22-24, God says this to you: "Turn to me and be saved, all you from the ends of the earth, for I am God and there is no other. By my own self I swear it, and what comes from my mouth is truth, a word that will not be revoked. Before me every knee will bend, by me every tongue will swear, saying, 'In Yahweh alone are righteousness and strength.'"

Here are some of your places and structures that will be destroyed:

Skyline of Motjheel

Sangsad Bhaban

Absan Manzil

Lalbagh Fort

Typical Neighbourhood in Dhaka

Aerial view of Dhaka's main CBD

North Dhaka

Nimtali

Nagar Bhaban

Bangladesh Bank Building

Uttara

Kawran Baza

Kamal Ataturk Avenue

Haturia House

Curzon Hall

Mirpur-Banani Flyover

Bangabandhu National Stadium

Bangla Academy

Mirpur Indoor Stadium

Dakar, Senegal

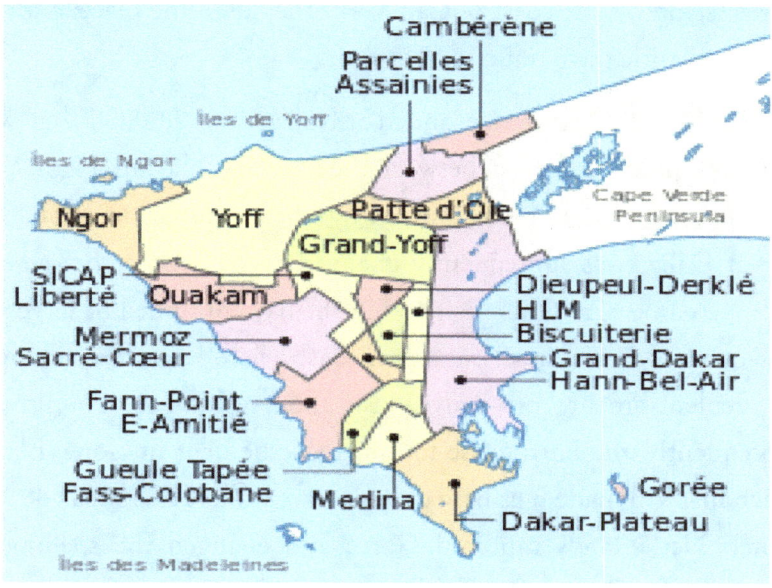

Map of Dakar

Dakar is the capital and the largest city of Senegal. With a land area of 83 square kilometers, Dakar city proper has a population of 1,030594 and 3.94 million in the metropolitan area based on a 2021 population survey.58

Dakar

In the early part of the 15th century, Portugal colonised the area around Dakar. Thereafter, the Portuguese established a stronghold on Goree Island off the coast of Cap-Vert. They used the place as a base for the Atlantic slave trade.

In 1444, the Portuguese landed at Dakar Bay.59,60,61 There was a friendly, peaceful contact between the natives (Ouakam, Ngor, Yoff, and Hann) and the Portuguese led by Diogo Gomes in 1456. The Bay of Dakar was subsequently changed to " *Angra de Bezeguiche*" after the name of a local chieftain.62 The bay continued to serve as a stop-over for Portuguese India Armadas, where large fleets stopped for replenishment of provisions and repair of equipment. Subsequently, the Portuguese founded a settlement in Goree Island, which in 1536 made it as base of their slave trade. Later, in 1588, the United Netherlands captured Goree and changed the spelling to Goeree, after Goeree-Overflakkee in the Netherlands. As the two combatants fought for supremacy over the island, the Portuguese and the Dutch switched control of the island several times until England, led by Admiral Robert Holmes, conquered the place on January 23, 1664.

Finally, in 1677, France, by its might, took control of the island and abolished the slave trade. Heretofore, France annexed the mainland area, including Dakar, and converted it into a major regional port and major city of the French Colonial Empire in the 19th century. Also in 1902, Dakar was made the capital of French West Africa, replacing Saint Louis. Between 1959 and 1960, Dakar was made capital by the Mali Federation for a short duration, as this federation did not last long. Eventually, upon gaining independence as a Republic, Senegal named Dakar as its official capital in 1960.

As scientifically observed, Dakar is one of 12 major African cities that would be most severely affected by future sea level rise.63,64 It is believed that this sea level rise will continue for many years as climate change worsens.64

Despite Dakar's geographical uncertainty, the city is already sighted by God to be destroyed in the last days because of its sinfulness and wickedness. The other cities near Dakar, like Kaolack, Thies, and St. Louis, will also be destroyed if they do not repent and go back to God's fold through our Lord Jesus Christ. **Dakar, your day will be on July 7, 2090, a Friday at 4:18 A.M. An earthquake and rain of consuming fire will fall on you, resulting in your total destruction.**

It says in Psalm 21:10, "You will make of them a blazing furnace, O Lord, when you appear. You will strike them down in your wrath, your fire will engulf and burn them up." For this, God has this to say in Isaiah 44:26: "I confirm the word of my servant and carry out the plan announced by my messengers…"

In Isaiah 45:22-24, God says this to you: "Turn to me and be saved, all you from the ends of the earth, for I am God and there is no other. By my own self I swear it, and what comes from my mouth is truth, a word that will not be revoked. Before me every knee will bend, by me every tongue will swear, saying, 'In Yahweh alone are righteousness and strength.

Here are some of your places and structures that will be destroyed:

Blaise Diagne International Airport

IFAN Museum of African Arts

Assenblee nationale

Grand Mosque of Dakar

Deux Mamelles

Residential area Mermoz

Dakar Central Station

Mosque of the Divinity

Ngor Beach

Gueule Tapee

London, England

Map of London, England

London is the capital and the largest city of England and the United Kingdom, with a population of more or less 8.8 million.65 It should be noted that London does not hold a city status in the same way as other cities in the United Kingdom granted by the crown. A major residence for nearly two thousand years, London is situated on the River Thames in South East England at the head of a 50-mile estuary down to the North Sea. It was founded by Romans as Londinium, where the financial center and trades were put up.66,67 Formerly, the seat of national government and parliament were held in Westminster City, situated in the western portion of London. The name "London" since the 19th century also pertains to the metropolis around the area and historically separated from counties of

Middlesex, Essex, Surrey, Kent, and Hertfordshire, which comprised largely Greater London since 1965.68,69 As a major global city,70 London serves as a strong influence in world art, entertainment, fashion, commerce and finance, education, health care, media, science and technology, tourism, transport, and communications.71,72

London has been in existence since 4800 B.C. based on discovered remains of Bronze Age artifact radiocarbon dated to 1750-1285 B.C. and the other timber discovered in 2010 with radiocarbon dated to 4800-4500 B.C.73,74,75 While London has tasted the fruit of its economic progress and advancement, it has also experienced several trials in the past that claimed lives of its residents. In 1848, cholera epidemics claimed the lives of 14,000 residents, and in 1866, there were 6,000 casualties due to the same epidemic.76 The city also became a target of bombing during the suffragette and arson campaign for two years, between 1912 and 1914, which destroyed Westminster Abbey and St. Paul's Cathedral.77 London was also bombed by German invaders during the First World War and during the Second World War, the Blitzkrieg style of the German *Luftwaffe*, which killed more than 30,000 residents and destroyed numerous houses and buildings across London.78 In a series of terrorist attacks, three London underground trains and a double-decker bus were bombed on July 7, 2005.79

City of London (Showing Houses of Parliament; Elizabeth Tower; London Eyer; the Shard and Canary Wharf

With the quantum leap of advancement and progress that London has achieved in the course of time, it also grows in its sinfulness and wickedness, which God detests. It is for this reason that London is doomed to be destroyed in the last days. **Your day, London, will be on July 6, 2090, a Thursday at 8:46 P.M. Your 32 boroughs will also be destroyed if you do not repent of your sin and continue committing sin before God's eyes. Earthquakes and rains of consuming fire will destroy you completely.**

It says in Psalm 21:10, "You will make of them a blazing furnace, O Lord, when you appear. You will strike them down in your wrath, your fire will engulf and burn them up." For this, God has this to say in Isaiah 44:26: "I confirm the word of my servant and carry out the plan announced by my messengers…"

In Isaiah 45:22-24, God says this to you: "Turn to me and be saved, all you from the ends of the earth, for I am God and there is no other. By my own self I swear it, and what comes from my mouth is truth, a word that will not be revoked. Before me every knee will bend, by me every tongue will swear, saying, 'In Yahweh alone are righteousness and strength.'"

Here are some of your places and structures that will be destroyed:

SIS Building

London, as seen from Primrose Hill

East Wing of Buckingham Palace

10 Downing Street, the official residence of Prime Minister

St. Paul's Cathedral

BAPS Shri Swaminarayan Mandir London

National Gallery

St. Maryle-Bow Church

London Stock Exchange at Paternoster

Bank of England

British Museum

Heathrow Airport

St. Pancras International

University College London

Imperial College London

Royal Central School of Speech & Drama

Royal Observatory, Greenwich

Harrods in Knightsbridge

Shakespeare's Globe

Sherlock Holmes Museum

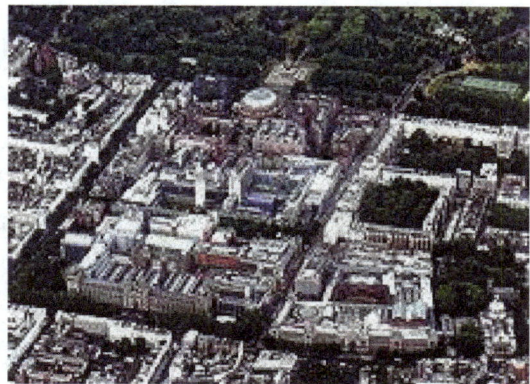

Aerial view of Albertopolis

Royal Albert Hall

Abbey Road Studios

Hyde Park

Wembley Stadium

Centre Court Wimbledon

Twickenham Stadium

Nelson's Column

Palace of Westminster

London Eye

Canary Wharf

Athens (Athinai), Greece

Map of Athens, Greece

Athens is a major coastal urban area in the Mediterranean. It is the largest city and the capital of Greece. As the eighth largest urban area in the European Union, Athens has a population of 3,059,764 in urban areas and 3,638,281 in metropolitan areas.[80] As the capital of the Attica region, Athens is one of the world's oldest cities with recorded history ranging more than 3400 years.[81] It is believed that Athens had been inhabited by people since the 11th century and 7th millennia B.C. The place is called "The City of Wisdom," named after Athena, the goddess of wisdom of ancient Greece.[82]

In classical Athens, it was one of the most powerful city-states in ancient Greece. Being the center of democracy, arts, education, and philosophy, it was highly influential in ancient Rome and in the European continent.[83,84,85] It is considered the cradle of Western civilisation and the natal place of democracy.[86,87] Today, Athens is a great cosmopolitan metropolis and the center of economy, finance, industry, maritime, politics, and culture in Greece.88 Based on observation and study of the Globalisation and World Cities Research Network, Athens is a Beta-status global city since it is one of the biggest economic centers in Southeastern Europe. Also, it has a large financial sector, and its port, Piraeus, is the second busiest passenger port in Europe and the 13th largest container port on earth.89,90 ,91 Still existing in Athens are the heritage of the classical period, such as the Parthenon, which is considered a landmark of Western culture. It also retains monuments from the Roman, Byzantine, and Ottoman periods. The Acropolis of Athens and the medieval Daphni Monastery are two UNESCO World Heritage Sites.

Acropolis of Athens

With the prosperity and advancement of Greece in the fields of arts, economy, finance, industry, politics, and culture, people in the city became sinful and wicked, which God dislikes the most. For this, Athens is set to be destroyed in the last days. Its neighbouring cities, such as Iraklion, Patras, Piraeus, and Thessaloniki, will also be destroyed if they do not repent. Thessaloniki has abandoned the teachings of Paul, whose teachings would be able to save them if applied in life. **Athens, your day is July 18, 2091, a Wednesday at 8:41 P.M. Earthquakes, tsunamis, and rains of consuming fire will destroy you completely.**

It says in Psalm 21:10, "You will make of them a blazing furnace, O Lord, when you appear. You will strike them down in your wrath, your fire will engulf and burn them up." For this, God has this to say in Isaiah 44:26: "I confirm the word of my servant and carry out the plan announced by my messengers..."

In Isaiah 45:22-24, God says this to you: "Turn to me and be saved, all you from the ends of the earth, for I am God and there is no other. By my own self I swear it, and what comes from my mouth is truth, a word that will not be revoked. Before me every knee will bend, by me every tongue will swear, saying, 'In Yahweh alone are righteousness and strength.'"

Here are some of your places and structures that will be destroyed:

Zappeion

Metropolitan Cathedral

Monastiraki

Old Royal Palace

Academy of Athens

Stavros Niarchos Foundation Cultural Center

The Acropolis Hill

Tower of the Winds

Byzantine Church of the Holy Apostles

Frankish Tower of the Acropolis

Tzistarakis Mosque

Entry of King Otto

Vila Atlantis

Ermou Street

OTE Headquarters in Marousi

Athens International Airport

National Archaeological Museum

Acropolis Museum

Museum of the Ancient Agora

Old Parliament House

Kallimarmaron

Stavros Niarchos

Agia Sophia Stadium

Athens Olympic Sports Complex

Valletta, Malta

Map of Velleta, Malta

Valletta is an administrative unit and capital of Malta. Situated on the main island between two harbors, Marsamxett Harbour to the west and Grand Harbour to the East, its population in the 2014 survey was 6,444.92 According to the record in 2020 of Eurostat, the urban area and metropolitan region, which covered the whole island, comprised a population of 480,134. 93,94 As the southernmost capital of Europe, Valletta occupies an area of 61 square kilometers or 24 square miles, making it the smallest capital city in the European Union.

The buildings in Valletta date back to the 16th century and were mainly erected by Knights Hospitaller. The city was named after Jean Parisot de Vallette, who successfully defended the island from Ottoman invaders during the Great Siege of Malta in 1565. It was officially declared a capital city on March 18, 1571, when Grand Master Pierre de Monte transferred his seat at Fort St. Angelo in Birgu to Grandmaster's Palace in Valletta.

The history of Valletta is one of being conquered all the time by strong forces. In 1798, Valletta was invaded by France and expelled therefrom the order of Malta. France occupied Valletta for a long time, making the place their military stronghold. The Maltese put up a revolt but to no avail, for the weapons of France were much heavier than those of the natives. In September 1800, France was booted out from the island by Britain. During the British rule, Valletta improved its structures. Some projects included widening gates, demolishing and rebuilding structures, widening new houses, and installing civic projects.

Small as it is, Valletta is being sighted by God to be completely destroyed in the last days as it has become sinful already and wicked. Its residents have not repented of their sins. Instead, they continue committing sin without respect for God. **Valletta, your day will be on July 4, 2091, a Wednesday at 7:41 P.M. Earthquakes, rains of consuming fire, and a tsunami will strike you, leading to your total destruction.**

It says in Psalm 21:10, "You will make of them a blazing furnace, O Lord, when you appear. You will strike them down in your wrath, your fire will engulf and burn them up." For this, God has this to say in Isaiah 44:26: "I confirm the word of my servant and carry out the plan announced by my messengers…"

In Isaiah 45:22-24, God says this to you: "Turn to me and be saved, all you from the ends of the earth, for I am God and there is no other. By my own self I swear it, and what comes from my mouth is truth, a word that will not be revoked. Before me every knee will bend, by me every tongue will swear, saying, 'In Yahweh alone are righteousness and strength.'"

Here are some of your places and structures that will be destroyed:

Saluting Battery

Grand Harbour

Barrakka Gardens

Grandmaster's Palace

City Walls

Royal Opera House

Auberge de Castille

Renzo Piano's Parliament House

Renzo Piano's Valletta City Gate

Mediterranean Conference Centre

Is-Suq tal-Belt

Auberge d'Italie

Tritons' Fountain

St. John's Co-Cathedral

Jakarta, Indonesia

Map of Jakarta

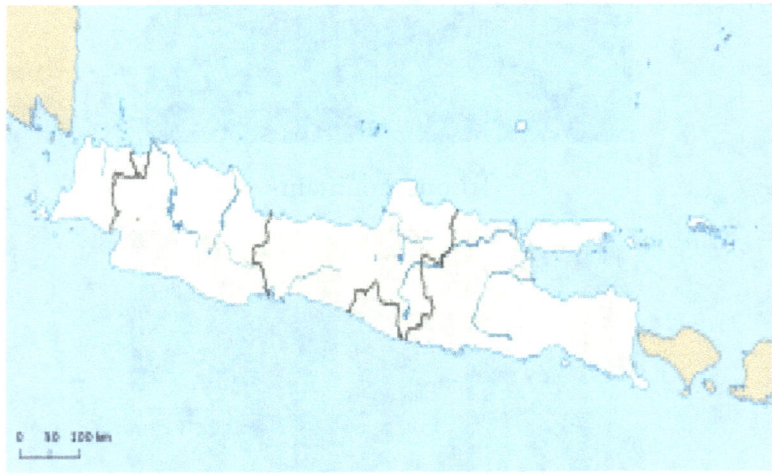

Map of Indonesia

Jakarta is a special capital region of Indonesia. In the years 397-1527, it was named Sunda Kelapa under the Sunda Kingdom; between years

1527-1619 inclusive, it was called Jayakarta; in years inclusive 1619-1942, it was called Batavia; in years inclusive 1942-1972, it was called Djakata. It has only been called Jakarta from 1972 up to the present. Situated on the northwest coast of Java, the world's most populous island, Jakarta is the largest metropole in Southeast Asia and presently acts as the diplomatic capital of ASEAN (Association of Southeast Asian Nations). It is bordered by two provinces: West Java to the south and east and, since the year 2000, Banten to the west. Its coastline faces the Java Sea to the north and shares a maritime border with Lampung to the west.

Special Capital Region of Jakarta

Jakarta is the center of Indonesia in terms of economy, culture, and politics. With a population of 10,679,951 in the year 2022, it achieves a province-level status in terms of number of residents.95 Jakarta covers only 661.23 square kilometers in land area, which is a comparably smaller area than any province of Indonesia. With its metropolitan area of 9,957.08 square kilometers, which includes the satellite cities of Bogor, Depok, Tangerang, South Tangerang, and

Bekasi, with an estimated population of 35 million residents as of 2022, it has become the largest urban area in Indonesia and second largest on Earth after Tokyo, Japan. In the Human Development Index, Jakarta ranks first among the provinces of Indonesia. With business and employment opportunities it can offer, coupled with its ability to provide a potentially higher standard of living compared to other parts of the country, Jakarta has attracted migrants from across the country, thus making the place a melting pot of diverse cultures.

As one of the oldest inhabited cities in Southeast Asia, Jakarta became an important trading port for the Sunda Kingdom in the fourth century. It was named Batavia by the Dutch East Indies as its de facto capital. It became a city within West Java until 1960 when its status was changed to a province with the distinction of a special capital region. As a province, its government comprises five administrative cities and one administrative regency. Being the seat of the ASEAN secretariat, Jakarta is categorised as an alpha world city.

Presently, Jakarta faces some problems that the government has to address quickly, such as rapid urban growth in population, ecological breakdown, gridlocked traffic, congestion, and flooding caused by subsidence. Jakarta is sinking up to 17 cm (6.7 inches) every year, being one of the fastest-sinking capitals on earth. The government has envisioned transferring Indonesia's capital to Nusantara, a province of East Kalimantan on Borneo Island. Such a move was already approved by the parliament on January 18, 2022.

For the country itself, Indonesia is the biggest country-archipelago in Southeast Asia, comprising 13,667 islands scattered across the Indian and Pacific Oceans. It is the world's fourth most populous country. The province of Kalimantan is the largest land mass located on Borneo Island. With 130 active volcanoes connected to the Pacific

Ring of Fire, the country always experiences frequent earthquakes, especially in southern islands. Politically, the country is seemingly unstable due to numerous human rights abuses and the illegal annexation of East Timor in 1975.

For Jakarta, as its economy grows, the sinfulness and wickedness of its residents grow also, which God extremely detests. Their predominant religion, which is Islam, hinders them from knowing God and our Lord Jesus Christ. For this, Jakarta will be destroyed by God in the last of days. Its neighbouring cities, which are parts of its metropolitan area, such as Bogor, Depok, Tangerang, South Tangerang, and Bekasi, will also be destroyed if they will not repent. **Jakarta, your day will be on August 4, 2091, a Saturday at 3:30 A.M. Strong, violent earthquakes, tsunamis, and a rain of consuming fire will strike you, leading to your total destruction.**

It says in Psalm 21:10, "You will make of them a blazing furnace, O Lord, when you appear. You will strike them down in your wrath, your fire will engulf and burn them up." For this, God has this to say in Isaiah 44:26: "I confirm the word of my servant and carry out the plan announced by my messengers…"

In Isaiah 45:22-24, God says this to you: "Turn to me and be saved, all you from the ends of the earth, for I am God and there is no other. By my own self I swear it, and what comes from my mouth is truth, a word that will not be revoked. Before me every knee will bend, by me every tongue will swear, saying, 'In Yahweh alone are righteousness and strength.'"

Here are some of your places and structures that will be destroyed:

Aerial view of North Jakarta

Betawi House at Taman Mini

Museum Bank Indonesia in Kota Tua

Wisma 46

Bundaran HI at Menteng District

Monas

Jakarta History Museum

Gelora Bung Karno Stadium

Istiqlal Mosque

Immanuel's Protestant Church

University of Indonesia

Polda Metro Jaya at Kebayoran Baru

SCBD South Jakarta

Jakarta City Hall

Jakarta, as seen from Monas

Jakarta Inner Ring Road

Headquarters Bank of Indonesia

CSW-ASEAN TOD

Jakarta Cathedral

Stockholm, Sweden

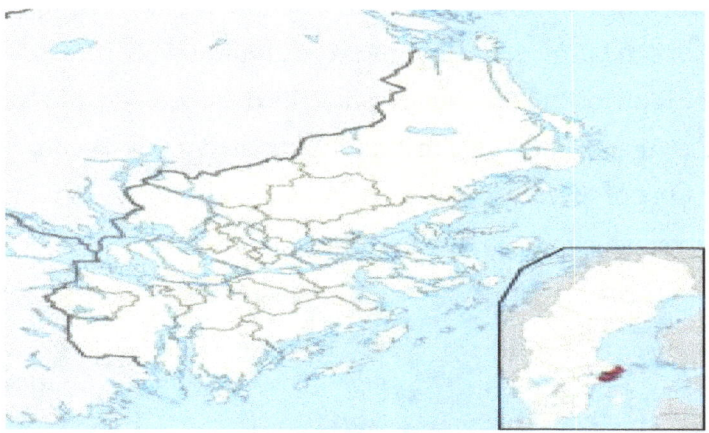

Map of Stockholm, Sweden

Stockholm is the capital of Sweden. It is the most populated city in Sweden and the largest urban area in Nordic countries. More or less, there are one million residents in the municipality,96 2.1 million residents in urban areas, and 2.4 million residents in metropolitan areas.97 The city extends across 14 islands where Lake Malaren flows toward the Baltic Sea. Stockholm archipelago is seen as an island chain outside the city going east along the coastline. History tells that Stockholm has been inhabited since the Stone Age Period, i.e., in the 6th millenium B.C., and was founded as a city in 1252 by Birger Jarl, a Swedish statesman. The city is the seat of the local government of Stockholm County. Further, history tells that after the Ice Age, estimated at around 8000 BC, there were already numerous inhabitants living in the Stockholm area. But when temperatures became the coldest, the residents transferred to the South. Thousands of years later, as the ground thawed, the climate became tolerable for occupancy, and the lands became fertile, people began to migrate back to the North. Then, in 1000 C.E., people began to build Stockholm under the Vikings' leadership in an archipelago between the Baltic Sea and Lake Malaren. They created trade routes that were conducive to business and commerce, thus improving their economy. The location of Stockholm was described in legends and sagas of Norse as Agnafit and in Heimskringla as related to the legendary King Agne. One of Sweden's major trade centers during the Vikings Age was Birka, which was located near Stockholm.98

View of STOCKHOLM from Avicii Arena

The earliest mention of Stockholm dates back to 1252, when time mines in Bergslagen made it an important place for the iron trade. "Stock" in Swedish means log; in German, it is fortification. The second word, "holm," means islet. Hence, Stockholm is the fortification of an islet, which refers to the fortification of the islet Helgeandsholmen, which is located in central Stockholm. The city was founded by Birger Jarl, according to Eric Chronicles, to protect Sweden from sea invasions by Karelians in the summer of 1187.99 As a consequence of the Baltic trade of the Hanseatic League, the city rose to economic prominence. In 1296, it established strong economic and cultural relations with Lubeck, Hamburg, Gdansk, Visby, Tallinn, and Riga.100 Half of Stockholm's 24-member city council were German-speaking burghers, which shows the utmost importance of the German language in medieval Nordic trade and commerce.

Today, Stockholm is the center of Sweden's culture, media, politics, and economy. It accounts for over a third of the country's Gross Domestic Product and is among the top 10 regions in Europe by GDP per capita.101,102 Being the largest in Scandinavia, it has developed into a prime center for corporate headquarters in the Nordic region.103,104 Stockholm is categorised as a global city. Many of Europe's top-ranking universities can be found in the city, such as Karolinska Institute, Stockholm School of Economics, KTH Royal Institute of Technology, and Stockholm University.105

With the advancement of Stockholm's technology and science and its progress in economy, banking and finance, and politics, Stockholm has become sinful and wicked before God's eyes. People in the city never stop doing sinful acts, because of which God decided that it would be destroyed in the last days. The only recourse for this city is to stop committing sin and always worship God, obeying his will, stopping venerating graven images or printed images, and worshiping God in spirit and truth. **Nearby cities, such as Goteborg, Malmo, Uppsala, and Orebro, will also be destroyed if they do not repent. Stockholm, your day will be on July 7, 2091, a Saturday at 4:30 P.M. An earthquake and rains of consuming fire will completely destroy you.**

It says in Psalm 21:10, **"You will make of them a blazing furnace, O Lord, when you appear. You will strike them down in your wrath, your fire will engulf and burn them up."** For this, God has this to say in Isaiah 44:26: **"I confirm the word of my servant and carry out the plan announced by my messengers..."**

In Isaiah 45:22-24, God says this to you: **"Turn to me and be** saved, all you from the ends of the earth, for I am God and there is no other. By my own self I swear it, and what comes from my mouth is truth, a word that will not be revoked. Before me every knee will bend, by me every tongue will swear, saying, 'In Yahweh alone are righteousness and strength.'"

Here are some of your places and structures that will be destroyed:

Gamla Stan

Stockholm City Hall

Kastellet

Kista Science Tower

Avicii Arena

Stockholm Palace

Victoria Tower

KTH Royal Institute of Technology

Aerial photo of Stockholm University

Strandvagen

Djurgardsbron Bridge

Norstedt Building

Royal Dramatic Theatre

Gamla Stan Station

Aula Medica, The Karolinska Institute

Friends Arena

Soder Torn

Ericsson Headquarters

Norra lanken

Tele 2 Arena

Stockholm Public Library

Stockholm Central Station

Oslo, Norway

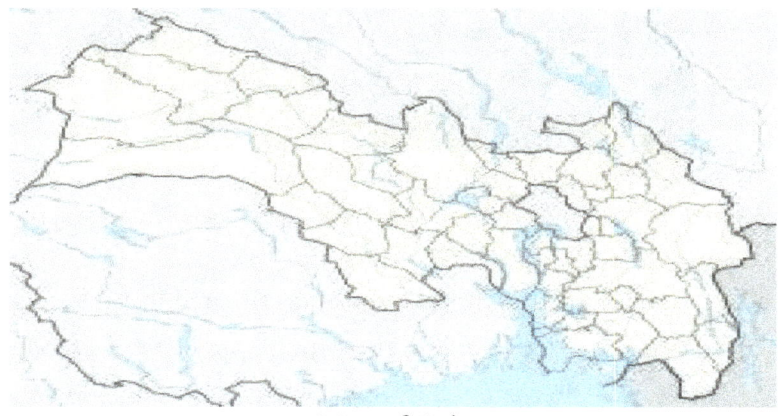

Map of Oslo

Oslo Surrounded by Viken county

Oslo is the capital and the most densely populated city in Norway. It is categorised as both a county and a municipality. As a municipality, it comprised 709,037 residents in the 2022 survey, while as a city urban area, it comprised 1,064,235 residents in 2022.106 In the metropolitan area, it has a population of more or less 1,546,706 in 2021. 107

The City of Oslo

The area that includes modern Oslo was situated in Viken during the Viking Age, a place in the northernmost province of Denmark. Such a place was alternately controlled by Danish and Norwegian kings during the Middle Ages. Denmark's claim on the area lasted only until 1241. Based on Norse sagas, Harald Hardrada founded Oslo in 1049.108 Unearthed archaeological finds, however, comprising burial remains carbon-dated 1000 A.D., deny beliefs that Oslo was founded in 1049 but instead in 1000 A.D. It was founded and named Anslo and was converted into *kaupstad,* or a trading center, by Harald Hardrada in the year 1048. It was raised to the bishopric category in 1070 and a capital under Haakon V of Norway around 1300. The city seemingly reduced its influence when it had a union with Denmark in the years 1397 to 1523 and again from 1536 to 1814. During the reign of King Christian IV in 1624, the city was destroyed by fire and rebuilt near Akershus Fortress and named Christiana in honor of the king.

Oslo commune

On January 1, 1838, it became a municipality or *formannskapsdistrikt*. It became the capital of Norway between the years 1814 and 1905 inclusive, including the time when there was a union between Sweden and Norway. At the beginning of 1877, the city was called Kristiana in government usage and was adopted by municipal authorities in 1897. It was only in 1925 that the city was renamed Oslo after incorporating the village, retaining its former name. In 1948, Oslo merged with Aker, a municipality surrounding the capital that was 27 times larger, thus creating a very much larger Oslo municipality.

In the course of time, Oslo became Norway's center of economy and government. Presently, it is a hub for Norwegian trade, banking, industry, commerce, and shipping. Consequently, it has become an important center for maritime industries and trade in Europe. Oslo is now the home to many companies in the maritime sector, some of which are among the world's largest shipping companies, shipbrokers, and brokers in maritime insurance. It is now the pilot city of the Council of Europe and European Commission intercultural cities program.

Considered a global city, Oslo was ranked "Beta World City" in studies made by the Globalisation and World Cities Study Group and Network in 2008.109 Also, it ranked number one in terms of quality of living among large European cities in the European Cities of Future 2012 report by *fDi* magazine.110 Likewise, a survey made by ECA International in 2011 ranked Oslo as the second most expensive city in the world for living expenses after Tokyo, Japan.111

With its excellent growth in economy, trade, banking, and finance, Oslo's residents are doing activities that depart them from God, making the place sinful and wicked. The city grows more sinful and multiplies its sinfulness through the activities of a group called LGBTQ. God expresses his extreme anger on this group as its members constantly do immoral, sinful acts and activities. The presence of LGBTQ in Oslo aggravates the sins of people there. As this proud city is already dirty and sinful before God's eyes, Oslo is doomed for destruction in the last of the days. In fact, of all the forty cities in the world that are eyed to be totally destroyed by God, Oslo ranks first to be entirely destroyed. No amount of repentance, as they have no sense of penitence, can ever change God's mind. Its neigbouring cities, Bergen, Trondheim, and Stavanger, will also be destroyed if they do not repent. **Oslo, pay attention to the message of God; your day will be on July 8, 2064, a Tuesday at 2:30 A.M. A Violent earthquake will strike you and will be followed by a rain of consuming fire.**

It says in Psalm 21:10, "You will make of them a blazing furnace, O Lord, when you appear. You will strike them down in your wrath, your fire will engulf and burn them up." For this, God has this to say in Isaiah 44:26: "I confirm the word of my servant and carry out the plan announced by my messengers..."

In Isaiah 45:22-24, God says this to you: "Turn to me and be saved, all you from the ends of the earth, for I am God and there is no other. By my own self I swear it, and what comes from my mouth is truth, a word that will not be revoked. Before me every knee will bend, by me every tongue will swear, saying, 'In Yahweh alone are righteousness and strength.'"

Here are some of your places and structures that will be destroyed:

National Theatre

Flytoghet

Victoria Terrasse

Uranienborg Church

MUNCH Museum

Trafikanten Tower

Norway Panorama

Mollergata 19

Tram

Frogner Park

Holmenkollen Ski Jump

Bryggetorget

Oslo Harbour

Oslo Central Station

Oslo Opera House

Akershus Fortress

Jembanetorget

Astrup Fearnley Museum

Royal Palace

Wessel Square

Fjerdingen

Stalverksparken

Lovenskiold

Meltzer

Parliament of Norway

Oslo City Hall

Bjorvika

University of Oslo, Faculty of Law

B.I. Norwegian Business School

Library, University of Oslo

Nobel Peace Center

National Theatre

Norway Supreme Court

Gronland Police Station

Oslo Central Station

National Theatre Station

Budapest, Hungary

Map of Budapest, Hungary

Budapest is the capital and the most densely populated city in Hungary. It is the ninth largest city in the European Union in terms of population within the city area and the largest city on the Danube River. 112,113,114 Comprising an area of about 525 square kilometers or 203 square miles, it has a population of 1,752,286 more or less.115 Being the center of the metropolitan area, Budapest serves as a city and a county at the same time. With an area of 7,626 square kilometers or 2,944 square miles and a population of 3,303,786, constituting 33% of the total population of Hungary, it is considered a primate city.116;117

Budapest's history started when the Celtic settlement, built before 1 A.D., was converted into the Roman town of Aquincum, 118;119, and made capital of Lower Pannonia.118 In the 19th century, 120 Hungarians settled in the area only to find out that Mongols had destroyed it in 1241-42.121 They re-established the place and converted it into the center of Renaissance humanist culture in the 15th century.122;123;124 In 1526, the Battle of Mohacs became the prelude of Ottoman rule, which lasted nearly 150 years. 125 Following Buda's reconquest in 1686, the region joined a new age of prosperity. Thereafter, Pest Buda became a global city as a result of the unification of Obuda and Pest on November 17, 1873, acquiring the name "Budapest" as the new capital.117; 126 Also, Budapest became co-capital of Austro-Hungarian Empire,127 a powerful empire that was dissolved after World War I in 1918. The city became an arena of bloodshed during the Hungarian Revolution of 1848, during the Battle of Budapest in 1945, and the Hungarian Revolution of 1956. 128;129

Panorama of Budapest

As a global city, Budapest has become the center of commerce, finance, media, art, fashion, research, technology, education, and entertainment. 130;131 Being Hungary's financial center, Budapest also serves as the headquarters of the European Institute of Innovation and Technology132, European Police College, 133 and the foreign office of China Investment Promotion Agency. 134 In the field of education, more than 40 colleges and universities are located in Budapest. 135;136

Having achieved prosperity in the course of time, Budapest and its people seemingly forgot God and performed acts and continuously commit acts that are sinful before God's eyes, thereby making the place a wicked city. For this, God has decided to destroy it in the last days. Its neighbouring cities of Debrecen, Miskolc, Pecs, and Szeged will also be destroyed if they do not repent. **Budapest, your day will be on August 11, 2091, a Saturday at 11:05 P.M. A Violent earthquake and a rain of consuming fire will fall on you, leading to your total destruction.**

It says in Psalm 21:10, "You will make of them a blazing furnace, O Lord, when you appear. You will strike them down in your wrath, your fire will engulf and burn them up." For this, God has this to say in Isaiah 44:26: "I confirm the word of my servant and carry out the plan announced by my messengers…"

In Isaiah 45:22-24, God says this to you: "Turn to me and be saved, all you from the ends of the earth, for I am God and there is no other. By my own self I swear it, and what comes from my mouth is truth, a word that will not be revoked. Before me every knee will bend, by me every tongue will swear, saying, 'In Yahweh alone are righteousness and strength.'"

Here are some of your places and structures that will be destroyed:

Hungarian Parliament

Buda Castle and the Chain Bridge

Fisherman's Bastion & Matthias Church

Heroes Square

St. Stephen's Basilica

Mary Magdalene Church

Aquincum

Hungarian National Galler

Tomb of Gul Baba

Gercse Parish Church

Kos Karoly Square in Wekerletelep

Budapest Bridge

Hungarian Parliament

Research and Development Center

Budapest Stock Exchange

MOL Campus

Hungarian Royal Curia

Sandor Palace

St Anne Parish, Matthias Church, Fisherman's Bastion,
Stigmatisation of St. Francis Church

University Church

Boscolo Budapest Hotel

Hungarian Stock Exchange Palace

Budapest Stock Exchange

City Park Ice Rink

Margaret Island

Gate of the Gellert Spa

Szechenyi Thermal Bath

Budapest International Airport

Green Line 4

Gerbeaud Café

Model United Nations

Dohany Synagogue

Western Railway Station

Arany Sas Patika Muzeum

Museum of Fine Arts Budapest

Museum of Applied Arts

Geological Museum of Budapest

Hungarian State Opera House

Puskas Arena

Budapest University of Technology and Economics

Danube Arena

Holy Trinity Square

Liszt Ferenc Academy of Music

Eotvos Lorand University

Main Façade of Eotvos Lorand

Night Panorama of Gellert Hill

National Athletics Centre

Budapest Business School

Megyeri Bridge

Szell Kalman Square

Brussels, Belgium

Map of Brussels, Belgium

Brussels is officially called the Brussels-Capital Region in Belgium, comprising 19 municipalities, including Brussels City, which is the capital of Belgium.137 Situated in the central part of the country, the Brussels-Capital Region is both part of the French Community of Belgium 138 and the Flemish Community.139 However, it is separate from the Flemish Region and Wallon Region.140

Northern Quarter Business District

Densely populated in Belgium, Brussels is known to have the highest GDP per capita 141 but has the lowest available income per household.142 Brussels region comprises an area of 162 square kilometers (63 square miles) and a population of 1.2 million.143 The metropolitan portion of Brussels, which comprises an area five times the region, has a population of more than 2.5 million residents, making it the largest in the whole country of Belgium.144;145;146

From a small settlement on the Senne River, Brussels became an important city region in Europe. By the end of the Second World War, it became a major center for international politics and a base for many international organisations, politicians, diplomats, and civil servants.147 As the de facto capital of the European Union, Brussels hosts numerous E.U. institutions, including administrative-legislative, executive-political, and legislative branches, though the judicial branch is located in Luxembourg, and the European Parliament sometimes meets in Strasbourg.148;149;150 Also located in Brussels are the Secretariat of Benelux and the headquarters of the North Atlantic Treaty Organisation. 151;152

With the political and economic growth of Brussels, its people and residents seemingly forgot to venerate God as they continuously commit abhorrent sins. For this reason, God has decided that this city will be totally destroyed in the last days. Its neighbouring cities, such as Antwerp, Ghent, Charleroi, and Liege, will also be destroyed if they do not repent. **Brussels, your day will be on July 17, 2091, a Tuesday at 2:10 A.M. You will be destroyed by a strong, violent earthquake and rains of consuming fire.**

It says in Psalm 21:10, "You will make of them a blazing furnace, O Lord, when you appear. You will strike them down in your wrath, your fire will engulf and burn them up." For this, God has this to say in Isaiah 44:26: "I confirm the word of my servant and carry out the plan announced by my messengers…

In Isaiah 45:22-24, God says this to you: "Turn to me and be saved, all you from the ends of the earth, for I am God and there is no other. By my own self I swear it, and what comes from my mouth is truth, a word that will not be revoked. Before me every knee will bend, by me every tongue will swear, saying, 'In Yahweh alone are righteousness and strength.'"

Here are some of your places and structures that will be destroyed:

Grand Place/Grote Markt

Mont des Arts/Kunstberg

Parc du Cinquantenaire/Jubelpark

Cathedral of St. Michael & St. Gudula

Congress Column

Anderlecht Municipality

Auderghem (Oudergem) Municipality

Royal Palace of Brussels (Palace of the King and Queen of the Belgians)

Berchem Saint Agathe Municipality

Municipality of the City of Brussels

Etterbeek Municipality

Evere Municipality

Forest (Vorst) Municipality

Ganshoren Municipality

Ixelles (Elsene) Municipality

Jette Municipality

Koekelberg Municipality

Molenbeek Saint Jean Municipality

Saint Gilles Municipality

Sint Joost-ten-Node Municipality

Schaerbeek Municipality

Uccle (Ukkel) Municipality

Watermeal-Boitsfort Municipality

Sint Lambrechts Woluwe Municipality

Sint Pieters Woluwe Municipality

Brussels Parliament Building

Aerial view of Brussels European Quarter

Place du Luxembourg/Luxemburgplein

Botanical Garden of Brussels

Berlaymont Building (European Commission)

Europa Building (European Council)

Espace Leopold (European Parliament)

Mont des Arts//Kunstberg

Headquarters of Eurocontrol in Haren

National Basilica of the Sacred Heart in Koekelberg

The Great Mosque of Brussels

Hotel Tassel

Grand–Place of Brussels — a UNESCO World Heritage Site

Hotel Albert Ciamberlani

Former Old England Dept.Store

Saint-Cyr House

Cauchie House

Stoclet Palace

Flagey Building

Atomium

Cinquantenaire/Jubelpark Memorial Arcade

Royal Theatre of La Monnaie

Brussels Summer Festival

Place du Jeu de Balle/Vossenplein

Constant Vanden Stock Stadium

Northern Quarter Business District

Brussels Stock Exchange

Universite libre de Bruxelles

Royal Library of Belgium

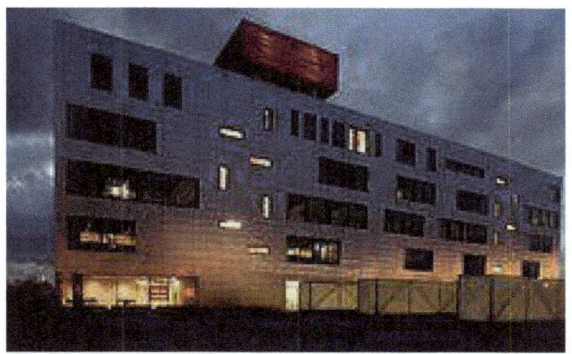

Erasmus Hospital in Anderlecht

Planetarium of Royal Observatory of Belgium

The Saint Catherine Dock

Main Hall of Brussels-South Railway Station

Rue de la Loi/Wetstraat

Parc du Cinquantenaire/ Jubelpark

Royal Greenhouses of Laeken

Ixelles Ponds

Cairo (El Qahira), Egypt

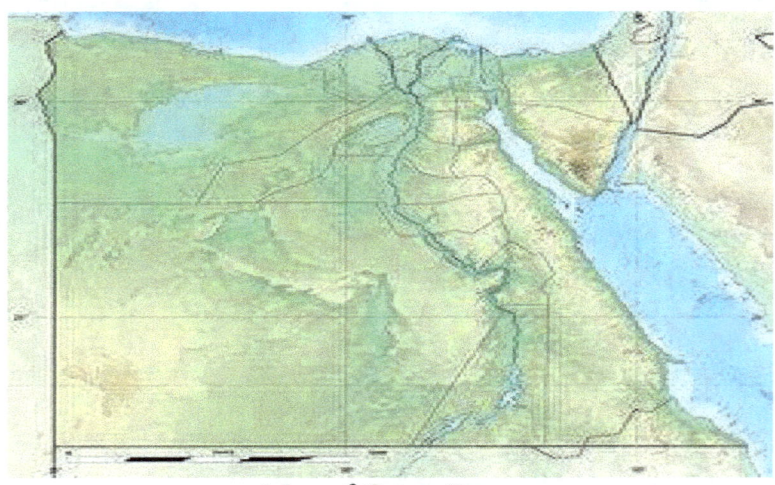

Map of Cairo, Egypt

Cairo is the capital of Egypt and the largest city within the Cairo Governorate. As the largest city in Egypt, it is a residential place of 10 million people.153 It is part of the largest urban agglomeration in Africa, the Arab countries, and the Middle East. Home to 22.1 million people, 154 the Greater Cairo metropolitan area ranks as the 12th-largest in the world in terms of population.

Due to its strategic location at Nile Valley and Nile Delta, modern-day Cairo has been the place of Ancient Egypt. As a strategic point, Cairo is at the crossroads of major routes between North Africa and the Levant. 155; 156 To the southwest of modern-day Cairo lies the city of Memphis, which became the capital during the Old Kingdom and remained a major city until the end of the Ptolemaic period.157 Another important city, a centre of religious activities, is Heliopolis, which was situated in what is now the districts of Matariya and Ain Shams in northeastern Cairo.157; 158 The place, however, was destroyed by Persian invaders in 525 BC and 343 BC and partly abandoned in the late first century BC.155

The roots of modern-day Cairo can be traced back to settlements during the first millenium A.D. As Memphis was slowly declining in importance in the 4th century,159 the Romans built a large fortress along the eastern portion of the Nile. This fortress was named Babylon, first built by emperor Trajan between 98 A.D. and 115 AD and was completed by emperor Diocletian in the year 285-305 AD. 160

Aerial view of Cairo, at the south, is Zamalek and Gezira District on Gezira Island

Cairo has long been the centre of the region's political and cultural life. For its Islamic architecture, Cairo is sometimes called the "city of a thousand minarets." It is also considered a world city attaining a "Beta +" classification according to GaWC.161

As this city is gradually improving its economy, politics, and culture, this place is growing prouder and prouder and sinful. People never venerate God of truth and spirit. For this, God has decided that this place will be destroyed in the last of days. We can recall that this place has held God's chosen people as slaves for four hundred thirty years (Exodus 12:40). The Pharaoh inhumanly treated the Israelites as slaves in Egypt.

In Exodus 3:7-8, we are informed of this: "Yahweh said 'I have seen the humiliation of my people in Egypt and I hear their cry when they are cruelly treated by their taskmasters. I know their suffering. I have come down to free them from the power of the Egyptians and to bring them up from that land to a beautiful spacious land, a land flowing with milk and honey...'"

Most probably, this is one reason why God wants this place destroyed. In Psalm 9:7, it says: "Your enemies lay in endless ruin, their cities trampled, their memory perished."

Cairo, your day will be on August 14, 2091, a Tuesday at 6:33 P.M. You will be completely destroyed by a strong, violent earthquake and rains of consuming fire. The earthquake that struck you in 1992, which resulted in 545 deaths, injuring 6,512 and leaving 50,000 people homeless, 162 was only insignificant compared to the earthquake that will strike you in the last days. The other cities near you, like Alexandria and Port Said, will also be destroyed if the people do not repent.

It says in Psalm 21:10, "You will make of them a blazing furnace, O Lord, when you appear. You will strike them down in your wrath, your fire will engulf and burn them up." For this, God has this to say in Isaiah 44:26: "I confirm the word of my servant and carry out the plan announced by my messengers..."

In Isaiah 45:22-24, God says this to you: "Turn to me and be saved, all you from the ends of the earth, for I am God and there is no other. By my own self I swear it, and what comes from my mouth is truth, a word that will not be revoked. Before me every knee will bend, by me every tongue will swear, saying, 'In Yahweh alone are righteousness and strength.'"

Here are some of your places and structures that will be destroyed:

Ibn Tulun Mosque

Metropolitan Cairo

Cairo Tower

Al-Muizz Street

Talaat Harb Square

Baron Empain Palace

Casiro Citadel; Cairo Opera House

NBE Towers

Statue of Talaat Pasha Harb

Faculty of Pharmacy/Ain Shams University

Mosque of Ibn Tulun

Mausoleum-Madrasa Hospital Complex of Sultan Qalawun

The Funerary Complex of Sultan Qaytbay

Library/American University of Cairo

Panorama of the Nile

Babylon Fortress

Egyptian Museum

Hanging Church in Old Cairo

Cemetery in Coptic Cairo

Ain Shams University/ Engineering

Faculty of Pharmacy/ Cairo University

Khan al-Khalili

Terminal 3 Cairo International Airport

Tahrir Square

Al-Azhar Mosque

Cairo Tower

Interior of Rameses Station

Cairo Opera House

6th October Bridge

Khedivial Opera House

Al-Muizz Street

Vilnius, Lithuania

Map of Vilnius, Lithuania

Formerly known in English as Vilna, Vilnius is the largest city and the capital of Lithuania. In the July 2023 survey, Vilnius had an estimated population of 593,436. 163 Vilnius urban area, extending beyond city limits, had a population of 718,507 based on a 2020 survey.164 In the Vilnius city and Vilnius district municipalities combined, there are 768,342 permanent residents based on the November 2023 survey. 165 166

Situated in the southeastern part of Lithuania, Vilnius is the second largest city in the Baltic states and the seat of Lithuania's national government. Historians identified the city of Vilnius with Voruta, one of the castles of Mindaugas, who was crowned king of Lithuania in 1253. From a trading settlement, Vilnius city started to become prosperous during the reign of Grand Dukes Batvydas and Vytenis. Archaeological discoveries indicate that Vilnius became the capital of the Kingdom of Lithuania and later of the Grand Duchy of

Lithuania. It remained the capital of Lithuania even after the dual confederation with the Kingdom of Poland. 167 Such dual confederation was extremely abhorred by the citizens of Lithuania. They protested, saying: *"Mes be Vilniaus nenurimsim!"* (English: We will not calm down without Vilnius). 168 In 1323, Vilna was specifically mentioned in the letters of Grand Duke Gediminas, which were sent to German cities inviting Germans, including Jewish Germans, to settle in Vilnius; a copy of such letter was also sent to Pope John XXII. One content of this letter refers to Vilnius as the capital of Lithuania. Today, Vilnius is already the European capital of culture, together with the city of Linz, Austria.

Skyline of New City Centre

A multi-lingual city where people speak different languages, such as Polish, German, Yiddish, Ruthenian, Lithuanian, Russian, Old Church Slavonic, Latin, Hebrew, and Turkic, has grown to become sinful and wicked. God detests this wickedness of Vilnius. Because of this, God decided to destroy this city in the last of days. In the absence of sincere repentance, the neighbouring cities of Vilnius, like Kaunas, Klaipeda, and Siauliai, will also be destroyed. **Vilnius, your day will be on September 14, 2095, a Wednesday at 10:30 P.M. A Violent earthquake and rains of consuming fire will strike you, resulting** in your total destruction.

It says in Psalm 21:10, "You will make of them a blazing furnace, O Lord, when you appear. You will strike them down in your wrath, your fire will engulf and burn them up." For this, God has this to say in Isaiah 44:26: "I confirm the word of my servant and carry out the plan announced by my messengers..."

In Isaiah 45:22-24, God says this to you: "Turn to me and be saved, all you from the ends of the earth, for I am God and there is no other. By my own self I swear it, and what comes from my mouth is truth, a word that will not be revoked. Before me every knee will bend, by me every tongue will swear, saying, 'In Yahweh alone are righteousness and strength.'"

Here are some of your places and structures that will be destroyed:

Gediminas Tower

311

Vilnius Cathedral

Vilnius Old Town

Vilnius Central Business District

Presidential Palace

Church of Saint Therese & Gate of Dawn

Town Hall Square

Palace of Grand Dukes of Lithuania

House of Signatories

Lithuanian National Philharmonic Society

Cathedral Square

Museum of Occupations and Freedom Fights

Gediminas Avenue

Neris River at Mindaugas Bridge

Independence Square

Vilnius at winter time

Vilnius Castle Complex

Vilnius Picture Gallery

Zawadzki Bookstore

Basilian Monastery

Vileisis Palace

Minor Radvilos Palace

Vingis Park

Lithuanian National Drama Theatre

Kaziuko mugė

Vilnius Town Hall

Vilnius City Municipal Building

Medininkai Castle

Seimas Plenary Chamber

Emergency Response Centre in Antakalnis

Skyline of Vilnius

St Anne's Church /Church of St. Francis St. Bernard

Church of St Peter & St. Paul

Chapel of St. Casimir

Apartments in Vilnius Old Town

Valakampiai Neighbourhood

Housing in Paupys

Dominican Church of the Holy Spirit

K29 Business Centre

Vilnius Modern Skyline

Vilnius University Astronomical Observatory

Green Hall Business Centre

Europa Tower

Scientific centres and universities

Bank of Lithuania Headquarters

Snipiskes hosts headquarters

Grand Courtyard of Vilnius University

National M.K. Ciurlionis School of Arts

Vilnius University Library

Church of Saint Nicholas

Church of Saint Casimir

Orthodox Cathedral of Theotokos

Choral Synagogue of Vilnius

Chapel of Gate of Dawn

Verkiai Calvary

Kalnai Par

Old Town of Vilnius

Republic of Uzupis

Siemens Arena

Grand Hotel Kempinski Vilnius

Vilnius International Airport

Teaching Hospital in Vilnius

Vilnius Medical Society

Katmandu, Nepal

Map of Kathmandu, Nepal

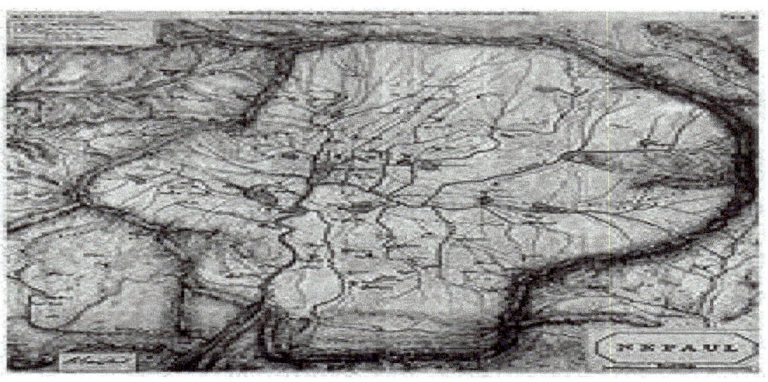

Map of Nepal, showing the location of Kathmandu

Kathmandu, officially called Kathmandu Metropolitan City, is the capital and most densely-populated city of Nepal, comprising 845,767 residents staying in 105,649 households and 2.9 million inhabitants in its urban agglomeration based on the 2021 Nepal census.169 It is situated in the Kathmandu Valley, a large valley in high plateaus in central Nepal with an altitude of 1,400 meters. Founded in the 2nd century A.D., Kathmandu is one of the oldest continuously inhabited places on Earth. Nepal Valley was originally called Nepal Mandala, which was home to the Newar people, a cosmopolitan urban civilisation in the Himalayan foothills. Kathmandu was the royal capital of the Nepal Kingdom established by the Nepali aristocracy. It has been the headquarters of the South Asian Association for Regional Cooperation since 1985. As part of Bagmati Province, Kathmandu is the seat of government of the Federal Democratic Republic of Nepal, which was established in 2008.

Skyline of Kathmandu from Swayambhu

Kathmandu has been the centre of the history, art, culture, and economy of Nepal. Although it is a multi-ethnic place, the majority of its inhabitants are Hindus and Buddhists. People's lives here are concentrated on religious and cultural festivities. Its economy is more dependent on tourism, which brings a high percentage of national income. Based on TripAdvisor, Kathmandu ranks first in Asia and third in the world. It is considered a gateway to the Nepal Himalayas and home to several World Heritage Sites, such as Durbar Square, Swayambhu Maha Chaitya, Bouddha, and Pashupatinath. According to the World Bank, in 2010, Kathmandu's population grew by 4 percent, which made it the fastest-growing metropolitan area in South Asia. Being the largest metropolitan area in the Himalayas, Kathmandu is the first region in Nepal that faces unprecedented challenges of rapid urbanisation and modernisation at a metropolitan scale.170

In some parts of Kathmandu, archaeological excavations resulted in findings of evidence of ancient civilisations. The oldest of these findings was a statue unearthed in Maligaon dated 185 AD. 171. Another archaeological find was the excavation of Dhando Chaitya, which uncovered a brick with an inscription in Brahmi script, which archaeologists believed to be two thousand years old already.171

Due to the religious beliefs of people in Kathmandu, which are centreed on Hinduism and Buddhism, of which they are susceptible to idolatry, this place is sighted by God to be destroyed in the last days. For sure, people in this place will laugh at this as they do not believe in God and in Jesus Christ. Therefore, I advise people in this place to multiply their laughter more and more on this message. **For your day, Kathmandu, will be on September 17, 2098, a Wednesday at 2:03 P.M. A Strong, violent earthquake will strike you and will be followed by rains of consuming fire, resulting in your total destruction.**

It says in Psalm 21:10, "You will make of them a blazing furnace, O Lord, when you appear. You will strike them down in your wrath, your fire will engulf and burn them up." For this, God has this to say in Isaiah 44:26: "I confirm the word of my servant and carry out the plan announced by my messengers…"

In Isaiah 45:22-24, God says this to you: "Turn to me and be saved, all you from the ends of the earth, for I am God and there is no other. By my own self I swear it, and what comes from my mouth is truth, a word that will not be revoked. Before me every knee will bend, by me every tongue will swear, saying, 'In Yahweh alone are righteousness and strength.'"

Here are some of your places and structures that will be destroyed:

Kathmandu Skyline w/ Gaurishankar

Ghanta Ghar

Dharahara

Pashupatinath Temple

Narayanhiti Palace

Katmandu Durbar Square

Dipawali

Kathmandu from Shivapuri Hills

Haphazard Settlement near Soyambhu

Araniko Highway

Northeastern Kathmandu

Office of Prime Minister of Nepal

Consulate of the Netherlands

Public Baths, Kathmandu

Kathmandu Durbar Market

Kathmandu Pashupatinath

Changunarayan

Boudhanath

Patan Durbar Square

Bhaktapur Palace

Naxal Bhagwati

Mahakaal Temple

Pashupatinath

Swayambhunath

Pashupatinath from Bagmati River

Boudhanath Stupa

Bouddha and Devotee

Chaitya at Bakunani

Nepal Museum

Buddha Statue

Asa Archives

Yenya

Samyak

Nepali Lakhe

Central Bank of Nepal

Hotel Shanker

Hyatt Regency Hotel

Dasharath Rangasala Stadium

SAARC Secretariat

Singha Durbar

Arch Bridges over Dhobi Khola

Basantapur Durbar Square

Goddess Kumari in chariot procession

Entrance to Durbar Square

Ghanta Hgar

Dharahara

Boudhanath

Czestochowa (Chenstokhov), Poland

Map of Czestochowa, Poland

Czestochowa is a city situated in southern Poland on the Warta River with a population of 214,342 and is the thirteenth largest city in the country.172 Although it is located in the Silesian Voivodeship, it is a part of the Lesser Poland region by history. Prior to 1795, it was a part of Krakow Voivodeship. Located in Krakow-Czestochowa Upland, it is the largest economic, cultural, and administrative hub in the northern portion of the Silesian Voivodeship.

Panorama of Czestochowa, Poland

Based on archaeological discoveries, it was in the 11th century within Piast-ruled Poland that the first medieval settlement in the location of Czestochowa was established. Historical records in 1220 revealed that when the Bishop of Krakow, Iwo Odrowaz, listed the properties of the Mstow monastery, two villages were specifically mentioned: Czestochowa and Czestochowa. These two villages belonged to the basic territorial unit of Slavic Polish tribes, with the capital at Mstow. Czestochowa was located on a hill where Jasna Gora Monastery was later built. Jasna Gora is the place where the Pauline monastery was constructed, which became the home of the Black Madonna painting in 1384, making the place a shrine of the Virgin Mary. Millions of pilgrims every year visit the shrine to see the Black Madonna. This is one reason why God is furious about this city because it promotes idolatry, which makes people going there sinful. The wickedness of this city is already registered before God's eyes, and it will be destroyed in the last days. In the absence of sincere repentance, neighbourting cities of Czestochowa, such as Gdansk, Cracow, Lodz, Wroclaw, and Warszawa (Warsaw), will also be totally destroyed.

Czestochowa, your day will be on August 28, 2094, a Saturday at 7:59 P.M. Earthquakes and rains of consuming fire will destroy you.

It says in Psalm 21:10, "You will make of them a blazing furnace, O Lord, when you appear. You will strike them down in your wrath, your fire will engulf and burn them up." For this, God has this to say in Isaiah 44:26: "I confirm the word of my servant and carry out the plan announced by my messengers..."

In Isaiah 45:22-24, God says this to you: "Turn to me and be saved, all you from the ends of the earth, for I am God and there is no other. By my own self I swear it, and what comes from my mouth is truth, a word that will not be revoked. Before me every knee will bend, by me every tongue will swear, saying, 'In Yahweh alone are righteousness and strength.'"

Here are some of your places and structures that will be destroyed:

Jasna Gora Monastery

St. Sigismund Church & Daszynskiego Square

City Hall & Pilsudski Monument

Saint Mary Avenue

Youth Culture Centre

Jasna Gora Monastery

Black Madonna of Czestochowa

Museum Zapa

Monument of Defenders of Poland

Huta Czestochowa Steelworks

Franke's House

Zapalkiewicz House

Polish Bank's Townhouse

Ulica 7 Kamienic

Mary Panny Avenue

Cathedral Basilica of the Holy Family

Interior of Basilica Jasna Gora Monastery

View on the Avenues

3rd avenue

Staszic Park

Sienkiewicz Avenue

Town Hall &Czestochowa Regional Museum

Halina Poswiatowska Museum

Archaelogical Reserve in Czestochowa

Iron Ore Mining Museum

Philharmonic of Czestochowa

Adam Mickiewicz Theatre

Regional Specialist Hospital-Parkitka Nowobialska

National Road Czestochowa

City Polyclinic Hospital-Mirowska

National Specialist Hospital-PCK

City Polyclinic Hospital Mickiewicz

Jan Dlugosz University

CKM Wlokniarz Czestochowa Stadium

Miejski Stadion Pilkarski "Rakow"

Municipal Office

St Barbara and St. Adrew Church

St. Sigismund Church

St. Roch and Sebastian Church

Katedra Polskokatolicka

Cerkiew Ikony

St. Jacob's Church

Sports Hall Czestochowa

Prague (Praha) Czech Republic

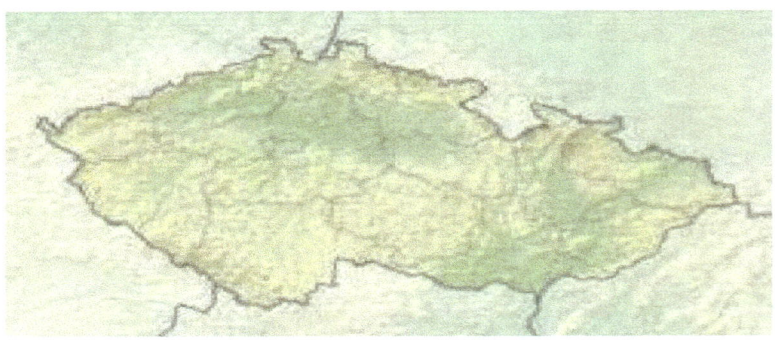

Map of Prague, Czech Republic

Prague is the capital and the most densely-populated city of the Czech Republic, 173 and the historical capital of Bohemia. Standing on the Vltava River, Prague is home to about 1.3 million people. 174 However, data obtained from mobile phone movements around Prague suggest that actual inhabitants in the city are 1.9 or 2.0 million.175 It has a temperate oceanic climate with relatively warm summers and chilly winters.

From a simple settlement stretching from Prague Castle in the north to Fort Vysehrad in the south, the place gradually became the capital of a modern European country. It is believed that the region has been inhabited since the early Paleolithic period.176 With reference to Cyriacus Spangenberg, Jewish historian David Solomon Ganz claimed the city. It was established as Boihaem in circa 1306 B.C. by the ancient king, Boyya.177 Between the fifth and fourth century B.C., a Celtic tribe inhabited the area, establishing settlements, including Zavist, the largest Celtic oppidum in Bohemia in the present-day south suburb Zbraslav in Prague, naming the place Bohemia, meaning "home of Boii people." 176; 177 The Celts,

370

however, were slowly driven away by Germanic tribes — Marcomanni, Quadi, Lombards, and Suebi — who then installed Maroboduus as the king of Marconi in Zavist. 177; 179 Within the area where present-day Prague stands, a Roman geographer by the name of Ptolemaios indicated a Germanic city, Casurgis, on a 2nd-century map.180

Prague Mrakodrapy Praze, Pankrac District

In the late 5th century A.D., following the fall of the Roman Empire, a great migration period took place when Germanic tribes staying in Bohemia moved westwards, and in the 6th century, Slavic tribes settled in the Central Bohemian region. For three consecutive centuries thereafter, Czech tribes built fortified settlements there, most notably in Sarka Valley, Butovice, and Levy Hradec.176

Prague is a political, cultural, and economic hub in Central Europe with a rich architectural history, such as Romanesque, Gothic, Renaissance, and Baroque. It became the capital of the Kingdom of Bohemia and the residence of several Holy Roman Emperors, like Charles IV (1346-13780) and Rudolf II (1575-1611).181

Being an important city during the time of the Habsburg

monarchy and Austro-Hungarian Empire, Prague played a major role in Bohemian and Protestant Reformations, the Thirty Years' War, and the 20th-century history of Czechoslovakia during the two World Wars and in the post-war Communist period.182

Today, Prague is home to numerous popular cultural attractions that survived the violence and destruction of the 20th-century Europe. Among these attractions are Prague Castle, Charles Bridge, Old Town Square, Prague astronomical clock, Jewish Quarter, Petrin Hill, and Vysehrad. Prague is home to numerous educational institutions, including Charles University in Prague, the oldest university in Central Europe.183

Prague is classified as an "Alpha" global city based on GaWC studies.184 In 2019, the city was ranked 69th most livable urban area in the world by Mercer.185 Likewise, in the same year, the PICSA Index ranked Prague as the 13th most liveable urban area in the world.186 Due to its interesting political history, which attracts tourists from all over the world, the city attracts 8.5 million international visitors every year. It is the fifth most visited European city after London, Paris, Rome, and Istanbul.187

Coupled with the economic and political advancement of Prague, the city and its people became wicked before God's eyes as they venerated statues. Their Roman Catholic religion drags them to engage in idolatry, which God vehemently detests. For this, Prague is already sighted by God to be destroyed in the last days. In the absence of sincere repentance, its neighbouring cities, such as Brno, Ostrava, and Plzen, will also be destroyed. **Prague, your day will be on January 9, 2092, a Wednesday, at 7:18 P.M. A strong, violent earthquake will strike you and will be followed by rains of consuming fire, causing your total destruction.**

It says in Psalm 21:10, "You will make of them a blazing furnace, O Lord, when you appear. You will strike them down in your wrath, your fire will engulf and burn them up." For this, God has this to say in Isaiah 44:26: "I confirm the word of my servant and carry out the plan announced by my messengers..."

In Isaiah 45:22-24, God says this to you: "Turn to me and be saved, all you from the ends of the earth, for I am God and there is no other. By my own self I swear it, and what comes from my mouth is truth, a word that will not be revoked. Before me every knee will bend, by me every tongue will swear, saying, 'In Yahweh alone are righteousness and strength.'"

Here are some of your places and structures that will be destroyed:

Panorama of Prague showing Prague Castle

National Theatre

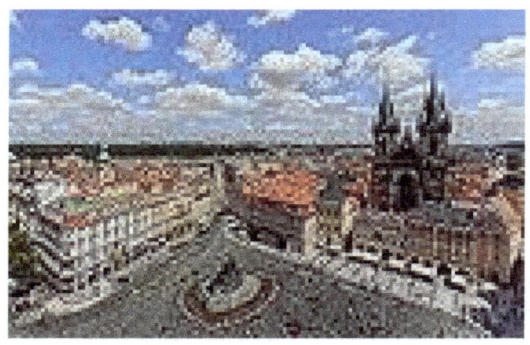

Old Town Square

Mala Strana

St. Vitus Cathedral

Prague Astronomical Clock

Prague from Powder Topwer

Veletrzni Palace National Gallery

Rudolfinum

Prague Congress Centre

U Medvidku

Na příkopě

Charles Bridge

Zizkov TV Tower

Petrin Observation Tower

Prague Panorama

Sunrise in Prague

Wenceslas Square

Gothic Powder Tower

Milunic's and Gehry

Library of Strahov Monastery

Charles Bridge

Prague Castle

Church of our Lady before Tyn

St. Nicholas Church

Basilica of St. Peter & St. Paul

Parizska Street

Church of St. Ludmila

National Theatre

Vystaviste

Olds New Synagogue

Charles University

Prague's Holesovice

University of Economics Prague

Barrandov Bridge

Vaclav Havel Airport

O2 Arena

Prague Main Train Station

Prague Zoo

National Monument on Vitkov

Minsk, Belarus

Map of Minsk, Belarus

Map of Europe

Minsk is the capital and the largest city in Belarus. It is located on the Svislach and Niamiha rivers. As a capital, Minsk has a special administrative status in Belarus. It is also the administrative centre of the Minsk region and Minsk district. Based on the 2023 population survey, Minsk is inhabited by 2 million people, making it the 11th most populous city in Europe.188 Minsk is one of the administrative capitals of the Commonwealth of Independent States (CIS) and the Eurasian Economic Union.

Minsk Business District

In the 9th and 10th centuries A.D.,189 Lithuanian people settled in the area where Minsk is located today. Svislach River valley was the boundary between two Slavic tribes, the Krivichs and Dregovichs. In 980 A.D., the area was included in the early medieval Principality of Polotsk, one of the earliest East Slavic principalities of Kievan Rus. In 1067 A.D., Minsk was first mentioned as Menesk in Primary Chronicle as related to the Battle of River Nemiga.190 City authorities unanimously agreed that the exact founding date of Minsk is March 3, 1067.191 This date is widely accepted, but there were some people who believed that the place had been in existence for quite some time, considering that there were areas fortified by wooden walls. There were several theories attached to the origin of the name Minsk.192

In the early 12th century, the Principality of Polotsk was divided into smaller fiefs. Later, one dynasty of the princes of Polotsk established the Principality of Minsk. In 1129, the Principality of

Minsk was annexed by Kiev, which was the dominant principality of Kievan Rus at that time. Polotsk dynasty, however, regained control of the principality in 1146 A.D. The princes of Minsk and Polotsk were continuously engaged in bloody struggle trying to unify all lands previously under Polotsk's rule.193

For two years, between 1237 and 1239, Minsk was able to escape the Mongol invasion of Rus. Three years later, in 1242, Minsk became the province of the Grand Duchy of Lithuania. It joined peacefully with Lithuania in exchange for lavish privileges enjoyed by local elites, such as high rank in society, among others. In 1413, there was a unification between the Grand Duchy of Lithuania and the Kingdom of Poland, which many disagreed with. As a consequence of such unification, Minsk became the centre of Minsk Voivodship (province). In 1441, Casimir IV, Grand Duke of Lithuania, included Minsk as one of the cities enjoying certain privileges. Again, in 1499, during the reign of Alexander I Jagiellon, Minsk received town privileges by virtue of Magdeburg law.195 In 1569, after the union of Lublin, the Grand Duchy of Lithuania and the Kingdom of Poland merged into one state called the Polish-Lithuanian Commonwealth.194 This commonwealth was part of territories annexed by the Russian Empire in 1793 following the Second Partition of Poland. After the Russian Revolution, from 1919 to 1991, Minsk was made the capital of the Byelorussian Soviet Socialist Republic, which later became a republic of the Soviet Union in 1922. After the dissolution of the Soviet Union, Minsk became the capital of the newly–proclaimed independent Republic of Belarus.

Considering that Minsk's predominant religion is Catholicism, which teaches veneration of graven images, idolatry has been deeply rooted in their culture. Idolatry is one thing that God dislikes most.

For this, Minsk has already been sighted by God to be totally destroyed in the last days. Its neighboring cities, such as Homyel' (Gomel'), Vitsyebsk, and Mahilyov, will also be destroyed if they do not repent. Minsk, your day will be on August 4, 2092, a Monday, at 8:17 P.M. An earthquake and rains of consuming fire will destroy you.

It says in Psalm 21:10, "You will make of them a blazing furnace, O Lord, when you appear. You will strike them down in your wrath, your fire will engulf and burn them up." For this, God has this to say in Isaiah 44:26: "I confirm the word of my servant and carry out the plan announced by my messengers…"

In Isaiah 45:22-24, God says this to you: "Turn to me and be saved, all you from the ends of the earth, for I am God and there is no other. By my own self I swear it, and what comes from my mouth is truth, a word that will not be revoked. Before me every knee will bend, by me every tongue will swear, saying, 'In Yahweh alone are righteousness and strength.'"

Here are some of your places and structures that will be destroyed:

Minsk Old Town

391

Belarus State University Rector's Office

National Opera & Ballet Theatre

Babrujskaja Minsk

Church of Saints Simon & Helena

Trajeckaje pradmiescie

The Saviour Church

Saints Peter and Paul Cathedral

Railway Station Square

Janka Kupala National Theatre

Independence Avenue

Panorama to the centre of Minsk

Svislac River

Apartment Buildings in Minsk

New Synagogue in Minsk

Minsk Central Bus Station

Minsk Geothermal Power Plant

The Jesuit Collegium

Church of St. Mary Magdalene

Belarusian State University

Church of Exaltation of the Holy Cross

Church of Holy Trinity

Church of All Saints

Church of St. Elisabeth Convent

Cathedral of Saint Virgin Mary

Minsk Catedral of the Holy Spirit

Minsk City Hall/ Freedom Square

Stadler Astra Train

National Arts Museum

Minsk State Linguistic University

Sofia, Bulgaria

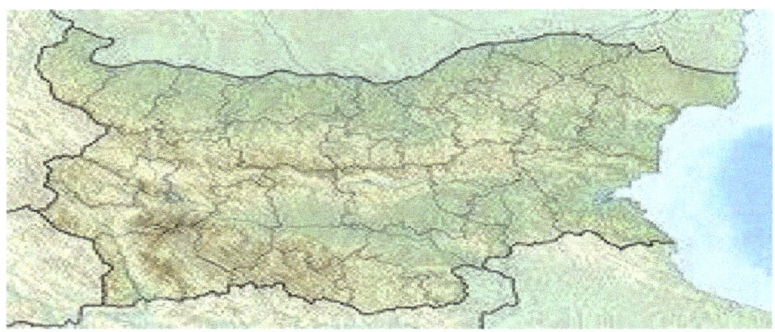

Map Sofia, Bulgaria

Sofia is the capital and largest city of Bulgaria. It is located in Sofia Valley at the foot of Vitosha mountain, the western portion of the country. The city was established west of the Iskar River with numerous mineral springs, such as Sofia Central Mineral Baths. Being situated in the centre of the Balkans, it is midway between the Black Sea and the Adriatic Sea and closest to the Aegean Sea.196; 197

Sofia, Bulgaria

Sofia has been inhabited since 7000 BC. It was popularly known as Serdica in past antiquity and Sredets during the Middle Ages. The recorded history of Sofia begins with an attestation of the conquest of Serdica by the Roman Republic in 29 B.C. from the Celtic tribe Serdi. Beginning in 476 A.D., when the Roman Empire declined and finally fell, the city was raided by several tribes, such as Huns, Visigoths, Avars and Slavs. In 809 A.D., Serdica was annexed into the Bulgarian Empire by Khan Krum and its name was changed to Sredets. In 1018, the Byzantine Empire ended its rule over Bulgaria, and the Bulgarian Empire regained its power. Starting in 1194, when it was reincorporated into the Bulgarian Empire, Sredets became a major administrative, economic, cultural, and literary hub until its conquest by the Ottoman Empire in 1382. Between the period 1530 and 1836, Sofia became the regional capital of Rumelia Eyalet, a key province of the Ottoman Empire in Europe. When Bulgaria was restored in 1878, Sofia was chosen as the capital of the Third Bulgarian State, paving the way for intense demographic and economic development.

Being the fourteenth largest city in the European Union, Sofia is surrounded by mountainsides, like Vitosha by the south, Lyulin by the west, and Balkan Mountains by the north, making it the third highest European capital after Andorra la Vella and Madrid. As the capital city, Sofia is home to many major universities, cultural institutions, and commercial companies.198 It was formerly described as a city of triangle religious tolerance due to the presence of churches such as Sveta Nedelya Church, Banya Bashi Mosque, and Sofia Synagogue. Later, this triangle was changed to a square by the construction of the Catholic Catedral of St. Joseph.199;200

Sofia has been included as one of the top ten best places for startup businesses, particularly in information technologies. 201 It is the capital city in Europe that is easy to visit due to its affordability.

202 In 1979, Bayona Church in Sofia, constructed during the Second Bulgarian Empire, was included in the World Heritage List for its patrimonial symbolism. With its cultural sites in Southeastern Europe, Sofia is home to the National Opera and Ballet of Bulgaria, the National Palace of Culture, the Vasil Levski National Stadium, the Ivan Vazov National Theatre, the National Archaeological Museum, and the Serdica Amphitheatre. To inform visitors about lifestyle in Communist Bulgaria, there are many sculptures and posters that can be seen in the Museum of Socialist Art.203

With regard to the population of Sofia, it steadily decreased in the late 18th century. From 70,000, it went down to 19,000 in 1870, and in 1878, it went further down to 11,649. After that year, it began increasing.204 Sofia has a population of 1.24 million,205 occupying a territory of 492 square kilometers,206 which represents a concentration of 17.9% of the country's population within the 200th percentile of the country's land area. Sofia's urban area comprises 1.54 million 207 residents within an area of 5723 square kilometers. This area includes Sofia City Province and parts of Sofia Province, representing 5.16% of the country's territory.208 The metropolitan area of Sofia, based on one-hour car travel time, stretches internationally and includes Dimitrovgrad in Serbia. 209 The metropolitan region of the city is resided by 1.66 million 210 inhabitants.

The city frequently experiences intensive and destructive earthquakes. In 1818 and 1858, it experienced destructive earthquakes. In 2012, the Pernik earthquake struck west of Sofia with a moment magnitude of 5.6, a much lower Mercalli intensity of VI. In 2014 Aegean Sea Earthquake was also felt in the city. These earthquakes are of very low intensity compared to eartthquakes that will strike the city in the last days. **Sofia is already destined by God to be destroyed in the last days because of its sinfulness and wickedness.** In the absence of genuine repentance, its neighbouring cities, such as Burgas, Plovdiv, Ruse, and Varna, will also be destroyed. Sofia, your day will be on September 16, 2093, a Wednesday, at 7:14 P.M. An earthquake and rains of consuming fire will totally destroy you.

It says in Psalm 21:10, "You will make of them a blazing furnace, O Lord, when you appear. You will strike them down in your wrath, your fire will engulf and burn them up." For this, God has this to say in Isaiah 44:26: "I confirm the word of my servant and carry out the plan announced by my messengers…"

In Isaiah 45:22-24, God says this to you: "Turn to me and be saved, all you from the ends of the earth, for I am God and there is no other. By my own self I swear it, and what comes from my mouth is truth, a word that will not be revoked. Before me every knee will bend, by me every tongue will swear, saying, 'In Yahweh alone are righteousness and strength.'"

Here are some of your places and structures that will be destroyed:

Cathedral of Saint Alexander Nevsky

Tsarigradsko shoes

Statue of Sveta Sofia, Bulgarian Academy of Sciences

Borisova gradina

National Palace of Culture.

St. Sophia Church

Polygraphia office centre

The National Assembly Building

Council of Ministers; Presidency; former Communist Party House

Ivan Vasov National Theatre

Banya Bashi Mosque

Bayona Church

Vitosha Boulevard

Aleksander Nevsky Cathedral

Arena Sofia

Business Park Sofia

Cherni Vrah Boulevard

Sofia University Faculty of Chemistry

Bulgarian State Railway

Port Louis, Mauritius

Port Louis is located in the Indian Ocean.

Port Louis is the capital city of Mauritius. It is situated in the Port Louis district with a small western portion in the Black River district. As a populous city, Port Louis is the country's financial and political centre. Based on a 2018 population survey conducted by Statistics Mauritius, the city is inhabited by 147,066 residents. 211

Aerial view of Port Louis

Known as Harbour of Tortoises,212 Port Louis was used by Dutch settlers as their harbour sometime in 1606. In 1736, under the

413

control of the French government, it became the administrative centre of Mauritius and a major replenishing point of French ships on their way to Asia and Europe around the cape of Good Hope.213 Named in honour of King Louis XV of France, Port Louis is the capital of Mauritius, known in France as Île-de-France. The French governor of the place was Bertrand-Francois Mahe' de La Bourdonnais, whose government contributed much for city development. As it was relatively protected from strong winds by the Moka Mountain Range, Port Louis was chosen to house the main harbour and fort of the country. Its importance as a port was continued by the British military during the Napoleonic Wars (1800-1815), which helped Britain control the Indian Ocean. Following the opening of the Suez Canal in 1869, port calls of ships in Port Louis began to drop. However, during the temporary closure of the Suez Canal in 1967, port activity increased for seven years. In order to maintain Mauritius's role in the importation and exportation of goods, the port has undergone steady modernisation since 1970. Following the modernisation of the port, the tourism industry expanded, which paved the way for the existence of many shops, hotels, and restaurants built on the Caudan Waterfront.

Small as it is, Port Louis is now being sighted by God for destruction in the last days due to its sinfulness and wickedness. Practically, the whole country will be erased from the world map when God's wrath falls on you on **October 6, 2093, a Tuesday, at 4:25 A.M. A series of volcanic eruptions followed by strong, violent earthquakes, tsunamis, and rains of consuming fire will totally blot you out of world map.**

It says in Psalm 21:10, **"You will make of them a blazing furnace, O Lord, when you appear. You will strike them down in**

414

your wrath, your fire will engulf and burn them up." For this, God has this to say in Isaiah 44:26: "I confirm the word of my servant and carry out the plan announced by my messengers…"

In Isaiah 45:22-24, God says this to you: "Turn to me and be saved, all you from the ends of the earth, for I am God and there is no other. By my own self I swear it, and what comes from my mouth is truth, a word that will not be revoked. Before me every knee will bend, by me every tongue will swear, saying, 'In Yahweh alone are righteousness and strength.'"

Here are some of your places and structures that will be destroyed:

Port Louis Waterfront

Port Louis Harbour

Panoramic view of Port Louis

Municipal City Council of Port Louis

Skyline of Port Louis/ Bank of Mauritius Tower

Wellington, New Zealand

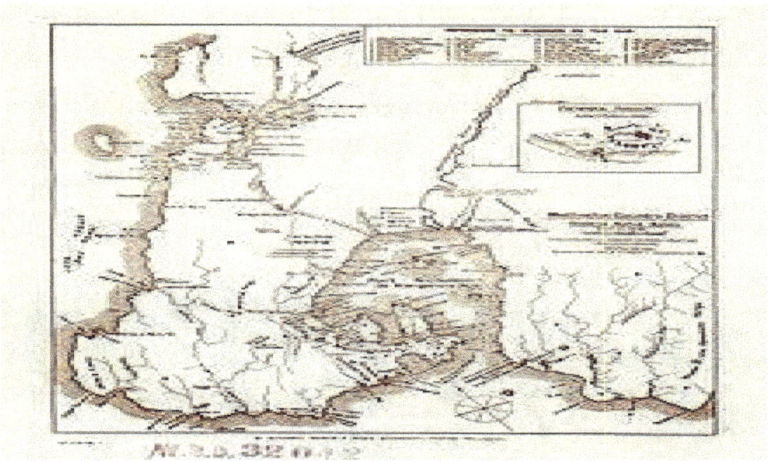

Map of Wellington

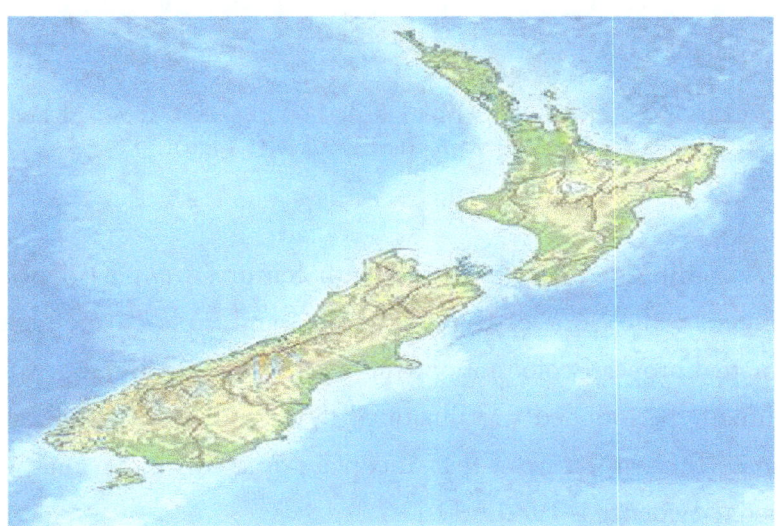

Map of New Zealand

Wellington is the capital of New Zealand. It is situated at the southwestern tip of North Island between Cook Strait and Remutake Range. As the third largest city in New Zealand, Wellington is the administrative centre of the Wellington Region. It is the world's southernmost capital of a sovereign state.214 As the world's windiest city by its average wind speed,215 Wellington features a temperate maritime climate.

Wellington from the top of Mt. Victoria

According to a legend, in the tenth century A.D., a Polynesian explorer by the name of Kupe discovered and explored the region. Prior to European colonisation, the place where Wellington would eventually be founded was inhabited by an indigenous tribe called Maori. The earliest year that the place was inhabited and with concrete evidence is 1280 A.D.216

In the early 12ᵗʰ century A.D., several Maori groups already occupied some parts of Wellington. Around 925 A.D., 217; 218 it is believed that Kupe, a legendary Polynesian explorer and chieftain from a neighbouring Island, had already stayed in Wellington harbour. Later, Whatonga,219 an explorer from the Maori tribe, named the harbour *Te Whanganui-a-Tara* after the name of his son. Before the 1820s, most of the residents of Wellington were descendants of Whatonga.220 After the year 1820, the descendants of Whatonga residing in Wellington were Ngati Ira, Rangitane, and Muaupoko.221 As time went on, these groups were forced out of *Te Whanganui-a-Tara* by waves of migration by other iwi (Maori tribes) coming from the Northern 221 portion of New Zealand. The migrating tribes were Ngati Toa from Kawhai, Ngati Rangatahi from nearby Taumarunui, Te Atiawa Ngati Tama, Ngati Mutunga Taranaki, and Ngati Ruanui from Taranaki. Later, Ngati Matunga transferred to the Chatham Islands. The Waitangi Tribunal has found that at the time of the signing of the Treaty of Waitangi in 1840, Te Atiawa, Taranaki, Ngati Ruanui, Ngati Tama, and Ngati Toa held mana whenua interest in the area by occupation and conquest.221

At the start of the year 1839, attempts to establish Pakeha or European settlement began upon the arrival of Colonel William Wakefield to purchase land for the New Zealand Company to sell to prospective British settlers.221 Related to this transaction, the Maori already had some contacts with Pakeha whalers and traders.222 On September 20, 1839, European settlement was initiated with the arrival of an advance party of the New Zealand Company on board the ship Tory. An additional 150 settlers arrived on ship Aurora on January 22, 1840. Prior to the official signing of the document *Treaty of Waitangi* for the purchase of the settlement area, British settlement was already established. These settlers constructed their first homes at Petone, which they called Britannia, for the meantime, located at the mouth of the Hutt River. Observing that the area was swampy and prone to flooding, most of the newcomers transferred their settlement across the harbour to Thorndon, which is now the present site of

Wellington city.223

Wellington's physical set-up was originally designed by Captain William Mein Smith, the first surveyor general for Edward Wakefield's New Zealand Company in 1840.224 Captain Smith's plan comprised a series of interconnected grid plans traversing valleys and lower hill slopes.225 Based on the 2023 population survey, 226 the residents in urban areas alone were 215,200 which included urbanised areas within Wellington city. The larger Wellington metropolitan area, which includes the cities of Lower Hutt, Upper Hutt, and Porirua, has a population of 440,900 residents as of June 2023.226 With no legislative basis, Wellington has been the capital city of New Zealand since 1865. It was only established by a convention that this city became the capital of New Zealand. Being the capital of New Zealand, the New Zealand Government, Parliament, the Supreme Court, and most public services are based in the city.227

Wellington's economy is anchored primarily on service-based with greater emphasis on finance, business services, government, and the film industry. It is the centre of New Zealand's film and special effects industries and progressively a hub for information technology and innovation 228 with two public research universities. Its airport, Wellington International Airport in Rongotai, is the country's second busiest airport.

As New Zealand's cultural capital, Wellington has a diverse culture centred mainly on youth, which has wielded influence across Oceania.229;230;231 Wellington and Tokyo tied in 4th rank 232 as the world's most liveable cities in the 2021 Global Livability Ranking. For two consecutive years, 2017 and 2018, Deutsche Bank ranked Wellington as first in the world both in livability and in non-pollution..233;234 As a global city, Wellington has grown from the simplest Maori settlement to a colonial outpost, then to the Australasian capital with an experience of remarkable creative resurgence. 235;236;237;238

Wellington is prone to earthquakes. In 1848, it experienced serious damage caused by a strong earthquake.239 Again, in 1855, the Wairarapa earthquake, with 8.2 on the moment magnitude scale, probably the most powerful earthquake that was ever experienced in New Zealand's recorded history, caused considerable damage in Wellington. When this strong earthquake of 1855 occurred, the majority of buildings were already made of wood. The largest wooden building in the Southern Hemisphere is a government building that was restored in 1996. 241

The Canterbury earthquakes of 2010 and 2011 have awakened the government to be prepared for such calamities,242;243 especially in terms of building specifications and standards 244;245 required for building. It was learned that every five years, there is always an occurrence of a year-long slow quake beneath the city, stretching from Kapiti to Marlborough sounds. It was first observed and measured in 2003, 2008, and 2013. 246 Such geologic movement releases an energy of a magnitude 7 quake but it brings no damage as it happens very slowly.247 The Seddon earthquake hit the city on July 21 2013, at 5:09 P.M. with a magnitude of 6.5, but it caused no damage.248

On August 16, 2013, a Friday at 2:31 P.M. Lake Grassmere earthquake struck with a strength of 6.6, but it also caused no damage, though people were forced to be evacuated from the buildings.249 Also, on January 20, 2014, a Monday at 3:52 P.M., a 6.2 magnitude earthquake struck the North Island, 15 km east of Eketahuna, and was felt in Wellington. The destruction recorded was only two giant eagle sculptures at Wellington airport. 250;251 Buildings in earthquake-prone areas were no longer rebuilt, but instead, they were demolished upon the decision of the insurer. The demolished buildings were NZDF headquarters 252;253 and the Statistics House at Waterfront.254 After the Earthquakes, docks were closed for safety reasons.255 In 1987, Edgecumbe was struck also by an earthquake that caused considerable damage. On December 9, 2019, White Island was also struck by a strong earthquake that caused the death of many tourists.

It is a good practice for the Wellington government and New Zealand to keep an updated record of earthquakes that strike their place because this city is destined to be destroyed by God in the last of days. As the city grows economically, politically, and culturally, it becomes sinful and wicked before God's eyes. **Hence, it is reasonable for God to destroy this city. Wellington, your day will be on April 4, 2087, a Friday, at 10:30 P.M. A strong, violent earthquake, never experienced by mankind, will strike you and will be followed by tsunamis and rains of consuming fire. In the absence of true repentance, other cities near you, like Aucland, Churchchrist, Dunedin, and Hamilton, will also be destroyed.**

It says in Psalm 21:10, "You will make of them a blazing furnace, O Lord, when you appear. You will strike them down in your wrath, your fire will engulf and burn them up." For this, God has this to say in Isaiah 44:26: "I confirm the word of my servant and carry out the plan announced by my messengers…"

In Isaiah 45:22-24, God says this to you: "Turn to me and be saved, all you from the ends of the earth, for I am God and there is no other. By my own self I swear it, and what comes from my mouth is truth, a word that will not be revoked. Before me every

knee will bend, by me every tongue will swear, saying, 'In Yahweh alone are righteousness and strength.'"

Here are some of your places and structures that will be destroyed:

Old High Court Building

Old Government Buildings

Old Saint Paul Church

Public Trust Office Building

Wellington Railway Station

Museum of Wellington City

Oriental Bay

Classic weatherboards in Wellington

Wellington Zoo

Te Papa Museum

Bucket Fountain

Entrance to the city Gallery

The Weta Cave

Wellington Town Hall

Victoria University Kelburn Campus

Te Wharewaka o Poneke

Wellington Regional Stadium

Te Auaha Performing Arts School

Te Ngakau Civic Square

Circa Theatre

Wellington Botanical Gardens

Reykjavik, Iceland

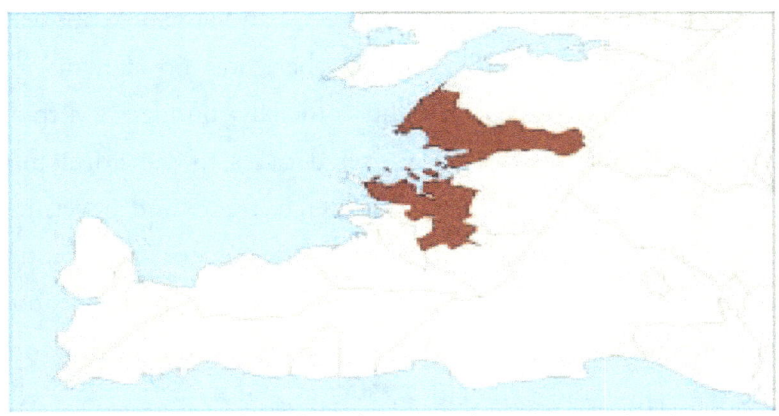

Location of Reykjavik in Southwestern Iceland

Reykjavik is the capital and largest city of Iceland. It is situated in Southwestern Iceland on the southern shore of Faxafloi Bay. It is the world's northernmost capital of a sovereign state. It has a population of 140,000 residents based on 2023 population survey. The capital region has a population of around 248,000.256

Panorama of Reykjavik seen from Perlan with the mountains Akrafjall ()middle) and Esja (right)

The place where Reykjavik is situated is believed to be the exact location of the first permanent settlement in Iceland, founded by Ingofr Arnarson in 874 A.D., according to Landnamabok, aborigines of Iceland. Even in the 18th century, there was no sign of urban development in the place. It was first officially founded as a trading town in 1786 and steadily grew over decades to transform into a regional and national centre of commerce, trade, and government centres. Presently, Reykjavik is the centre of Iceland's cultural, economic, and governmental activities and a popular tourist destination among foreigners. Also, it is ranked as one of the world's cleanest, greenest and safest cities.257;258;259

As written in the Book of Settlement, the first permanent Norse settlement in Iceland was founded by Ingofr Arnarson in 870 AD. It is believed that Ingolfr decided on a place to be settled using a traditional Norse method; that is, when the land was in sight, he cast his high seat pillars overboard and promised to settle where the gods decided to bring them ashore. He then instructed his two slaves to search the coastal areas to look for the pillars. After three years of searching, his two slaves were able to find the pillars on the site where Reykjavik 260 is now situated.

In the 19th century, the idea of Icelandic independence became prevalent as nationalist sentiment gained influence. Being the only city in Iceland, Reykjavik became the centre of nationalistic ideas. Advocates of Iceland's independence realised the importance of the city to realise such an objective. The general assembly, formed in 930 A.D., was reestablished in 1845 in Alþingi. Such general assembly was suspended several decades earlier when it was transferred to Pingvellir. Its function was only advisory assembly giving advises to the king about Icelandic affairs. As Alþingi is situated in Reykjavik, it follows that Reykjavik becomes automatically the capital of Iceland. In 1874, Iceland adopted a constitution giving Alþingi limited legislative powers. The next step was to transfer executive power to Iceland. In 1904, home rule was granted when the office of the minister of Iceland was established in Reykjavik. On December 1, 1918, Iceland became a sovereign country, i.e., the Kingdom of Iceland was in personal union with the Crown of Denmark.

On the morning of May 10, 1940, after the German occupation of Denmark and Norway on April 9, 1940, four British warships arrived in Reykjavik harbour, for this allied occupation of Reykjavik was realised in a matter of hours without resistance. Iceland received several requests from Britain to consent to occupation. But by reason of the Neutrality Policy, such requests were refused. For the remaining parts of the war, British, American, and Canadian forces formed a garrison in Iceland. 261

The presence of allied forces in Iceland proved to be advantageous to residents as unemployment caused by the great depression was consequently remedied. Several constructions were undertaken in the country. Reykjavik Airport, which remains functional today, was built by the British government. The Americans, likewise, built Keflavik Airport, situated 31 miles west of Reykjavik, which consequently became Iceland's primary international airport. 262 In 1944, the Republic of Iceland was formed, and a president was elected, replacing the king and with offices stationed in Reykjavik.

As Reykjavik grows economically, politically, and culturally, its residents also grow in their sinfulness and wickedness. For this, this place is already sighted by God to be destroyed in the last days. **Reykjavik, your day will be on December 16, 2091, a Sunday, at 7:42 P.M. A strong, violent earthquake will strike you and will** be followed by rains of consuming fire.

It says in Psalm 21:10, "You will make of them a blazing furnace, O Lord, when you appear. You will strike them down in your wrath, your fire will engulf and burn them up." For this, God has this to say in Isaiah 44:26: "I confirm the word of my servant and carry out the plan announced by my messengers..."

In Isaiah 45:22-24, God says this to you: "Turn to me and be saved, all you from the ends of the earth, for I am God and there is no other. By my own self I swear it, and what comes from my mouth is truth, a word that will not be revoked. Before me every knee will bend, by me every tongue will swear, saying, 'In Yahweh alone are righteousness and strength.'"

Here are some of your places and structures that will be destroyed:

Hallgrimskirkja from Perlan; Reykjavik, Frikirkjan

434

Central Reykjavik

Panorama of the Northern seashore of Reykjavik, as seen from Orfirisey

Old Harbour

Safnahusio

Austurvollur, Reykjavik Cathedral & Parliament House

Skolavoroustigur

Embassy of Denmark

Laugardalsvollur

Residential area of Reykjavik

Austurstraeti Street

Laugavegur

Tiornin in Central Reykjavik

King of Atlantis Statue in Reykjavik

As keenly observed, those cities that were chosen to be destroyed by God in the last days are those cities whose residents became sinful by their activity of venerating idols. Whether a city is small or big, prosperous or poor, and new or old, it is targeted for destruction if its inhabitants have committed sins before God's eyes.

In Psalm 9:6, it says: "You have turned back the nations, you have beaten down the wicked and blotted out their names forever." The names of cities, dates, and times of destruction, as specifically stated here, are meticulously double-checked and confirmed by God as correct, exact, precise, accurate, and final by God's infinite wisdom. In Isaiah 45:19, God says this: "…I, Yahweh, speak the truth. What I declare is always right." So, I likewise declare this truth as what God has said to me. I cannot say any untruthful statement as God warns this in Psalm 101:7: "No double-dealer shall live in my house, no one who utters falsehood shall stand before my eyes."

All that will happen to these cities is a fulfilment of what was written long ago by Apostle John in Patmos in Revelation 16:17-19, which states: "The seventh angel emptied his cup into the air. Then a voice came forth from the throne and was heard outside the sanctuary, saying, "It is done." And there were flashes of lightning, peals of thunder and a violent earthquake. No, never has there been an earthquake so violent since people existed on earth. **The Great City was split into three, while the cities of the nations collapsed.**" This is also a fulfilment of Revelation 16:20-21 which states: "Then the continents withdrew and the mountain ranges hid. Great hailstones from heaven, as heavy as stones, dropped on the people, and the people insulted God because of this disastrous hailstorm, for it was truly a terrible plague."

But God, as he has promised, will readily relent in his plan if residents of that city change their ways and reject the evil that God denounces. For, it says in Jeremiah 18:7: "At times I warn a nation or a kingdom that I will uproot or destroy it. But if they change their ways and reject the evil I denounce, I then relent and refrain from doing the harm I had intended to do." In Revelation 9:17-19, it says: "In my vision, I saw those horses and their riders: they wear breastplates the colour of fire, hyacinth and sulphur. The heads of the horses look like lions' heads and fire, smoke and sulphur come out of their mouths. Then a third of humankind was killed by these plagues: fire, smoke and sulphur which the horses released through their mouths, for the power of the horses was both in their mouths and in their tails. Their tails, in fact, look like serpents, and their heads are able to inflict injury as well." It says further in Revelation 9:20-21: "However, the rest of humankind who were not killed by these plagues did not renounce their way of life: they went on worshipping the demons, keeping those idols of gold, silver, bronze, stone and wood that cannot see, hear or walk. No, they did not repent of their crimes, or their sorcery, or their sexual immorality or their theft."

By God's infinite wisdom, he has sealed in utmost secrecy the names of the last five cities to be destroyed so that all other places and cities would have time to reflect if they are included. In Revelation 10:4, it says: "Then the seven thunders sounded their own message. I was about to write what the seven thunders had sounded, when a voice from heaven said to me, 'Keep the words of the seven thunders secret and do not write them down.'"

So they will aspire to verify closely if their city is included by weighing their day-to-day activities if these are abhorrent before God's eyes. If they worship idols made of wood, stone, gold, and silver; if they continue committing sins and wickedness; if their men marry men and if their women marry women; if they do not recognise our Lord Jesus Christ as their personal savior; if they kill fetus inside mother's womb; if they do not observe Sabbath according to God's will; if they do not practise honest living and take advantage of their fellow men; and if they do not obey God's will, then their city is included and worthy to be destroyed in the last days. In any way, they will be able to know and feel that their city is soon to be completely destroyed. For God's people, they have to depart from that place immediately and settle in a safe place.

Isaiah 1:28 says: "But rebels and sinners alike will be destroyed and those who desert the Lord will likewise perish." Depart away from Sodom! By God's rich grace and mercy, he revealed to me that these last five cities consist of three populous cities in Asia, one city in America, and one city in Europe. It says in Psalm 9:21: "Bring terror, O Lord, strike at them, let the people realise that they are human."

That is true, humans are frail and easy to be destroyed. In Psalm 9:17-18, it says: "The Lord has made himself manifest in the execution of his judgment- the wicked plotters have been trapped by the work of their own hands. To the netherworld, the wicked will depart, all the nations that turn away from God." These unnamed cities will be destroyed, respectively, on January 8, 2078; February 9, 2083; August 9, 2093; February 14, 2069; and August 4, 2094. For this, the righteous should nurture a seed of faith in God Almighty through our Lord Jesus Christ in order to gain salvation and everlasting life.

God says to these cities in Ezekiel 7:5-11 "Thus says the Lord Yahweh: Disaster! Disaster is coming! The end is near! It is your tun, you who live in the country. The time has come, the day is near! No joy, only panic on the mountains! Now I am unleashing my fury against you; my anger will exhaust itself on you. I will judge you according to your ways and your detestable practices. I will not look on you with pity; I will be without mercy. I will judge you according to your conduct and call you to account for your detestable practices. I will not look on you with pity and I will show you no mercy. I will give you what your conduct deserves. And you will know that I am Yahweh when I strike you for your abominable practices. This is the day, the end is coming, the die is cast. For insolence has blossomed, pride bears its fruits and violence reigns. No one will escape."

In Joel 1:19-20, it says: "To you, Yahweh, I call. Fire has razed the open pasture; flames have burned the trees. Even wild beasts cry out to you for the streams have dried up, for the pastures have been devoured by fire."

Also, Ezekiel 13:13-14 says: "In my fury I will make a violent wind break out and in my anger I will send a torrential downpour, and my wrath will hurl destructive hailstones. I will destroy the wall you daubed with whitewash. I will level it to the ground and its foundation will be laid bare. It will fall and beneath it you will be utterly destroyed and you will know that I am Yahweh."

In Jeremiah 44:29, it says: "And this is the sign that I will punish you in this place, says Yahweh that you may know that my threatening words to you will be fulfilled." In Joel 1:15, it says: "What a dreadfdul day- the day of Yahweh that draws near and comes as ruin from the Almighty." After the cities are destroyed, they will become desolate and devoid of inhabitants. In Zephaniah 3:6, it says: "I have wiped out the nations, demolished their watchtowers, left their streets abandoned, and no one walks in them; their cities have been levelled, without even a man or an inhabitant to be seen."

For sinners who want to repent even if their sins have piled up like a mountain, God has this to say in Tobit 13:8: "…Be converted, you sinners, and live justly before him, certain that he will be pleased with you and show you mercy." The only salvation is for you to be converted and accept our Lord Jesus Christ as your personal savior. Have an unwavering faith in God Almighty through our Lord Jesus Christ so that you will be saved. Other than that is already destruction.

Isaiah 30:15 says: "For thus said the Lord Yahweh, the Holy One of Israel: 'Conversion and calmness are your salvation, quietness and trust will be your bravery.'" Even how sinful you are, you can still be forgiven and inherit God's kingdom. It says in Isaiah 1:18-20, "Come, say the Lord, let us reason together. Though your sins be like scarlet, they will be white as snow; though they be as crimson red, they will be white as wool. If you are willing and obedient, you eat the good things of the earth; but if you resist and rebel, the sword will eat you instead…"

God's wrath will bring total destruction to these cities. "For the mountains with the waters will be shaken to their foundations, the rocks will melt like wax before you, but to those who fear you, you will always show mercy." (Judith 16:15). "For the Lord, the Most High, is to be feared; he is a great king all over the earth" (Psalm 47:3). If God sees righteous people in their land, they will be forgiven. In Ezekiel 14:13-14, it says: "Son of man when a nation sins against me by being unfaithful, I will stretch out my hand against it deprived it of bread, and famine destroy men and animals. But if there were found in the land these three men, Noah, Daniel and Job, they would save their lives because of their righteousness..."

Furthermore, God tells you in Ezekiel 26:19-21: "...When I make you into a city of ruins like uninhabited towns, when I make the ocean rise against you and the mighty waters cover you, then I will thrust you down with those who descend to the pit, to the people of long ago. I will throw you into the netherworld, into everlasting loneliness, like those who go down to the pit that you may not return to the land of the living. Then you will be an object of horror, and even if sought, you will not be found-word of the Lord Yahweh."

Your unfaithfulness to God is explicit and transparent, as shown in your ways, words, and actions. You delight in worshipping creations instead of the Creator. You worship people dead long ago who are declared saints by the Roman Catholic Church instead of a true, living God. You venerate the Blessed Virgin Mary instead of God, who chose her as an instrument for Christ's coming into this world. You worship Jupiter, the highest pagan god, instead of our Lord Jesus Christ by celebrating Christmas every December 25. Let it be made known to all that Jupiter's feast day is December 25. Early Christians used December 25 to celebrate Christ's feast day to conceal from Roman authorities to avoid being persecuted. Because, at that time, teaching about Jesus Christ was considered a crime with a severe penalty attached to it, like nailing on trees, sawing in two from head to buttocks, feeding to hungry lions, cutting into several pieces, and reducing bodies into a torch.

The birth of our Lord Jesus Christ was not December 25 — it was rather April 14, 12 B.C., a Sunday, at 9:41 P.M. as revealed by Almighty God to me. You worship graven images and statues made of wood and stone, adorned with silver and gold, as dictated by your religion, instead of true God. You love money and eventually worship it as your "god." You worship handsome men and beautiful ladies, idolising them because of their being popular actors and actresses or singers and by reason of their looks instead of God. Your actions, activities, and practices are entirely works of Satan, who always waylays people to worship anything or anyone other than God Almighty. Without you knowing it, Satan used you as his instrument, tool, employee, and slave for his evil design. You are also used by Satan to obey your religion that worships idols made of wood and stone adorned with gold and silver.

Our Lord Jesus Christ is the only way toward salvation, for He is the way, the truth, and the life. No one comes to the Father except through Him. Our Lord Jesus Christ is the vine, and we are the branches. If we detach from Him, we are nothing — death engulfs us. With Him and in Him, we have everlasting life that even if we die, we will live again in resurrection. Do not believe in your religion. If your religion requires you to venerate images and statues, throw them away the same way a menstrual cloth is thrown in a garbage can. If your religion believes in the infallibility of its leader, throw it away as garbage. If your religion believes that its priests or pastors can mediate you to God, throw it away the same way as rubbish is thrown. Just believe in Our Lord Jesus Christ, and your salvation is already complete.

These are the people you wrongfully believe can save you: 1) The Blessed Virgin Mary, 2) The popes of Rome 3) Buddha, 4) Zoroaster, 5) Confucius, 6) the Emperor, 7) The author of Baghavad-Gita Zarathustra 8) Other gods and goddesses. They cannot save you nor mediate you to God Almighty. Only our Lord Jesus Christ can save you and mediate you to God Almighty. He alone. None else.

In Hebrews 9:14-15, it says: "…He, moved by the eternal spirit, offered himself as an unblemished victim to God and his blood cleanses us from dead works, so that we may serve the living God. So Christ is the mediator of a new covenant or testament. His death made atonement for the sins committed under the Old Testament and the promise is handed over to all who are called to the everlasting inheritance." In 1st Timothy 2:5-6, it states: "As there is one God, there is one mediator between God and men, Christ Jesus, true man, who gave his life for the redemption of all." Build a strong foundation of faith in God through our Lord Jesus Christ to be saved and have everlasting life.

You, believers and followers of Catholicism; you celebrate feasts of saints to adore them, but you never venerate God. That practice is a complete disregard of your duty to God which is to worship him alone, to love him alone, and to serve him alone. For this, you rebel against God. What are you doing in your feasts? You celebrate it with DISCO (Dancing in Satan's Company Overnight), playing satanic songs, chants, and Satan-inspired music, and you dance in satanic movements and style. You prepare food and liquor in your feast and be a glutton and drunk, making foolishness and evil. You celebrate Christmas, making Santa Claus the centre of celebration instead of our Lord Jesus Christ. You are insulting God and our Lord Jesus Christ. Do not worship any other god. Worship only God Almighty through our Lord Jesus Christ. Remember, our God is a jealous God. He does not want you to worship any other gods.

Following the destruction of these forty cities, there will be a scarcity of goods, foods, resources, and other basic needs. Those with money cannot easily buy food and other necessities if they have no mark of the beast. As their names are not written in the Book of Life, those who worship the beast can buy food and will not go hungry.

Revelation 13:5-8 says: "The beast was given speech and it spoke boastful and blasphemous words against God; it was allowed to wield its power for forty-two months. It spoke blasphemies against God, his name and his sanctuary, that is, those who already dwell in heaven. It was allowed to make war on the saints and to conquer them. It was given authority over people of evey tribe, language and nation; this is why all the inhabitants of the earth will worship before it, those whose names have not been written in the book of life of the slain Lamb, since the foundation of the world."

God's saints, whose names are written in the Book of Life and destined for eternal life, will suffer a lot. Many of them will go to prison to be tortured and die, while some will be killed right away.

Revelation 13:10 says: "If your lot is the prison, to prison you will go, if your lot is to be killed by the sword, by the sword you will be slain." These God's saints will suffer for forty-two months. In Isaiah 13:15, it says: "Whoever is captured will be slain, whoever is caught will be slaughtered." Only a few of them will survive. Those who will die will be raised to life in Christ's second coming.

There will be another beast who will help the first beast. It will mark the right hand or forehead of people with the name of the beast. Those who refuse to be marked and will not worship the beast will be put to death. Revelation 13:15-17 says: "It has been allowed to give a spirit to this statue; the statue of the beast speaks and those who refuse to worship it are killed. So this second beast makes everyone great and small, rich and poor, free and enslaved-be branded on right hand or on the forehead, and no one can buy or sell unless he has been branded with the name of the beast or the number of its name."

Those who belong to God will prefer to suffer than be marked with the number of beast, which is 666. They cannot buy or sell anything. They will go hungry. They will suffer because of love to God Almighty through our Lord Jesus Christ. It would be better for those who have died earlier for they no longer experience hardship. It says in Revelation 14:12-13, "This is the time for patient endurance among saints, for those who keep the commandments of God and faith in Jesus. I heard someone from heaven say, "Write this: Happy from now are the dead who have died in the Lord. The Spirit says: Let them rest from their labours; their good deeds go with them." The beast, 666, will be discussed further in Chapter 7. As they are already identified and pinpointed, God's people should take the necessary steps to reject them.

CHAPTER III
THE ALMIGHTY FATHER AND OUR LORD JESUS CHRIST

Since most of God's redeemed people still lack knowledge about Him, I have to tell you what I know about our God, hoping that I can add to your knowledge about Him so you may have some information about him when you come to His eternal glory. He is our only God: the God of all creation, the Master of the Universe, the God of Abraham, Isaac, and Jacob, the God of truth and spirit, the everlasting, infinite God of eternity. Our only God is an infinite God. He has no beginning and no end. Out of nothing, he made the Heavens, the Earth, and the entire universe by his will.

In 2nd Maccabees 7:28, it says: "I ask you now, my son, that when you see the heavens, the earth and all that is in it, you know that God made all this from nothing, and the human race as well." Also, Psalm 104:24 says: "How varied O Lord are your works! In wisdom you have made them all – the earth full of your creatures."

He is a merciful God. He is merciful to all people of all generations. He is merciful not only to righteous people but also to sinners. He gives time to sinners to repent that they will be saved together with righteous people so that everyone would attain eternal life. In Psalm 145:9, it says: "The Lord is merciful to everyone; his love is for all his creation."

In order to obtain mercy from Him, you have to be humble in heart and spirit. You have to take note of prayer in Psalm 57:1, which says: "Have mercy on me, O God, have mercy, for my soul takes refuge in you; I will find shelter in the shadow of your wings till the disaster has passed."

God is infinite. He has no beginning and no end. Isaiah 45:21 says: "Take counsel together come here and declare: who announced this from the beginning, who foretold it in the distant past? Am I not Yahweh? There is no other God besides me, a Savior, a God of justice- there is no other one but me." In Malachi 1:14, it says: "...For I am a great King and my name will be respected through all the nations, says Yahweh of hosts." In Isaiah 44:6, God says: "I am the first and I am the last, and there is no other God besides me..."

He is limitless. Let us praise him forever. Psalm 67:3-4 says, "May your way be known on earth and your salvation among the nations. May the peoples praise you, O God, may all the peoples praise you."

Our God is perfect. As he is perfect, he wants us also to follow his example. Many people say and argue that man can't be perfect as nothing can compare to God. Yes, it is possible to achieve perfection in this world, but the people who do do not realise that they are perfect. Those people whose prayers are answered by God are perfect. In Job 12:4, it says: "The man who calls and whom God answers, the just and perfect man..."

His wisdom cannot be fathomed by anyone in Heaven and on Earth. He is all-loving, all-faithful, holy, eternal, and the Almighty

God. Our Lord is compassionate and slow to anger. In Deuteronomy 3:2-4, it says: "He is the Rock and perfect are all his works, just are all his ways. A faithful God he is, upright and just and unerring." In Psalm 145:8, it says: "Compassionate and gracious is the Lord, slow to anger and abounding in love." In Psalm 100:5, it says: "For the Lord is good: his love lasts forever and his faithfulness through all generations."

Words alone are inadequate to describe our Eternal God. But still, I have to tell you what I know about Him. I have not seen Him with my naked eye, as it is impossible for man to see God and live, but I have heard His heavenly voice several times, which makes my tears drop in great joy that cleanses my eyes and my whole being and cures my illnesses.

I am pretty sure that it is the same voice heard by Abraham, Isaac, Jacob and his servants who obeyed and have faith in him. It is the same voice heard by Noah when He commanded Noah to build an ark one hundred years before the great flood (Genesis 6:9-22). It is the same voice heard by Moses when He commanded Moses to liberate his people from the bondage in Egypt (Exodus 3: 4-22). Only a few men had seen our Lord God Almighty. Moses was able to come face to face with God at Mount Horeb, but he hid his face for no man could be alive seeing God's face (Exodus 3:115). Any flesh cannot sustain God's flame. For God is a consuming fire (Hebrews 12:29, Deuteronomy 4:24). Enoch had seen God Almighty, and he was taken up to heaven (Genesis 5:21-24). He left no account of his encounter with God Almighty. Isaiah only saw God in a vision.

Isaiah 6:1-7 says: "In the year that King Uzziah died I saw the Lord seated on a throne, high and exalted; the train of his robe filled the Temple. Above him were seraphs, each with six wings: two to cover the face, two to cover the feet, and two to fly with. They are calling to one another: "Holy, holy, holy is Yahweh Sabaoth. All the earth is filled with his Glory!" At the sound of their voices the foundations of the threshold shook and the Temple was filled with smoke. I said, 'Poor me! I am doomed! For I am a man of unclean lips living among people of unclean lips, and yet I have seen the King, Yahweh Sabaoth.' Then one of the seraphs flew to me; in his hands was a live coal which he had taken with tongs from the altar. He touched my mouth with it and said, 'See, this has touched your lips; your guilt is taken away and your sin is forgiven.'" Elijah saw God Almighty when he was taken up by a whirlwind of flames in a chariot drawn by fiery horses. (Sirach 48:9).

We, the redeemed God's people, will also see God's face in the last days. Before this event, we must know more about Him. To know more about God, we must always talk to him in spirit — as he is spirit — through prayer. We are very lucky that we have Him as our God, as He is the only One in the whole universe.

It says in Deuteronomy 6:4-9, "Listen, Israel: Yahweh, our God, is One Yahweh. And you shall love Yahweh, your God, with all your heart, with all your soul and with all your strength. Engrave on your heart the commandments that I pass on to you today. Repeat them over and over to your children, speak of them when you are at home and when you travel, when you lie down and when you rise. Brand them on your hand as a sign, and keep them always before your eyes. Engrave them on your doorposts and on your city gates."

Yahweh, being our only God, we have to worship him alone, love him alone, and serve him alone and none else. We should not replace Him with any other gods or, worse, with graven images or statues, for Exodus 20:4-6it says: "Do not make yourself a carved image or anything in heaven, or on earth beneath, or in the waters under the earth; you shall not bow down to them or serve them. For I Yahweh your God, am a jealous God; for the sin of the fathers, when they rebel against me, I punish the sons, the grandsons and the great-grandsons; but I show steadfast love until the thousandth generation for those who love me and keep my commandments."

Likewise, God sternly warns us on this: "Therefore do not become corrupted: do not make an idol or a god carved in the form of man or of a woman, or in the form of animal that lives on the earth, or of any kind of bird that flies in the sky, or of any reptile that crawls on the earth, or of any fish that lives in the water under the earth. When you look at the heavens and you see the sun, the moon, the stars, and all the heavenly bodies, do not prostrate yourselves to adore and serve them as gods" (Deuteronomy 4:16-19).

As a shining example, God punished the Israelites for worshipping idols by making them captives in Babylon for seven generations.

Our God is holy. Revelation 15:4 says: "Lord, who will not give honor and glory to your Name? For you alone are holy." It means that He is faultless, guiltless, spotless, unblemished, and undefiled. For this, we have to venerate Him with deep respect by bowing our heads low when we talk to Him in spirit as He is spirit. His name should be revered as Holy and never to be mentioned if unnecessary. You have to mention His Holy Name only in complete reverence in moments of praising Him. You have to implant His Holy Name deep in your heart, deep in your mind, and deep in your soul. Do not in any way profane His Holy Name (Leviticus 20:3).

God's Holiness is exclusively for Him alone and not to be extended to anyone in this world. No person is Holy in this world unless God's Holiness is bestowed on him. When someone says that he is holy and that such holiness does not come from God, it means that that holiness is fake. No one should be addressed in this world as "Your Holiness" as the way popes of Rome are addressed. The popes of Rome, who are securely guarded and surrounded by bodyguards in black uniforms wherever they go, are addressed as "Your Holiness" and professed to be infallible. This is a clear rivalry with God's Holiness. For this, the popes of Rome, who need not be guarded by angels as they have strong bodyguards around them, have deliberately defiled God's sanctuary and profaned His Mighty Name.

By God's Holiness, it means that He abides by those who have a contrite heart and are humble in spirit. In Isaiah 57:15, it says: "For thus says the Most High, he who is enthroned forever, he whose name is holy, 'I reign exalted and holy but I am also with him who is contrite and humble in spirit, to give the contrite heart revived and the humble in spirit a new life.'"

By God's Holiness, it means that no unholy person can come face to face with him. Any unholy person who meets God will instantly die. During Moses' time, the Israelites were afraid of seeing God lest they die right away. Only Moses, who was holy, could come near God. In Exodus 19:16-22, it says: "On the morning of the third day there was thunder and lightning and a dense cloud over the mountain and a very loud trumpet blast was heard. All the people in the camp trembled Moses then made the people leave the camp to meet God and stand at the foot of the mountain. Mount Sinai was completely covered in smoke because Yahweh had come down in fire, and the smoke rose as from a furnace. The whole mountain shook violently, while the blast of the trumpet became louder and louder. Moses spoke and God replied in thunder. When Yahweh had come down to the summit of Mount Sinai, God called Moses who went to the summit where Yahweh said to him, 'Go down and give warning to the people, lest they rush to see Yahweh and many of them perish.' Even the priests who come near Yahweh must purify themselves lest Yahweh break out against them."

This is the reason why no person can meet God if he is unholy and unpurified. He must first be purified before he can see God. Before praying, a person should first be clean and pure so that his prayer is heard by God. By God's Holiness, it means that no person can ever see his face; otherwise, that person will die right away. In Exodus 33:20-23, it says: Then Yahweh said, 'You cannot see my face because man cannot see me and live.' And he added, 'See this place near me, you shall stand on the rock and when my Glory passes I will put you in a hollow of the rock and cover you with my hand until I have passed by. Then I will take away my hand and you shall see my back, but my face shall not be seen."

The only one who has seen God is the one who came from Heaven, and that is our Lord Jesus Christ. John 1:18 says: "No one has ever seen God, but God-only Son made him known: the one who is in and with the Father." Our Lord Jesus Christ has seen the Father as he is the image of God. Colossians 1:15-16 says: "He is the image of the unseen God, and for all creation he is the firstborn, for in him all things were created, in heaven and on earth, visible and invisible: thrones, rulers, authorities, powers… All was made through him and for him."

By God's Holiness, it means that no one can judge his actions and decisions. His judgments are always right and just. In Daniel 3:26-27, it says: "Blessed and worthy of praise are you, O Lord God of our fathers! Your name is glorious forever! Justice is in all that you do; your acts are faultless, your ways are right, your judgments always true." As He is perfect and holy, God is always right in His decisions. In Ezekiel 18:29, it says: "But you, Israel, say: 'Yahweh's way is not just!' Is my position not just? Is it not rather yours that is wrong? That is why I will judge you, Israel, each one according to his ways, word of Yahweh. Come back, turn away from your offenses, that you may not deserve punishment."

God's Holiness is manifested by his conversation with Job. He reprimanded Job for being ignorant of his words to him as no one in this world can ever obscure divine plans. In Job 38:1-7, it states: "Then Yahweh answered Job out of the storm: 'Who is this that obscures divine plans with ignorant words? Gird up your loins like a man; I will question you and you must answer. Where were you when I founded the earth? Answer, and show me your knowledge. Do you know who determined its size, who stretched out its measuring line? On what were its bases set? Who laid its cornerstone, while the morning stars sang together and the sons of God shouted for joy?'"

Also, Job 42:1-6 states: "This was the answer Job gave to Yahweh: I know that you are all powerful; no plan of yours can be thwarted. I spoke of things I did not understand, too wonderful for me to know. My ears has heard of you, but now my eyes have seen you. Therefore I retract all I have said, and in dust and ashes I repent." To human beings, God's decisions may not sound just but in deepest thoughts, they are absolutely correct and true. Romans 11:33 says: "How deep are the riches, the wisdom and knowledge of God! His decisions cannot be explained, nor his ways understood!"

Our God is a jealous God. In Nahum 1:2-4, it says: "Yahweh is a jealous and avenging God, Yahweh takes vengeance in his wrath; Yahweh is slow to anger though immense in power. Yahweh punishes the guilty. In storm and whirlwind is his path; clouds are the dust of his feet. He rebukes the sea and dries it; he drains rivers of their water." He punishes sons, grandsons, and great-grandsons of sinners but shows steadfast love until limitless generations for those who love him and keep His commandments. God's jealousy is seen when his people, who were just taken out of captivity in Egypt, made a molten calf and declared that that was the god who brought them out of Egypt. God said to Moses: "I see that these people are a stiff-necked people. Now just leave me that my anger may blaze aginst them. I will destroy them, but of you I will make a great nation" (Exodus 32:9-10).

For this, Moses intervened to calm God's anger. It says in Exodus 32:11-13, "But Moses calmed the anger of Yahweh, his God, and said, 'Why O Yahweh, should your anger burst against your people whom you brought out of the land of Egypt with such great power and with a mighty hand? Let not the Egyptians say: 'Yahweh brought them out with evil intent, for he wanted to kill them in the mountains and wipe them from the face of the earth.' Turn away from the heat of your anger and do not bring disaster on your people. Remember your servants Abraham, Isaac and Jacob, and the promise you yourself swore: I will multiply your descendants like the stars of heaven, and all this land I spoke about I will give to them as an everlasting inheritance."

For this, let everybody know that God has commanded all His redeemed people not to make any kind of image or idols for worshipping. He alone is worthy to be praised and worshipped. Deuteronomy 4:24 says: "Know that Yahweh, your God, is a devouring fire. Yahweh is a jealous God." Also, Hebrews 12:29 says: "Our God is indeed a consuming fire."

Our Almighty Father is just. Whenever His servants commit sins, He is always ready to forgive. But He does not just leave it without punishment, which is to give a lesson to his servants. In Psalm 99:8, it says: "O Lord our God, you responded to them; you were a forgiving God for them, but you punished their wrongs."

Like in the case of Ahab, the king of Samaria. Ahab wanted to possess the vineyard of Naboth. But Naboth does not want to sell his vineyard to Ahab. Ahab killed Nabot through the manipulations of Jezebel, Ahab's wife. God wanted to punish Ahab for this. But because of Ahab's deep repentance, God did not bring disaster during his reign, but the disgrace was given to his son who ruled after him (1st Kings 21:1-27).

Also, in the case of David, he sent Uriah the Hittite to a very fierce battle to be killed by the enemy and took his wife for himself. This was not acceptable to God. Yet David was forgiven of his sins. But the child whom Uriah's wife bore to David was struck by God and became sick and later died. But before the child died, David appealed to God by fasting and sleeping on ashes. Yet God still went on with his decision that that child would die, but He forgave David for what he had done. David instead comforted his wife Bathsheba and slept with her. She bore a son whom he named Solomon. Yahweh loved Solomon and named him Jedidiah through Nathan on Yahweh's behalf (2nd Samuel 12:1-25). Indeed, our God is just, and He wants us to be just in our dealings as he is.

Hence, since our Almighty Father is our only God, the Holy God is a jealous God. We must love Him with all our heart, with all our mind, and with all our strength. In Hosea 6:6, it states: "For it is love that I desire, not sacrifice; it is knowledge of God not burnt offerings."

As God is love, the opening greetings to him should be: "I love you, Father" or "I love you, Lord." There is no such thing to Him as good morning, good afternoon, or good evening as He is light, and there is no darkness in him. He is love and the only source of perfect love. So the appropriate greeting to him is: "I love you, Father." It would be better if you say to Him this: "I love you, Father, with all my heart, with all my mind, with all my soul, with all my spirit, and with all my strength forever through our Lord Jesus Christ." The love that God gives humanity is true love, says the Lord. So believe and compensate him also with true love.

In 1st John 4:16-19, it says: "We have known the love of God and have believed in it. God is love. He who lives in love, lives in God and God in him. When do we know that we have reached a perfect love? When in this world, we are like him in everything, and expect with confidence the Day of Judgment. There is no fear in love. Perfect love drives away fear, for fear has to do with punishment, he who fears does not know perfect love. So let us love one another, since he loved us first." Amen.

The Divinity of Our Lord Jesus Christ

Our Lord Jesus Christ has been with God Almighty long before all things in this world came into being.

In Proverbs 8:22-31, we are reminded of this: "Yahweh created me first, at the beginning of his works. He formed me from of old, from eternity, even before the earth. The abyss did not exist when I was born, the springs of the sea had not gushed forth; the mountains were still not set in their place nor the hills, when I was born before he made the earth or countryside, or the first grains of the world's dust. I was there when he made the skies and drew the earth's compass on the abyss, when he formed the clouds above and when the springs of the ocean emerged; when he made the sea with its limits that it might not overflow. When he laid the foundations of the earth, I was close beside him, the designer of his works, and I was his daily delight, forever playing in his presence, playing throughout the world and delighting to be with the sons of men."

Being with God in the beginning of time, our Lord Jesus Christ also acquired what is in the Father. The divinity of the Father is also with the Son. For, in Colossians 2:9-10, it says: For in Him dwells the fullness of God in bodily form. He is the head of all cosmic power and authority, and in him you have everything."

The Father and the Son are one. Colossians 1:15 says: "He is the image of the unseen God and for all creation he is the firstborn …" Likewise, in Hebrews 1:3, it says: "He is the radiance of God's Glory and bears the stamp of God's hidden being, so that his powerful word upholds the universe. And after taking away sin, he took his place at the right hand of the divine Majesty in Heaven."

Those who have seen the Son have also seen the Father because the Father and the Son are one. Happy are those who have seen the Son because, in so doing, they have also seen the Father. But it is more blessed for those who have not seen the Son yet believe in His divinity and believe in the Father. Those who have not seen the Son have not also seen the Father. However, those who have not seen the Father and the Son but have unwavering faith in the Father through the Son will be saved and have everlasting life forever.

The divinity of our Lord Jesus Christ is confirmed in John 1:1-2, which says: "In the beginning was the Word. And the Word was with God and the Word was God; he was in the beginning with God." The actual beginning is not the creation of all things in the universe. It is beyond eternity to eternity, the limitless of time. It is beyond man's understanding but is well understood by faith. The Son is not merely a part of the Father; He is the Father himself, as all divine qualities of the Father are all in Him. In John 16:15, it says: "All that the Father has is mine; because of this I have just told you, that the Spirit will take what is mine and make it known to you." The purpose why the signs of our Lord Jesus Christ's divinity are recorded is for everyone to believe that they may have life and have it more abundantly. John 20:31 says: "These are recorded so that you may believe that Jesus is the Christ, the Son of God; believe and you will have life through his Name." Those who find our Lord Jesus Christ have found life and that they are blessed by God the Father. But those who hate our Lord Jesus Christ find death all throughout eternity. Proverbs 8:35-36 says: "Those who find me find life; theirs Yahweh's blessing. Those who offend me will undergo affliction; they hate me for they love death."

Our Lord Jesus Christ's divinity was clearly manifested when John the Baptist baptized Him in the Jordan River. In Mattherw 3:13-17, it says: "At that time Jesus arrived from Galilee and came to

John at the Jordan to be baptized by him. But John tried to prevent him, and said: 'How is it you come to me: I should be baptized by you!' But Jesus answered him, 'Let it be like that for now. We must do justice to God's plan.' John agreed. As soon as he was baptized, Jesus came up from the water. At once, the heavens opened to him and he saw the Spirit of God come down like a dove and rest upon him. At the same time a voice from heaven was heard, 'This is my Son, the Beloved; he is my Chosen One."

Also, in Mark 1:11, it says: "And these words were heard from Heaven, 'You are my Son, the Beloved, the One I have chosen." John the Baptist also attests to our Lord Jesus Christ's divinity. Mark 1:6-8 says: "John was clothed in camel's hair and wore a leather garment around his waist. His food was locusts and honey. He preached to the people, saying, 'After me comes one who is more powerful than I am; I have baptized you with water, but he will baptize you in the Holy Spirit. As for me, I am not worthy to bend down and untie his sandals."

Another clear evidence of our Lord Jesus Christ's divinity is the annunciation to the Blessed Virgin Mary by Archangel Gabriel that she would give birth to a child who would become the saviour and that she should name him Jesus. And during Christ's birth in Bethlehem, where there were angels who announced to shepherds tending their sheep camping in an open field on that night of his birth.

In Luke 1:26-35, it says: "In the sixth month, the angel Gabriel was sent from God to a town of Galilee called Nazareth. He was sent to a young virgin who was betrothed to a man named Joseph of the family of David; and the virgin's name was Mary. The angel came to her and said, 'Rejoice, full of grace, the Lord is with you.' Mary was troubled at these words, wondering what this greeting could mean. But the angel said, 'Do not fear Mary, for God has looked kindly on you. You shall conceive and bear a son and you shall call him Jesus. He will be great and shall rightly be called Son of the Most High. The Lord God will give him the kingdom of David, his ancestor, he will rule over the people of Jacob forever and his reign shall have no end.' Then Mary said to the angel, 'How can this be if I am a virgin?' And the angel said to her, 'The Holy Spirit will come upon you and the power of the Most High will overshadow you; Therefore, the holy child to be born shall be called Son of God." Our Lord Jesus Christ's divinity was announced in advance before He came into the world.

In response to a decree of the emperor for a census of the empire, the Holy Family was in Bethlehem to be registered. As there were many people who were to be registered and there was no room to stay, the Holy Family only settled in a stable. This reflects Christ's extreme humility coming into the world. In Luke 2:6-7, it says: "They were in Bethlehem when the time came for her to have her child, and she gave birth to a son, her first born. She wrapped him in swaddling clothes and laid him in the manger, because there was no place for them in the living room." The Son of God, the owner of all things in the universe, came into this world in extreme humility to show everyone that the wealth of this world is nothing compared to the salvation of souls. Similarly, Christ showed unprecedented humility when he was buried in a borrowed tomb. In Matthew 27:57-60, it says: "It was now evening and there arrived a wealthy man from Arimathea, named Joseph, who was also a disciple of Jesus. He went to Pilate and asked for the body of Jesus, wrapped it in a clean sheet and laid it in his own new tomb which had been cut out of the rock. Then he rolled a huge stone across the entrance of the tomb and left."

Another indication of Christ's extreme humility is the fact that the first ones to visit the nativity site were poor shepherds who were tending their flocks on the night of Christ's birth, which, according to divine revelation, took place on **April 14, 12 B.C., at 9:41 P.M.** Our Lord Jesus Christ was not born on December 25 as the Roman Catholic Church insists. December 25 is the feast day of the highest pagan god, Jupiter. The Roman Catholic Church has inculcated upon people's minds for more than two thousand years already that Christ was born on December 25. God is furious at this pagan religion for distorting the truth. God is likewise angry with people who are docile to the teachings of this religion, which are all lies. Nothing but wanton lies. The Roman Catholic Church, being pinpointed as the great harlot in the Book of Revelation, repeatedly thwarted truth by teaching blatant lies all throughout its existence. Those who follow its teachings are doomed to eternal damnation as they are susceptible to idolatry being encouraged by their church hierarchy. Those who practice idolatry by venerating carved statues and images as Catholics do will be condemned in the last days. Eternal fire awaits them in hell. I have to frankly tell you that you will never be saved if you do not depart from such kind of worship. I advise you to change your religion to James I:27 and be saved.

Luke 2:8-16 says: "There were shepherds camping in the countryside, taking turns to watch over their flocks by night. Suddenly an angel of the Lord appeared to them, with the Glory of the Lord shining around them. As they were terrified, the angel said to them, 'Don't be afraid; I am here to give you good news, great joy for all the people. Today a Saviour has been born to you in David's town; he is the Messiah and the Lord. Let this be a sign to you: you will find a baby wrapped in swaddling clothes and lying in a manger.' Suddenly the angel was surrounded by many more angels, praising

God and saying, 'Glory to God in the highest; peace on earth for God is blessing humankind.' When the angels left them and gone back to heaven, the shepherds said to one another, 'Let us go as far as Bethlehem and see what the Lord has made known to us.' So they came hurriedly and found Mary and Joseph with the baby lying in the manger."

This event leads us to the conclusion that our Lord Jesus Christ comes from Heaven and that His divinity comes from God. In 1st Peter 1:8-9, it states: "You have not seen him and yet you love him; even without seeing him, you believe in him and experience a heavenly joy beyond all words, for you are reaching the goal of your faith; the salvation of your souls."

Another clear evidence of our Lord Jesus Christ's divinity was shown when he died. In Matthew 27:51-54, it says: "Just then the curtain of the temple sanctuary was torn in two from top to bottom, the earth quaked, rocks were split, tombs were opened, and several holy people who had died raised to life. They came out of the tombs after the resurrection of Jesus, entered the Holy City and appeared to many. The captain and the soldiers who guarded Jesus were greatly terrified when they saw the earthquake and all that had happened, and said, 'Truly, this man was a Son of God.'" Those dead who came to life again at the resurrection moment of our Lord Jesus Christ partook with his rising from death because they lived their previous life in holiness. Similarly, God's people who lived a holy life while on earth will surely be resurrected and redeemed. Those who lived in Jesus and died in him will have their share in resurrection.

Our Lord Jesus Christ's divinity is clearly shown before his crucifixion when he fervently prayed to God. The prayer says: "Father, the hour has come; give glory to your Son, that the Son may give glory to you. You have given him power over all mortals, and you want him to bring eternal life to all you have entrusted to him" (John 17:1-2).

Our Lord Jesus Christ addressed God as "Father," which connotes that the Father and the Son are one. Our Lord Jesus Christ had known beforehand his mission, which was to sacrifice and die for humanity's salvation since animal sacrifice, which had been practised for centuries after the fall of man, cannot suffice to ransom mankind from sin. Man's salvation needs the sacrifice of the only begotten Son of God, our Lord Jesus Christ. That is why our Lord Jesus Christ says: "The hour has come," and he himself asks the Father for him to pass the cup for him to drink, which is the cup of crucifixion and death for salvation and atonement of sins of the world. Yet because of his faith in God, he has to obey him even going to death. In 1st Peter 2:24, it says: "He went to the cross burdened with our sins so that we might die to sin and live an upright life." Also, in Philippians 2:8, it says: "He humbled himself by being obedient to death, death on the cross."

The relationship of the Father to the Son is mutual, such that the glory of the Father is upon the Son, and the glory of the Son is upon the Father in saying these words: "Give glory to your Son, that the Son may give glory to you." Our Lord Jesus Christ is entrusted with power over all people, such that their salvation and eternal life will be brought by Christ by dying for them. It is, therefore, God's will that Christ will bring eternal life to all by sacrificing himself on the cross.

As a continuation to the prayer, our Lord Jesus Christ utters this: "I have glorified you on earth and finished the work that you give me to do. Now, Father, give me in your presence the same Glory I had with you before the world began" (John 17:4-5). Before the creation had begun, Christ already possessed an innate Glory derived from the Father. It goes to say that God's glory is also Christ's glory, which connotes that God's divinity is the same as Christ's divinity. Christ had glorified God the Father when he accomplished his mission, i.e., by his death on the cross. For this, Christ asks God to give him the same glory as he had before. This shows that Christ's divinity is inherent in God the Father in the infinity of time.

In succeeding verses, our Lord Jesus Christ continues his prayer: "I have made your name known to those you gave me from the world. They were yours and you gave them to me, and they kept your word. And now they know that all you have given me comes indeed from you. I have given them the teaching I received from you, and they received it and know in truth that I came from you; and they believe that you have sent me" John 17:6-8). Succinct in Christ's prayer that all teachings he has given mankind come from God. Hence, those who receive them and believe that such teachings come from God also affirm that Christ comes from God as Christ's divinity. Those who receive Christ's teaching also receive God's teachings. And that they believe that Christ comes from God. Hence God's divinity is also Christ's divinity, as the Father and the Son are one.

In John 17: 9-11, our Lord Jesus Christ continues this prayer: "I pray for them; I do not pray for the world but for those who belong to you and whom you have given to me- indeed all I have is yours all you have is mine- and now they are my glory. I am no longer in the world, but they are in the world whereas I am going to you. Holy Father, keep them in your name..." The oneness of God with his Son and the oneness of the Son with the Father is manifested in the prayer of our Lord Jesus Christ: "All I have is yours, and all you have is mine." As God's glory is also Christ's glory and God's possessions are also Christ's possessions, it goes to say that God's divinity is also Christ's divinity. "Whereas I am going to you." This part of prayer connotes Christ's divinity, which comes from God the Father should go back to the Father.

Our Lord Jesus Christ continues his prayer to God the Father in verses 12-16, which states: "When I was with them, I kept them safe in your Name, and not one was lost except the one who was already lost, and in this the Scripture was fulfilled. But now I am coming to you and I leave these my words in the world that my joy may be complete in them. I have given them your message and the world has hated them because they are not of the world; just as I am not of the world."

This continuation of Jesus' prayer signifies that the message he has given to people comes from God. This also supports Christ's divinity as he comes from God, who has given him a message to be preached to people. Such prayer refers to Judas Iscariot, who betrayed Jesus to fulfill Christ's mission to redeem mankind from sin in fulfillment of the Scripture. Likewise, it is a true fact that those who sincerely follow our Lord Jesus Christ become an object of the world's hatred. Those who follow Jesus, though they are in the world, must not belong to the world by detaching oneself from worldly things as Jesus was not in the world and he did not love worldly things.

In verses 17-21, it states: "Consecrate them in the truth-your word is truth-for I have sent them into the world as you sent me into the world. For their sake, I go to the sacrifice by which I am consecrated, so that they too may be consecrated in truth. I pray not only for these but also for those who through their word will believe in me. May they all be one as you Father are in me and I am in you. May they be one in us; so the world may believe that you have sent me."

Christ's divinity is clearly shown by his fulfillment of the mission given by God to be a sacrifice for the redemption of mankind. So, as God sent him, he also sent his disciples to people so that they may be one with God. As the Father and the Son are one, so the people who spread the teachings are one with the Father and the Son.

Our Lord Jesus Christ continues his prayer to God the Father in verses 22-24, which states: " I have given them the Glory you have given me, that they may be one as we are one: I in them and you in me. Thus they shall reach perfection in unity and the world shall know that you have sent me and that I have loved them just as you loved me. Father, since you have given them to me, I want them to be with me where I am and see the Glory you gave me, for you loved me before the foundation of the world."

This part of Jesus' prayer concludes his divinity, that where he is, he would bring with him the redeemed to let them see the Glory that God had given him before the world was made. "I have loved them just as you loved me," a phrase that connotes that our Lord Jesus Christ comes from God the Father and that his divinity also comes from him.

The last portion of Jesus' prayer to God the Father is stated in verses 25-26, which says: "Righteous Father, the world has not known you but I have known you that you have sent me. As I revealed your Name to them, so will I continue to reveal it, so that the love with which you loved me may be in them and I also may be in them." This strongly manifests Christ's divinity as he addresses God as "Father." He has known God as he came from him and carried the same qualities and divinity of God the Father. Our Lord Jesus Christ came into the world bringing with him joy, peace, and love to all the peoples of all generations.

In Ephesians 2:14-16, it says: "For Christ is our peace, he who has made the two peoples one , destroying in his own flesh the wall-- the hatred – which separated us. He abolished the Law with its commands and precepts. He made peace in uniting the two peoples in him, creating out of the two one New Man. He destroyed hatred and reconciled us both to God through the cross, making the two one body."

Here are some miracles and events supporting Christ's Divinity:

Wedding At Cana.

It was not yet the right hour for our Lord Jesus Christ to perform any miracle. But by the necessity of circumstance — as there was no more wine and to save the face of the bridegroom to the guests — Christ, upon the intercession of his mother, Mary, ordered the servants to fill with water to the brim the six stone water jars used for ritual cleansing. As soon as the jars were filled, Jesus transformed the water into wine. It was not an ordinary wine. It was rather the best wine as tasted by guests and steward. This miracle has not been duplicated by anyone on Earth since then. Hence, this is a divine work (John 2:1-11) that clearly supports Christ's divinity.

Jesus Drives Away the Devil

At Capernaum, when our Lord Jesus Christ began to teach in the synagogue during Sabbath assemblies, a man possessed by an evil spirit shouted: "What do you want with us Jesus of Nazareth? Have you come to destroy us? I know who you are: You are the Holy One of God." Then Jesus faced him and said with authority, "Be silent and come out of this man!" The evil spirit shook the man violently and, with a loud shriek, came out of him (*Mark 1:21-26). These demons, who came from Heaven and were cast down to Earth as fallen angels know very well that Jesus is divine and that his divinity comes from the Almighty Father.

Jesus Cures a Leper.

Matthew 8:1-4 tells us that when our Lord Jesus Christ came down a mountain and was followed by a large crowd, a leper came to him asking for favour to cure him. Then, Jesus touched him, saying that he would be clean. At once, the leper was healed. This miracle could have only been possible by God's power. It supports Christ's divinity, as the cleansing of a leper in an instant would never again be done in history. This event is recorded in Mark 1:40-44, which states: "A leper came to Jesus and begged him, 'If so will, you can make me clean.' Moved by pity, Jesus stretched out his hand and touched him, saying, 'I will; be clean.' The leprosy left the man at once and he was made clean. As Jesus sent the man away, he sternly warned him, 'Don't tell anyone about this, but go and show yourself to the priest and for the cleansing bring offering ordered by Moses; in this way you will make your declaration.'" Likewise, Luke 5:12 confirms this event. It shows here that God wants us to be healed of our illnesses immediately without medical or pharmaceutical intervention. This supports Christ's divinity.

Jesus Cures a Paralytic.

In Matthew 9:1-2, it states: "Jesus got back into the boat, crossed the lake again and came to his hometown. Here they brought a paralyzed man to him, lying on bed. Jesus saw their faith and said to the paralytic, 'Courage, my son! Your sins are forgiven." Then, the paralyzed man was cured. Upon hearing what our Lord Jesus Christ has said, the teachers of the Law criticised our Lord Jesus Christ, saying that he was insulting God. For God alone can forgive sins.

471

Then, our Lord Jesus Christ answered them this: "You must know that the Son of Man has authority on earth to forgive sins." Christ's answer manifests his divinity, which comes from God the Father.

Who should be criticised here are the popes of Rome as well as the cardinals and priests of the Roman Catholic Church who, without an iota of authority from God, easily forgive sins. Another thing the pope of Rome openly declares himself is infallible. It is very wrong. Only God Almighty and our Lord Jesus Christ are infallable and none else.

This miracle performed by our Lord Jesus Christ is also stated in Mark 2:1-5 which states: "After some days Jesus returned to Capernaum. As the news spread that he was at home, so many people gathered that there was no longer room even outside the door. While Jesus was preaching the Word to them, some people brought a paralyzed man to him. The four men who carried him couldn't get near Jesus because of the crowd, so they opened the roof above the room where Jesus was and through the hole, lowered the man on his mat. When Jesus saw the faith of these people, he said to the paralytic, 'My son, your sins are forgiven." This event is also confirmed in Luke 5:17-21. Christ's divinity is supported by his authority to forgive sins.

Our Lord Jesus Christ Raises the Dead.

A great display of Christ's divinity was performed in Naim, a town in Israel where he raised the dead. No person in this world can raise the dead as that divine feat belongs only to God Almighty and our Lord Jesus Christ. In Luke 7:11-16, it says: "A little later Jesus went to a town called Naim and many of his disciples went with him — a great number of people. As he was the only son of his mother and she was a widow, there followed a large crowd of townspeople. On seeing her the Lord had pity on her and said, 'Don't cry.' Then he came up and touched the stretcher and the men who carried it stopped. Jesus then said, 'Young man, awake, I tell you.' And the dead man got up and began to speak, and Jesus gave him to his mother. A holy fear came over them all and they praise God..." This event proves Christ's divinity.

Our Lord Jesus Christ Multiplies Bread.

Out of five loaves of bread and two fishes, our Lord Jesus Christ was able to feed five thousand men, not counting women and children. In Matthew 14:15-21, it says: "Late in the afternoon, his disciples came to him and said, 'We are in a lonely place and it is now late. You should send these people away, so they can go to the villages and buy something for themselves to eat.' But Jesus replied, 'They do not need to go away; you give them something to eat.' They answered, 'We have nothing here but five loaves and two fishes.' Jesus said to them, 'Bring them here to me.' Then he made everyone sit down on the grass. He took the five loaves and the two fishes, raised his eyes to heaven, pronounced the blessing, broke loaves and handed them to the disciples to distribute to the people. And they all ate, and everyone has enough; then the disciples gathered up the leftovers, filling twelve baskets. About five thousand men had eaten there without counting women and children." This miracle performed by our Lord Jesus Christ is echoed and confirmed in Mark 6:34-44, Luke 9:10-17, and John 6:1-13.

This multiplication of bread was repeated once more in Matthew 15:29-38, which says: "From there Jesus went to the shore of Lake Galilee, and then went up into the hills where he sat down . Great crowds came to him, bringing the dumb, the blind, the lame, the crippled, and many with other infirmities. The people carried them to the feet of Jesus, and he healed them. All were astonished when they saw the dumb speaking, the lame walking, the crippled healed and the blind able to see, so they glorified the God of Israel. Jesus called his disciples and said to them, 'I am filled with compassion for these people, they have already followed me for three days and now have nothing to eat. I do not want to send them away fasting, or they may faint on the way.' His disciples said to him. 'And where shall we find enough bread in this wilderness to feed such a crowd?" Jesus said to them, 'How many loaves do you have?' They answered, 'Seven, and a few small fish.' So Jesus ordered the people to sit on the ground. Then he took the seven loaves and the small fish and gave thanks to God. He broke them and gave them to his disciples, who distributed them to the people. They all ate and were satisfied, the leftover broken pieces filled seven wicker baskets. Four thousand men had eaten, not counting the women and children."

This miracle of our Lord Jesus Christ has never been duplicated by anyone since time immemorial. This is like the manna in the desert given to Israelites every day of their life after they left Egypt. It shows the vast riches of God stored in heaven, preserved for his people. This miracle supports Christ's divinity.

The Divinity of Our Lord Jesus Christ Is Strongly Supported by His Transfiguration From Human Form to Divine Form.

Matthew 17:1-9 tells us this: "Six days later, Jesus took with him Peter and James and his brother John and led them up a high mountain where they were alone. Jesus' appearance was changed before them: his face shone like the sun and his clothes became bright as light. Just then Moses and Elijah appeared to them, talking with Jesus. Peter spoke and said to Jesus, 'Master it is good that we are here. If you so wish, I will make three tents: one for you, one for Moses and one for Elijah.' Peter was still speaking when a bright cloud covered them in its shadow, and a voice from the cloud said, 'This is my Son, the Beloved, my Chosen One. Listen to him.' On hearing the voice, the disciples fell to the ground, full of fear. But Jesus came touched them and said, 'Stand up, do not be afraid.' When they raised their eyes, they no longer saw anyone except Jesus. And as they came down the mountain, Jesus commanded them not to tell anyone what they had just seen, until the Son of Man be raised from the dead." This event, witnessed by Peter, James, and John, shows that our Lord Jesus Christ is really the Son of God as He and the Father are One. This event strongly supports Christ's divinity. This is also confirmed in Mark 9:1-10 and in Luke 9:28-36.

Our Lord Jesus Christ as a Mediator Between God and Man.

In John 14:1-4, it states: "Do not be troubled; trust in God and trust in me. In my Father's house there are many rooms. Otherwise I would not have told you that I go to prepare a place for you. After I have gone and prepared a place for you, I shall come again and take you to me, so that where I am, you also may be. You know the way to where I am going." It strongly indicates that our Lord Jesus Christ is divine as he will go to God to prepare a place for us in Heaven. What Christ is driving at is we have to maintain faith in Him and with our Almighty Father and remain unblemished and undefiled until he comes back to usher us toward eternal life. This also signifies that our Lord Jesus Christ will have His Second Coming to the world. But we do not know the exact hour, day, or year. Only God knows this. It is very near already. So we have to be clean, undefiled, and unblemished until he comes.

The Prayer of Our Lord Jesus Christ at Gethsemane.

Our Lord Jesus Christ showed His divinity in the garden of Gethsemane. In Matthew 26:36-41, it says: "Jesus came with them to a place called Gethsemane, and he said to His disciples, 'Sit here while I go over to pray.' He took Peter and the two sons of Zebedee along with him, and he began to be filled with anguish and distress. And he said to them, 'My soul is filled with sorrow even to death. Remain here and stay awake with me.' He went a little farther and fell to the ground, with his face touching the earth, and prayed, 'Father, if it is possible, take this cup away from me. Yet not what I want, but what you want.' He went back to His disciples and found them asleep, and he said to Peter, 'Could you not stay awake with me for even an hour? Stay awake and pray, so that you may not slip into temptation. The spirit indeed is eager, but human nature is weak.'" The prayer of our Lord Jesus Christ signifies two aspects. First, our Lord Jesus Christ knows very well that His coming into the world is to redeem mankind from sin as a lamb to be sacrificed in order to regain life for all. Second, it signifies his divinity as he called God as Father, and he begs Him if it is possible that he will not drink the cup. His total obedience to God's will prevails so that the divine plan to save mankind is fulfilled.

Jesus Is Risen.

Christ's divinity is supported by his resurrection. In John 20:1-18, it says: "Now, on the first day after the Sabbath, Mary Magdala came to the tomb early in the morning, while it was still dark and she saw that the stone blocking the tomb had been moved away. She ran to Peter and the other disciple whom Jesus loved. And she said to them, 'They have taken the Lord out of the tomb and we don't know where they have laid him.' Peter then set out with other disciple to go to the tomb. They ran together but the other disciple outran Peter and reached the tomb first. He bent down and saw the linen cloths lying flat, but he did not enter. Then Simon Peter came following him and entered the tomb; he, too, saw the linen cloths lying flat. The napkin, which had been around his head was not lying flat like the other linen cloths but rolled up in its place. Then the other disciple who had reached the tomb first also went in; he saw and believed. Scripture clearly said that he must rise from the dead, but they had not understood that...

"Mary stood weeping outside the tomb, and as she wept she bent down to look inside; she saw two angels in white sitting where the body of Jesus had been, one at the head, and the other at the feet. They said, Woman, why are you weeping? She answered, 'Because they have taken my Lord and I don't know where they have put him.' As she said this, she turned around and saw Jesus standing there, but she did not recognize him. Jesus said to her, 'Woman, why are you weeping? Who are you looking for?' She thought it was the gardener and answered him, 'Lord if you have taken him away, tell me where you have put him, and I will go and remove him.' Jesus said to her, 'Mary.' She turned and said to him, 'Rabboni' — which means Master. Jesus said to her, 'Do not cling to me; you see I have not yet ascended to the Father. But go to my brothers and say to them: I am ascending to my Father, who is your Father, to my God, who is your God.' So Mary of Magdala went and announced to the disciples, 'I have seen the Lord, and this is what he said to me.'"

This event precedes Christ's ascension to Heaven. This strongly supports Christ's divinity.

Based on facts presented as supported by relevant Biblical verses, we can safely conclude that our Lord Jesus Christ is unquestionably divine and his divinity comes from God the Almighty Father.

CHAPTER IV
GOD'S PEOPLE

The Definition of the "Children of God"

They are those people who have unwavering faith in God Almighty and in our Lord Jesus Christ irrespective of creed, race, sex, culture, country and faith and worship God through our Lord Jesus Christ in truth and spirit without the aid of graven or printed images. God himself declared in Malachi 3:17-18, saying: "They will be mine on the day I make my choice. I will have mercy on them as a father has on his obedient son. Then you can distinguish the good from the bad, those who obey God from those who disobey him." You must be obedient to God's will so that His mercy will be upon you.

You committed sins in the past, but by God's grace, you were forgiven, as our God is a forgiving and merciful God. His love is abounding. He knows that your sins were not committed deliberately. You were repentant of your past sins that is why God forgives you as you come to His divine fold. In Colossians 1:21-23, it says: "You yourselves were once estranged and opposed to God because of your evil deeds, but now you have been reconciled. God reconciled you by giving up to death the body of Christ, so that you may be without fault, holy and blameless before him. Only stand firm, upon the foundation of your faith, and be steadfast in hope. Keep in mind the

Gospel you have heard, which has been preached to every creature under heaven…"

You are only enticed and deceived by evil that you have committed sin. You are not a born sinner. You belong to God. Even how sinful you are, even if your sin is as red as crimson, you will be forgiven by the Lord. In Sirach 2:11, it states: "For the Lord is compassion and loving-kindness; he forgives our sins and saves us in time of distress."

So return to God because you are his people. Instill in your life faith in him through our Lord Jesus Christ so that everlasting life will be yours. Whose fault was your sin? It was not your fault. It was Satan, the enemy, who caused you to sin. Satan continues even up to this time, day in and day out, on his evil deeds by destroying people and families. As he cannot destroy God, so he only destroys God's creatures, i.e., people and families. In many ways, Satan employs all kinds of strategies to destroy people.

Satan, through his minions who held powers in Europe, on several occasions in past history, attempted to destroy the word of God by burning thousands of copies of the Holy Bible. But he failed. He was able to burn the Holy Bible, but he was not able to burn the word of God. In Matthew 24:35, it says: "Heaven and earth will pass away, but my words will not pass away." Isaiah 40:8 says: "The grass withers, the flower fades, but the word of our God will forever stand."

There were also numerous attempts by Satan to destroy the Holy Bible by changing its wordings. Satan employs several groups to thwart the wordings of the Holy Bible, transforming them into Satan's cohorts. Nevertheless, there are bold men of God who are ready to check these evil deeds. These bold men of God are not afraid of whatever consequence they will get for doing service to God. They are not afraid of being hurt or killed as long as the word of God will come as pure and perfect — free of any dilution. They are equipped with sharp weapons in Job 39:22, which states: "afraid of nothing, laughing at fear, not shying away from the sword."

They are not afraid to die and be killed defending the word of God, for in dying for God and Christ, they will find eternal life. In Matthew 10:39, it says: He who cares only for his own life will lose it; he who loses his life for my sake will find it."

People of God, pay attention. "You do not lack any spiritual gift and only await the glorious coming of Christ Jesus, our Lord. He will keep you steadfast to the end, and you will be without reproach on the day of the coming of our Lord Jesus" (1ˢᵗ Corinthians 1:7-9). So let us rally behind the God of Truth and Spirit through our Lord Jesus Christ in the last days in order to be saved, for the time is at its end. We have to establish a seed of faith in God through our Lord Jesus Christ and be awarded everlasting life. These are what we should do:

First, pray constantly to God Almighty and worship Him in spirit and truth as He is Spirit and Truth. In Colossians 4:2, it says: "Be steadfast in prayer and even spend the night praying and giving thanks." In your prayer, you should always give thanks to God. He is the One who has transferred us from darkness to the kingdom of light in our Lord Jesus Christ. Colossians 1:12-14 says: "Constantly give thanks to the Father who empowered us to receive our share in the inheritance of the saints in his kingdom of light. He rescued us from the power of darkness and transferred us to the kingdom of his beloved Son. In him we are redeemed and forgiven."

In Psalm 18:7, it says: "But I called upon the Lord in my distress, I cried to my God for help; and from his temple he heard my voice, my cry of grief reached his ears." Have faith in God Almighty through our Lord Jesus Christ and be surely saved.

In Isaiah 8:13, it says: "Only Yahweh Sabaoth must you hold in veneration, only him must you fear, only him must you dread." In James 4:8, it says: "Draw close to God and he will come close to you."

Always course your prayer through our Lord Jesus Christ so that at the end of your prayer, you have to say: "This I pray through our Lord Jesus Christ, who lives and reigns with you in the unity of the Holy Spirit, One God forever and ever, Amen." Or, you may say, "Through our Lord Jesus Christ. Amen," or you may say, "Through Ieshua Mosha Amen Amen Amen Rak to the Rabbah to the Abbah."

In Colossians 3:17, it says, "And whatever you do or say, do it in the Name of Jesus, the Lord, giving thanks to God the Father through him." In Psalm 25:3, it says: "Those who hope in you will never be humbled; those who turn away from you will suffer disgrace."

If possible, pray together with your family. "For where two or three are gathered in my name, I am there among them" (Matthew 18:20). But you must also have an individual personal prayer to God to establish a strong personal relationship with Him. "He will give everlasting life to those who seek glory, honour, immortality and persevere in doing good" (Romans 2:7).

If you hear a voice after your individual prayer that "I do not know you" or "Do not be saddened," it means that that is the beginning of your personal relationship with God Almighty. I also experienced hearing such a voice saying, "I do not know you." But I just continued every night my prayer to Him until such time when He blessed me in truth and spirit. Make your prayer short and concise.

In 1st Chronicles 28:9, it says: "And you Solomon my son, know the God of your father serve him with undivided heart and a willing mind; for Yahweh knows all our thoughts and desires. If you seek him, he will let you find him; but if you turn away from him, he will abndon you forever." Also in Ecclesiastes 5:1, it says: "Don't be impulsive and hasty with words in the presence of God, for God is in heaven and you are on earth. For that reason let your words be few." In Colossians 4:2, it states: "Be steadfast in prayer and even spend the night praying and giving thanks."

So I advise you to just continue praying every night alone in your room and have faith in God Almighty through our Lord Jesus Christ. "Place your burden on the Lord, and he will sustain you, for he never allows the upright to fall" (Psalm 55:23). "Humble yourselves before the Lord and he will raise you up" (James 4:10). In 1ˢᵗ Peter 5:6-7, it says: "Bow down, then, before the power of God so that he will raise you up at the appointed time. Place all your worries on him since he takes care of you."

So bow your head low when praying to God Almighty. And when you pray, you have to face East where Jerusalem is located, that your prayers may be answered. In 1ˢᵗ Kings 8:44, it says: "… and they pray to Yahweh in the direction of the city which you have chosen and the House which I have built for your name, then from Heaven hear their prayers and supplications and defend their cause." It begins with a very little seed of faith, as small as the mustard seed. Then, it will grow into a very large tree of faith that will influence others to attain the seed of faith. Strictly, there must be no image or graven statue of any kind. No need for you to light candles as God Almighty is Light that no amount of darkness can withstand. But if you choose to light candles during your prayer, you may do so.

In Psalm 91:9-10, it says: "If you have made the Lord your refuge, the Most High your stronghold, no harm will come upon you, no disaster will draw near your home."

Second. Stay away from cities mentioned in Chapter II of this book that are doomed to be destroyed. In Acts of the Apostles, it says: "...Since I am with you, no one will harm you." Take the example of Lot, who immediately departed from Sodom after he was informed by an angel who saved his life and his family's lives. Do not turn back to where you came from. Lot's wife did not follow this instruction and she became salt. By not turning back, it means that you should not go back to the place you left behind to get anything that you failed to bring with you. Leave the place very quickly. Never mind those things you left behind.

In Mark 13:15, it says: "If you are on the housetop, don't come down to take anything with you. If you are in the field, don't turn back to fetch your cloak. How hard it will be then for pregnant women and mothers with babies at breast." By not turning back, it also means that you will leave behind your sinful vices and ways and never go back to them again. In Ephesians 4:22-26, it says: "You must give up your former way of living, the old self, whose deceitful desires bring self-destruction. Renew yourselves spiritually, from inside, and put on the new self, or self-according to God, which is created in true righteousness and holiness. Therefore, give up lying; let everyone speak the truth to his neighbour for we are members of one another. Be angry but do not sin: do not let your anger last until the end of day, lest you give the devil a foothold."

Save yourself and your family. "May the God of Peace make you holy and bring you to perfection. May you be completely blameless, in spirit, soul and body, till the coming of Christ Jesus, our Lord; he who called you is faithful and will do it" (1ˢᵗ Thessalonians 5:23-24).

Third. Do not join any cult or group which assures that it can save you. It cannot save you. In Colossians 2:8, it says: "See that no one deceives you with philosophy or any hallow discourse; these are merely human doctrines not inspired by Christ but by the wisdom of this world." The only one who can save you is our Lord Jesus Christ, who is the Way, the Truth and the Life. Have faith in God through our Lord Jesus Christ and be saved. Cults are antichrists. Do not join them. In 1ˢᵗ John 2:18, it says: "My dear children, it is the last hour. You were told that an antichrist would come; but several antichrists have already come, by which we know that it is now the last hour."

How will you know that that is an antichrist? If their teachings contradict Biblical teachings, then they are an antichrist. If it leads you to destruction, then it is an antichrist. If its leader insists on being infallible, like the popes of Rome and the Vatican, then it is an antichrist. If it venerates people who are long dead and declared saints, then it is an antichrist. If its teachings never consider our Lord Jesus Christ as God, then it is an antichrist. If its teachings are mixed with idolatry, then it is an antichrist. If it believes that its priests can pardon sins, then it is an antichrist. The ones who can pardon sins are those in heaven: God Almighty and our Lord Jesus Christ.

In Mark 2:10 and in Matthew 9:6, it says: "You must know that the Son of Man has authority to forgive sins ..." Our Lord Jesus Christ also delegated authority to forgive sins to his disciples but not to the popes, bishops, cardinals, priests of Roman Catholic Church. In John 20:21-23, it says: "Again Jesus said to them, 'Peace be with you. As the Father has sent me, so I send you.' After saying this he breathe on them and said to them, 'Receive the Holy Spirit; for those whose sins you forgive, they are forgiven; for those whose sins you retain, they are retained."

Those who forgive the sins of other people but are not authorised to forgive sins will only add up their sins because the authority to forgive sins is divine. These are priests, bishops, cardinals, and popes of the Roman Catholic Church who oftentimes make a sign of the cross in their hands, saying: "Your sins are forgiven." They are not authorised to do that. Do not believe what the priest says. It is a lie. Believe in what the Holy Bible says. Have your own personal Bible and read every detail.

In 2nd Timothy 3:15-17, it says: "Besides, you have known the Scriptures from childhood, they will give you the wisdom that leads to salvation through faith in Christ Jesus. All Scripture is inspired by God and is useful for teaching, refuting error, for correcting and training in Christian life. Through Scripture the man of God is made expert and thoroughly equipped for every good work."

In selecting a Bible, do not use a Bible in which the publisher specifically requires permission for using quotations from the Bible. It is sheer hypocrisy on their part to require permission to quote the words of God. They do not own God's words. It is God who owns His words. If there is a need to ask permission, we have to ask it from God, who is the rightful owner of the words in the Bible, not the publisher. This is true for the Holy Bible, New International Version, which requires specific permission to quote God's words taken from that version. This is hypocrisy in a larger sense. Do not be misled by the teachings of the Roman Catholic Church. That is not a true church. It only replaced the despotic rule of the Roman Empire after its fall in 476 A.D., using inquisition and excommunication to punish heretics or those who championed ideas that were against their teachings.

The true religion in this world can be found in James 1:27, which states: "In the sight of God, our Father, pure and blameless religion lies in helping the orphans and widows in their need and keeping oneself from the world's corruption."

Fourth: do not join any activities like yoga, transcendental meditations, magic, be it white or black and sorcery. These activities can not save you. In Hebrews 13:9, it says: "Do not be led astray by all kinds of strange teachings." Stay away from the Roman Catholic Church and those religions that worship graven images and statues. Do not join any of their organisations whether your status is an affiliate or regular member. In Jeremiah 15:19, it says: "Then Yahweh spoke to me, 'If you return, I will take you back, and you will serve me again. Draw the gold from the dross and you will be as my own mouth. You must draw them to you and not go over to them." In Philippians 4:8, it says: "Finally, brothers and sisters, fill your minds with whatever is truthful, holy, just, pure, lovely and noble. Be mindful of whatever deserves praise and admiration."

The prayer Hail Mary by Catholics is not a valid prayer. Do not pray the Rosary, for it only praises the Virgin Mary, not God. Any prayer that praises anybody other than God is absolutely invalid and useless prayer. A prayer that extols God and coursed through our Lord Jesus Christ is heard and positively answered. You have to worship and praise God only and none else. Do not worship God's creation or people who were servants of God or anything that is in Heaven or on Earth. Praise only Him. Him alone. Remember, our God Almighty is a jealous God. Rosary is basically designed by the Roman Catholic Church as dictated by the enemy, satan, for the purpose of diverting worship from God. Satan wants people to worship anything, anybody, including even graven images of saints other than

God. The only valid and acceptable prayer is one taught by our Lord Jesus Christ—the OUR FATHER (Pater Noster; Padre Nuestro).

The prayer of the Roman Catholic Church entitled 'Apostle's Creed' is not likewise a valid prayer to God. It is merely a recital of events in church history that dogmatises God's words, but it is not really God's words. It states: "I believe," which is devoid of faith in God. For, believing is far different from having faith in God. But having faith in God connotes a personal relationship with God. The purpose of a prayer is to talk to God and establish a relationship with Him through our Lord Jesus Christ. Hence, it should not be prayed by God's people. The best prayer to God must spontaneously be drawn from the heart.

Gather your family every night and make a simple prayer praising Yahweh, God of Israel. In Philippians 4:5-6, it says: "…The Lord is near: do not be anxious about anything. In everything resort to prayer and supplication together with thanksgiving and bring your requests before God." In Colossians 3:16, it says: "…With thankful hearts sing to God psalms, hymns and spontaneous praise." Pray to him through our Lord Jesus Christ. End your prayer with the Universal Symphony that is in Psalm 150. You may arrange a simple tune for this for your whole family to sing. The wordings of this Universal Symphony are these:

Alleluia!
Praise God in his sanctuary;
Praise him in the vault of Heaven.
Praise him for his mighty deeds;
Praise him for his own greatness.
Praise him with trumpet blast;
Praise him with lyre and harp.
Praise him with dance and tambourines;

Praise him with pipe and strings.
Praise him with clashing cymbals;
Praise him with clanging cymbals.
Let everything that breathes sing praise to the Lord.
Alleluia!

You and your family members should also sing praises to God Almighty, which are in Psalms 146, 147 and 148. It says in Ephesians 5:19, " Gather together to pray with psalms, hymns and spiritual songs. Sing and celebrate the Lord in your heart, giving thanks to God the Father in the name of Christ Jesus, our Lord, always and for everything." You may assign simple tunes to these praises. For, in Psalm 92:2-5, it says: "It is good to give thanks to the Lord, to sing praise to your name, O Most High, to proclaim your love in the morning, to declare your faithfulness at night, accompanied by music from the lyre and the melody of lute and harp. For you make me glad with your deeds, O Lord, and I sing for joy at the work of your hands." Here are the wording:

Psalm 146
Alleluia!
Praise the Lord, my soul!
I will sing to the Lord all my life;
I will sing praise to God while I live.
Do not put your trust in princes,
In a great man who cannot save.
Not sooner his spirit has left,
that he goes back to the earth;
on that very day, any plan comes to nothing.
Blessed are they whose help is the God of Jacob,
Whose hope is in the Lord their God,
maker of heaven and earth,
the sea and all they contain.

The Lord is forever faithful;
he gives justice to the oppressed
and gives food to the hungry.
The Lord sets the prisoners free
And gives sight to the blind.

The Lord straightens the bent,
and loves the virtuous.
The Lord protects the stranger,
sustains the widow and the orphan;
but the way of the wicked he brings to ruin.
The Lord will reign forever,
your God, O Zion,
from generation to generation. Alleluia!

Psalm 147
Alleluia!
How good it is to sing to our God,
how sweet and befitting to praise him!
The Lord rebuilds Jerusalem;
he gathers the exiles of Israel;
he heals their broken hearts
and binds up their wounds.

He determines the number of stars'
he calls each of them by name.
The Lord is great and mighty in power;'
his wisdom is beyond measure.
The Lord lifts up the humble,
but casts the wicked to the ground.

Sing to the Lord with thanksgiving,
make music on the harp for our God.
With clouds he covers the sky,
he waters the earth with rain

and makes grass grow upon the hill.
He provides food for the cattle
and the young ravens when they call.

He is not concerned with the strength of a horse;
nor is he pleased with men's bravery;
The Lord delights in those who fear him
and who put their hope in his constant love.
Exalt the Lord, O Jerusalem;
praise your God, O Zion!
For he strengthens the bars of your gates
and blesses your children within you.
He grants peace on your borders
and feeds you with the finest grain.
He sends his command to the earth
and swiftly runs his word,
He spreads snow like wool;
he scatters frost like ashes.
He hurls down hail like pebbles;
his icy blasts make water freeze.

But he sends his word and melts the snow;
he makes his breeze blow,
and again the waters flow.
He proclaimed his word to Jacob,
his laws and decrees to Israel.
He has done this for no other nation,
So his laws remain unknown to them.
Alleluia!

Psalm 148
Alleluia!
Praise the Lord from the heavens;
praise him in the heavenly heights.

Praise him, all his angels;
praise him, all his heavenly hosts.
Praise him, sun and moon;
praise him, all shining stars.

Praise him, you highest heavens
and you waters above the skies.

Let them praise the name of the Lord,
at whose command they were made.

He established them forever
and gave each a fixed and lasting duty.

Praise the Lord from the earth,
you sea creatures and all the depths,
clouds and snow, hail and lightning,
storm winds that do his bidding,
you mountains and all you hills,
you fruit trees and cedars,
you wild beasts and tame animals,
you creeping things and winged fowl.
Kings of the earth and nations,
princes and all rulers of the world,
young men and maidens,
old men and children-
let them praise the name of the Lord.

For his name alone is exalted;
his majesty is above earth and heaven;
and he has given his people glory.
This is his praise from his faithful,
from the children of Israel,
the people close to him.
Alleluia!

As redeemed and saved by God, we, God's people, must also sing the song of the saved in Chapter 12 of Isaiah. Simple tunes should be arranged on this. Here are the wordings of this song:

> *On that day, you will say:*
> *'I give thanks to you, O Lord.*
> *Although you have been angry with me*
> *your anger has been appeased*
> *and you have consoled me.*
> *God is indeed my salvation;*
> *in him I trust and am not afraid,*
> *for the Lord God is my strength.*
> *He is my song:*
> *he has become my salvation.'*
>
> *You will draw water with joy from the*
> *fountain of salvation.*
> *On that day you will say:*
> *'Give thanks to the Lord, acclaim*
> *his name; among the nations proclaim*
> *his work and make known*
> *how exalted is his name.*
> *Sing to the Lord, the Magnificent;*
> *wonders he has done all over the earth.*
> *Sing for joy,*
> *shout with exultation,*
> *O people of Zion,*
> *For great in your midst*
> *is the Holy One of Israel."*

After you are through with these songs, all family members should make a reconciliation with each other. Parents and children should reconcile their differences before going to bed. For, in Malachi 4:23-24, it says: "I am going to send you the prophet Elijah before the day of Yahweh comes, for it will be a great and terrible day. He will reconcile parents with their children, and the children with their parents, so that I may not have to curse this land when I come."

It is also commanded of children to obey their parents and for parents to educate their children well by correcting their attitudes. For, in Ephesians 6:1-4, it says: "Children, obey your parents for this is right: Honour your father and your mother. And this is the first commandment that has promise: that you may be happy and enjoy long life in the land." And you, fathers, do not make rebels of your children, but educate them by correction and instruction which the Lord may inspire."

A family will join up to four other families with their children and grandchildren to do such activity of praising Yahweh, God of Israel, once a week, most preferably on Saturday, the Lord's Day. Reconciliation must be done after singing of songs. This Universal Symphony will be one of your distinctive marks when our Lord Jesus Christ returns. The other distinctive marks of your being God's people are your belief and practice of the Sabbath and your distinctive mark on your forehead upon the arrival of God's Holy Angels. In Revelation 7:3, it says: "Do not harm the earth or the sea or the trees until we have sealed the servants of our God upon their foreheads." In the act of reconciliation, you have to take note of Paul's advice in Romans 16:16, which says: "Greet one another with brotherly embrace." And also, in 2nd Corinthians 13:12, which says: "Greet one another with a holy kiss."

Our God Almighty always put a distinctive mark on his people that they will not be destroyed. In Passover in Egypt, God Almighty instructed the Israelites to place the blood of the lamb they sacrificed on their doorposts for them to be saved so that the cloud of death would just pass them by. Those who obeyed were saved. Those who did not obey, although they were Israelites, experienced the death of their firstborn humans and animals alike.

God instructed his people Israel in Exodus 12:6-7 this: "On that evening all the people will slaughter their lambs and take some of the blood to put on the doorposts and on top of the doorframes of the houses where you eat." And so Yahweh explained to Israel in Exodus 12:13, which says: "The blood on your houses will be the sign that you are there. I will see the blood and pass over you; and you will escape the mortal plague when I strike Egypt and when he sees the blood on the lintel and the doorposts, he will pass over the door and not allow the destroyer to enter your houses and kill."

Also in Jericho's seige, God put a distinctive mark on those to be saved. Rahab was instructed by the men of Joshua to place scarlet cords in their windows as a sign that they would be spared. Rahab invited her relatives to join her in her house to be saved. Those who followed were spared of their lives. Those who did not follow were all killed during the siege. In Joshua 2:18-19, it says: "When we enter this land, tie this scarlet cord as a sign on the window through which we have escaped. Bring into your house your father, mother, brothers and sisters, and all your relatives. If any of them leaves the house, he shall be the one responsible for his death, and the guilt will not be ours. But if anyone who is with you is killed, then may the punishment for his death come upon us." So you are now instructed to have a distinctive mark that you and your family will be saved. All these advices come from God Almighty. In Isaiah 28:29, it says: "All comes from Yahweh Sabaoth whose advice is excellent, whose wisdom is wonderful."

Fifth: do not be afraid. In Joshua 1:9, it says: "It is I who command you; be strong then, and be valiant. Do not tremble or be

494

afraid, because Yahweh, your God, is with you wherever you go." In John 12:26, it says: "Whoever wants to serve me, let him follow me and wherever I am, there shall my servant be also. If anyone serves me, the Father will honor him."

Our Lord, God Almighty, assures you to be steadfast, for you are saved. No harm will fall on you. In Isaiah 43:1, it says: "...Fear not, for I have redeemed you; I have called you by your name; you are mine."

Take the advice of Peter and apply it in your life. In Peter 5:6-11, it states: "Bow down, then, before the power of God so that he will raise you up at the appointed time. Place all your worries on him since he takes care of you. Be sober and alert because your enemy the devil prowls about like a roaring lion seeking someone to devour. Stand your guard, firm in your faith, knowing that our brothers, scattered throughout the world, are confronting similar persecutions. God, the giver of all grace, has called you to share in Christ's eternal Glory and after you have suffered a little he will bring you to perfection: he will confirm, strengthen and establish you forever. Glory be to him forever and ever. Amen."

To your neighbours, encourage them to be courageous and persevere in their faith. "Say to those who are afraid: 'Have courage, do not fear. See, your God comes, demanding justice. He is the God who rewards, the God who comes to save you" (Isaiah 35:4).

Jesus says in Matthew 28:20, it says: "...I am with you always until the end of this world." In the last days, do not be afraid of the devil even if you are imprisoned or killed. In Psalm 123:4, it says: "Too long have our souls been filled with the scorn of the arrogant, with the ridicule of the insolent." Just remain faithful to God Almighty through our Lord Jesus Christ until death. In Revelation

2:10-11, it says: "Do not be afraid of what will happen to you. The devil will throw some of you into prison to test you and there wil be ten days of trials. Remain faithful even to death and I will give you the crown of life. If anyone has ears, let him listen to what the Spirit says to the Churches: The victor has nothing to fear from the second death." In Psalm 121:1-2, it says: "I lift up my eyes to the mountains from where shall come my help? My help comes from the Lord, maker of heaven and earth."

Sixth: do not imitate the works of these people, as they are not at God's side. Do not associate with them. In 2nd Corinthians 6:14-15, it says: "Do not make unsuitable covenants with those who do not believe: can justice walk with wickedness? Or can light coexist with darkness, and can there be harmony between Christ and Satan? What union can there be between one who believes and one who does not believe?"

Stay away from them. They are:

Those whose mouths are full of curses and deceit. In Psalm 5:10, it says: "Not a word of their mouth can be trusted, for their heart is full of mischief. Their throat is an open grave; their tongue flatters with deceit."

Those who pray in public to be seen by other people. In Matthew 6:5-6, it says: "When you pray, do not be like those who want to be seen. They love to stand and pray in the synagogues or on street corners to be seen by everyone. I assure you, they have already been paid in full. When you pray, go into your room, close the door and pray to your Father who is with you in secret; and your Father who sees what is secret will reward you."

Those who play music with satanic chants, dance, and

movements. Those who lend money for interest even if such interest is minimal. In Psalm 15, it says: "O Lord who will dwell in your tent and reside on your holy mount? They who walk blamelessly and do what is right, who speak truth from their heart and control their words, who do no harm to their neighbours and cast no discredit on their companions, who look down on evildoers but highly esteem God's servants; who at all cost stand by a pledge word, **who do not lend money at interest** and refuse a bribe against the innocent. Those who do all this will never be shaken."

Also, in Psalm 112:5-6, it says: "It will be well with him who lends freely, who leads a life of justice and honesty. For the righteous will never be moved; he will be remembered and loved forever."

Those who produce movies depicting Satan and devils, those who patronise these movies, those who spend too much time viewing television, and those who are addicted to computer games designed by Satan, for they have no more time left for themselves and for their families. In Galatians 6:8-10, it says: "The person who sows for the benefit of his own flesh shall reap corruption and death from the flesh. He who sows in the spirit shall reap eternal life from the Spirit. Let us do good without being discouraged; in due time we shall reap the reward of our constancy. So while there is time, let us do good to all and especially to our family in the faith."

Those who venerate images and graven statues. Isaiah 44:9-10 says: "Good-for-nothing are all idol makers, and useless are the works they prize so much. Their witnesses, blind and ignorant, will be put to shame. Whoever fashioned a god or cast an idol without hope of gain? See how its devotees will be ridiculed, for its craftsmen are but men. Let them assemble, let them come to court; they will be both terrified and scorned."

Those who practice sorcery *('kulam,' 'hiwit,' 'barang,' 'paktol,' etc.) witchcraft, magic, séance divination or astrology.* For these people have no place in God's kingdom. (Revelation 21:8)

Those who eat the blood of animals, making it as viands. It is a clear instruction of our Lord in Deuteronomy 12:16, which states: "Only you must not eat the blood but pour it out upon the earth like water." Also, in Deuteronomy 12:23, it says: "Only take care not to eat the blood because blood and life are one and you must not eat the life with the flesh. Do not eat it but pour it as water is poured upon the land, that all may go well with you and with your children after you, doing what is pleasing in the eyes of Yahweh." Do not eat the fat of animals. In Leviticus 3:17, it says: "All the fat belongs to Yahweh. This is a law forever for all your descendants wherever they may live: never eat fat or blood." Also, in Leviticus 17:10-11, it says: "If any man from the house of Israel or any alien living among them eats blood, I will set my face against that person and I will cut him off from among his people. For the life of the flesh is in the blood, and I have given it to you to rescue your life on the altar."

Those who eat the meat of strangled animals. In Acts of the Apostles 15:29, it says: "You are to abstain from blood from the meat of strangled animals…"

Those who eat foods offered to idols. In Acts of the Apostles 15:20, it says: "Let us just tell them not to eat food that is unclean from having been offered to idols."

Those who clip off the edges of their beard (Leviticus 19:26-28). In Colossians 1:10, it says: "May your lifestyle be worthy of the Lord and completely pleasing to him. May you bear fruit in every good work and grow in the knowledge of God."

Those who have tattoos, as God Almighty prohibits this (Leviticus 19:26-28).

Those who are disrespectful to their parents and elders. In Matthew 15:4, it says: "For God commanded: Do your duty to your father and your mother, and whoever curses his father or his mother is to be put to death." In Proverbs 20:20, it says: "Whoever strikes his father or mother shall be put to death." Also, in Exodus 21:17, it says: "He who curses his father or mother shall be put to death."

Those who drink too much intoxicating liquors and who are usual drunkards. In Romans 13:13, it says: "As we live in the full light of day, let us behave with decency; no banquets with drunkeness…"

Those who use prohibited drugs or are addicted to such drugs, like Shabu or methamphetamine hydrochloride, LSD or Lysergic Acid Diethylamide, morphine, heroin, opium, marijuana or cannabis, or party drugs, as these drugs are associated with the enemy, Satan. Every time there are crimes committed or accidents caused by these drugs, Satan becomes happy. In Luke 21:34-36, it says: "Be on your guard; let not your hearts be weighed down with a life of pleasure, drunkenness and worldly cares, lest that day catch you suddenly as a trap. For it will come upon all the inhabitants of the whole earth. But watch at all times and pray that you may be able to escape all that is bound to happen and to stand before the Son of Man."

Those who are unfaithful to their spouses. In Ephesians 4:17-19, it says: "…Do not imitate the pagans who live an aimless kind of life. Their understanding is in darkness and they remain in ignorance because of their blind conscience, very far from the life of God. As a result of their corruption, they have abandoned themselves to sensuality and have eagerly given themselves to every kind of immorality."

Those who do not show resolute repentance. Sinners should not remain in sinful life. They have to renew themselves and obey God's will. In Ephesians 4:22-24, it says: "You must give up your former way of living, the old self, whose deceitful desires bring self-destruction. Renew yourselves spiritually, from inside, and put on the new self, or self, according to God, which is created in true righteousness and holiness."

Those who do not observe Sabbath day. Genesis 2:2-3 states: "By the seventh day the work God had done was completed, and he rested on the seventh day and made it holy, because on that day he rested from all the work he had done in his creation."

Those who are members of LGBTQ+ (Lesbian, gay, bisexual, transgender, queer, and so on) and practice acts, actuation, speech, language, gestures and lifestyle of LGBT, except those who have already repented and accepted our Lord Jesus Christ and have faith in God Almighty in which case they will be made children of God and be welcome to God's Glory in Heaven. Being converted to the ways of God, they will behave in accord with God's will. They will leave their old self and put on virtues of God into their life.

"And since you are holy, there must not be among you even a hint of sexual immorality or greed, or any kind of impurity: these should not be named among you. So too for scandalous words, nonsense and foolishness, which are not fitting..." (Ephesians 5:3-4). Members of the LGBT who will not repent and continue their sinfulness and wickedness, they have to prepare themselves for eternal damnation in hell. Their strong organisation in this world cannot save them.

Those who commemorate the feast day of the highest pagan god,

Jupiter, in the guise of celebrating Christ's birth and those who observe Christ's birth knowing or without knowing that such date, December 25, is, in reality, the feast of the highest pagan god, Jupiter.

Those who devote their time to computers, cell phone/computer games, and social media activities, for they have no more time to attend to their personal needs and the needs of their families, thus destroying family relationships. In Ephesians 5:16, it says: "Try to make good use of the present time, because these days are evil."

Those who are perverse, greedy, evil, murderers, deceitful, gossipers, haughty, proud, liars, clever in doing evil, senseless, disloyal, cold-hearted, merciless, rebellious toward parents, and those who applaud the works of these people.

In Psalm 36:2-4, it says: "Wickedness speaks to the wicked in the depths of his heart: there is no fear of God before his eyes. Blinded by conceit, he fails to see his guilt. With mouths full of malice and deceit, they no longer think of doing good." Remember that there are things that God Almighty abhors. They are found in Proverbs 6:16-19, which says: "There are six things Yahweh hates; seven his inner being detests: the proud look, the lying tongue, hands which spill innocent blood, the depraved heart, feet which speed towards evil, a false lying witness and the man who sows discord among people."

Seventh. Persevere in doing good. In Colossians 4:5-6, it says: "Deal wisely with those who do not belong to the Church; take advantage of every opportunity. Let your conversion be pleasing with a touch of wit. Know how to speak to everyone in the best way." Do not participate in any useless discussions. In 2nd Timothy 2:16, it says: "Do not take part in useless conversations, alien to the faith. This leads to a greater lack of faith." Also, in 2nd Timothy 2:23, it says: "Avoid stupid and senseless discussions, since such are the cause of misunderstanding."

In Titus 3:9, it says: "Avoid stupid arguments, discussions about genealogies and quarrels about the law, for they are useless and unimportant." Walk in God's Spirit. Romans 8:14-17 says: "All those who walk in the Spirit of God are sons and daughters of God. Then, no more fear; you did not receive a spirit of slavery, but the Spirit that makes you adopted children and every time we cry, Abba Father! the Spirit assures our spirit that we are children of God. If we are children, we are heirs, too. Ours will be the inheritance of God and we will share it with Christ; for if we now suffer with him, we will also share Glory with him." In Mark 8:34-35, it says: "Then Jesus called the people and his disciples and said, 'If you want to follow me, deny yourself, take up your cross and follow me. For if you choose to save your life, you will lose it; and if you lose your life for my sake and for the sake of the Gospel, you will save it.'"

Also, in Galatians 3:26 and 29, it says: "Now in Christ Jesus, all of you are sons and daughters of God through faith. And because you belong to Christ, you are of Abraham's race and you are to inherit God's promise." Try your best to attain honour, glory, and immortality. "You also be patient and do not lose heart, because the Lord's coming is near" (James 5:8).

Walk uprightly, speak righteously, spurn profit from oppression, shake your fists at graft and corruption, stop your ears against suggestions of bloodshed, and close your eyes to opportunities for committing evil deeds so that you will be worthy of being called children of God Almighty (Isaiah 33:15). "Do not do to another what you would hate done to yourself" (Tobit 4:15). Love one another, and that should love be sincere. Indulge in the wishes of the spirit and shun the desires of the flesh. Be fervent in the Spirit and serve God;

love God with all your heart, with all your mind, and with all your soul. "The Lord hears the cry of the righteous and rescues them from all their troubles" (Psalm 34:18).

Embrace the truth, which is our Lord Jesus Christ and God Almighty. "In obeying the truth, you have gained interior purification from which comes sincere love for our brothers. Love one another, then, with all your heart, since you are born again, not from mortal beings, but with enduring life, through the Word of God who lives and remains forever" (1st Peter 1:22-23). "Do not worry over evil people nor be envious of wrongdoers. For they will fade as any green herb and soon be gone like withered grass. Trust in the Lord and do good, dwell in the land and be at peace. Make the Lord your delight, and he will grant your heart's desire. Commit your way to the Lord; put your trust in him and let him act" (Psalm 37:1-5).

In Jeremiah 17:7-8, it says: "Happy the man who trusts in Yahweh and whose confidence is in him! He is like a tree planted near water that thrusts its roots toward the stream. He has no fear when the heat comes, his leaves are always green; the year of draught is no problem and he can always bear fruit." Many of you will be taken up to Heaven by the holy angels during the rapture, after which you will have eternal life right away, transforming your earthly body into an incorruptible heavenly body that will sustain you for all eternity.

In the song of Moses and the Israelites to Yahweh, Exodus 15:13, it says: "In unfailing love you guided the people you redeemed, in strength you led them to your holy house." But some of you will remain in this world to witness and experience unconscionable, hardest trials that will take place for forty-two months. Persevere in all these trials, for a great reward awaits you in heaven. In Revelation 2:10, it says: "Do not be afraid of what will happen to you. The devil will throw some of you into prison to test you and there will be ten days of trials. Remain faithful even to death and I will give you the crown of life."

Remember that God Almighty has destined you to remain in this world to defend heaven's cause. Your steadfastness in these trials would represent your brother's steadfastness, who is already ahead of you in Heaven. In 1st Corinthians 10:13, it says: "No trial greater than human endurance has overcome you. God is faithful and will not let you be tempted beyond your strength. He will give you, together with the temptation, the strength to escape and to resist."

At all costs, do not surrender to the beast. Do not allow the beast to mark your right hand or forehead with 666 (Please read Chapter 7 of this book about the real 666). Once you are marked with 666, you will lose your right to inheritance of the saints. You have to prefer death than be branded with the beast's mark so you will be a victor before God's eyes. In James 5:8, it says: "You also be patient and do not lose heart, because the Lord's coming is near."

The slight affliction that quickly passes away prepares us for an eternal wealth of glory so great and beyond comparison. So we no longer pay attention to the things that are seen, but to those that are unseen, for the things that we see last for a moment, but that which cannot be seen is eternal. For your victory over evil, as you have unwavering faith in God Almighty through our Lord Jesus Christ, you will be rewarded. In 1st Peter 1:4-5, it says: "This inheritance is kept in the heavens for you, since God's power shall keep you faithful until salvation is revealed in the last days." In Sirach 36:15, it says: "Reward those who wait for you and fulfill the words of your prophets." Here are the rewards:

"…To the victor I will give to eat of the tree of life which is in

God's Paradise" (Revelation 2:7);

"I will give you the crown of life"..."The victor has nothing to fear from the second death" (Revelation 2:10-11);

"...To the victor I will give the hidden manna. I will also give him a white stone with a new name written on it which no one knows except the one who receives it" (Revelation 2:17);

"To him who is victor and keeps to my ways to the end, I will give power over the nations; he will rule them with an iron rod and shatter them like earthen pots; he will be like me, who received this power from my Father. Moreover, I will give him the Morning Star" (Revelation 2:26-27);

"The victor will be dressed in white and I will never erase his name from the book of life; instead, I will acknowledge it before my Father and his angels" (Revelation 3:5);

"I will make the victor into a column in the sanctuary of my God where he will stay forever..."

"I will let the victor sit with me on my throne just as I was victorious and took my place with my Father on his throne" (Revelation 3:21).

The start of the great suffering of God's people here on Earth before Christ's Second Coming will be on December 1, 2119, a Friday and will end on Friday 14, 2123. It will comprise 1,260 days or three and a half years. For the next day, which is May 15, 2123, the Second Coming of our Lord Jesus Christ will take place. In 2nd Timothy 3:12-13, it says: "All who want to serve God in Christ Jesus will be persecuted, while evil persons and impostors will go from bad to worse, deceiving and being deceived." In James 1:12, it says: "Happy the one who patiently endures trials, because afterwards he will receive the crown of life which the Lord promised to those who love him." In Romans 5:3-5, it says: "Not only that, we feel secure even in trials, knowing that trials produce patience, from patience comes merit, merit is the source of hope, and hope does not disappoint us because the Holy Spirit has been given to us, pouring into our hearts the love of God."

The Almighty Father reveals to me this: In a clear blue sky of May 15, 2123, a Saturday, the Lord's Day, the mouth of Heaven will open, and people will witness a spectacular event, says the Almighty Father. **Millions and millions of angels will visit the Earth,** added the Lord.

It is written by John in Revelation that there will be about 200 million angels. Revelation 9:16 says: "The number of the soldiers on horses was two hundred million." This is the number I heard. They will be here for a harvest. This is a fulfilment of what is said in John 1:51: "Truly, I say to you, you will see the heavens opened and the angels of God ascending and descending upon the Son of Man."

It is expected that those whose names are not written in the Book of Life will surely scoff at this revelation. Their mockeries are brought about by their ignorance and foolishness.

In Proverbs 1:22, it says: "You ignorant people, how long will you continue to cling to your foolishness? How long mockers revel in their mockery, and fools have contempt or knowledge?" In 2nd Peter 3:3-4, it says: "Remember, first of all, that in the last days, scoffers will appear, their mockery serving their evil desires. And they will say, 'What has become of his promised coming? Since our Fathers in faith died, everything still goes on as it was from the beginning of the world.'"

We have to ignore such mockeries and instead cling steadfastly to the truth as revealed by God. For, in Proverbs 9:7-9, it says: "He who corrects a mocker gains insults; and he who reprimands an evildoer receives abuse. Do not rebuke the mocker lest he hates you, but counsel the wise who will be grateful. Give to the wise man and he will become wiser each day; teach an upright man and he will increase his wisdom. So, then, the Lord knows how to free from trial those who serve him and keep the wicked for punishment on the Day of Judgment."

(2nd Peter 2:9). In Jude 14-16, it says: "…The Lord comes with thousands of angels to judge everyone and call the wicked to account for all the evil deeds they committed; he will punish all the injurious words the impious sinners uttered against him. All these are discontented who curse their lot and follow their passions. Their mouth is full of arrogant words, and they flatter people for their own interest."

As God Almighty requests me to pray fervently for the world's salvation, I am earnestly inviting you also to pray every night. Wherever you may be, say a prayer to God Almighty for the world's salvation. I asked the Father about the content of the prayer, and he instructed me to jot down this:

"ALMIGHTY FATHER, IN YOUR LOVING KINDNESS AND MERCY, WE FERVENTLY PRAY FOR FORGIVENESS OF THE SINS THE WORLD HAS COMMITTED AND PAVE THE WAY FOR ITS SALVATION. GRANT THAT WE BE RECONCILED WITH YOU THROUGHOUT ETERNITY. SAVE ALL THE PEOPLE OF ALL GENERATIONS AND BRING US INTO YOUR ETERNAL HOME FOREVER. NEVER ALLOW US TO SUFFER

CONDEMNATION INTO THE LAKE OF FIRE. ENDOW US EVERLASTING LIFE THROUGH IESHUA MOSHA. AMEN AMEN AMEN RAK TO THE RABBA TO THE ABBA."

This prayer should be followed by "OUR FATHER", the prayer taught by our Lord Jesus Christ. The wordings of this prayer are as follows:

"OUR FATHER WHO ART IN HEAVEN HALLOWED BE THY NAME THY KINGDOM COME, THY WILL BE DONE ON EARTH AS IT IS IN HEAVEN. GIVE US THIS DAY OUR DAILY BREAD; FORGIVE US OUR TRESPASSES AS WE FORGIVE THOSE WHO TRESPASSED AGAINST US AND LEAD US NOT INTO TEMPTATION BUT DELIVER US FROM EVIL. AMEN."

This prayer was given to me by God Almighty on the night of December 26, 2019. This was revised on the night of January 16, 2020. This is the final revised version. You may translate this prayer to your native dialect and language so that this can be well understood by everyone. This prayer also applies to the atonement of the sins of people of long ago before our Lord Jesus came into the world. This can be said also for dead relatives who died long ago. Praying this for their intention can give pardon for their sins.

In Nahum 1:7, it says: "Yahweh is good for those who hope; in the day of trouble he shelters them. He remembers those who trust in him…"

What God wants is the salvation of as many souls as possible so they have everlasting life.

In John 10:9, it says: "I am the gate. Whoever enters through me will be saved…" For, there are many rooms prepared already by God Almighty Father in heaven for us to dwell on. If there are people, who will not be saved because of sinfulness, who will occupy the empty rooms in Heaven which are already assigned to us?

John 14:2-3 says: "In my Father's house there are many rooms. Otherwise I would not have told you that I go to prepare a place for you. After I have gone and prepared a place for you, I shall come again and take you to me, so that where I am, you also may be."

A little while before His Ascension to Heaven, our Lord Jesus Christ said in John 13:36, "Where I am going you cannot follow me now, but afterwards you will." It goes to say that our Lord Jesus Christ will come back to this world and bring us with Him. There will be heavenly happiness to live with our Lord in heaven. In Psalm 84:5, it says: "Happy are those who live in your house, continually singing your praise."

For the redeemed and saved, entice others also to go back to God's fold so that they will be saved. Never allow them to be drowned in sinfulness and wickedness so that Satan cannot conquer them. We have to grieve over those people who still live in sin so that they may change their ways and be saved. In 2nd Corinthians 12:21, Paul grieved for sinful people: "I have to grieve over many of those who live in sin, on seeing that they have not yet given up an impure way of living, their wicked conduct and the vices they formerly practised."

For God's people here is the blessing that they have to receive from God based on Numbers 6:24-26 which states: (Bow your head low and say this blessing) **"May Yahweh bless you and keep you! May Yahweh let his face shine on you, and be gracious to you! May Yahweh look kindly on you, and give you his peace!" through Ieshua Mosha, Amen, Amen, Amen rak to the Rabba to** the Abba.

CHAPTER V
SABBATH DAY

The existence of humanity and Sabbath occurred almost at the same time in creation. Humanity was created on sixth day while Sabbath occurred on seventh day when God rested in His creation. One day to God is 1000 years to mankind. It states in Genesis 2:2-3: "By the seventh day the work God had done was completed, and he rested on the seventh day from all the work he had done. And God blessed the seventh day and made it holy, because on that day he rested from all the work he had done in creation" Reason dictates that since man was created ahead of Sabbath, therefore Sabbath was made for humanity and not humanity for Sabbath. In Mark 2:27-28, it says: "Then Jesus said to them, 'The Sabbath was made for man, not man for the Sabbath. So the Son of Man is Master even of the Sabbath." God made Sabbath as holy to shape mankind to pure holiness with God Almighty. Sabbath makes man holy, pure and perfect as God wants man to be perfect as himself. It is a safeguard for humanity to remain pure, perfect and worthy before God's eyes. God, being perfect, cannot face man nor answer man's prayer if such man is imperfect. It is pre-requisite for man to purify himself first through correct observance of Sabbath in order to be worthy of God's presence. A man who observes Sabbath purifies himself.

Though presently, perfect persons are hard to find, God possibly talks to man who has contrite heart having purified himself through right observance of Sabbath. If God answers your prayer you are a perfect man. In Job 12:4, it says: "The man who calls and whom God answers, the just and perfect man". The observance of Sabbath can make a person a perfect man before God's eyes. In Hebrews 4:9-10, it says: "Then some other rest, or Sabbath, is reserved for the people of God. He who enters this rest of God rests from all his works as God rests from his work." It follows then that only those people who observe Sabbath are considered God's people and those who do not observe Sabbath do not belong to Him. In 2nd Maccabees15:4, it says: They answered, 'It is the Living God himself, the Sovereign in heaven, who has commanded us to celebrate the seventh day."

Sabbath, which makes man pure and perfect before God's eyes, will be one of distinctive marks of salvation when our Lord Jesus Christ returns to this world. Those who are conscientiously observing Sabbath in their hearts will be known to angels of salvation and they will be the ones to be marked as saved and redeemed by God's angels and be raised to eternal life. God's enemy, Satan knows this. That is why Satan grabs billions of people away from observing Sabbath so that they will not be saved. Those who will not be saved will be with Satan for one millennium. Then they will be destroyed in lake of fire together with Satan. How does Satan operate to drive away people from observing Sabbath? Satan used Roman Catholic Church to entice people away from Sabbath by changing Sabbath from original Saturday to a fake Sunday. Satan succeeded on this. But in the last days before the second coming of our Lord Jesus Christ, people would regain consciousness of truth and return to God by observing Saturday as Sabbath day. Here is the basic law on Sabbath: What God Almighty has established, no one in heaven or on earth, no principality or kingdom can ever change it. Catholicism wrongfully justified that the seventh day is Sunday and not Saturday. It further erroneously argued that only Jewish people should observe Sabbath on Saturday. While the Gentiles should observe Sabbath on Sunday. The Council of Laodicea (a city in Asia Minor now the country of Turkey near Colossae) which justified such change in the year 336 A.D. made it a basis that Paul had performed a Eucharist at Troas on Sunday, the first day of the week. In Acts of the Apostles 20:7, it says: "On the first day of the week we were together for the breaking of the bread, and Paul, who intended to leave the following day, spoke at length. The discourse went on until midnight..." We must be reminded that when Laodicea Council was convened in 336 A.D., the pillars of true Christianity were no longer around as they were already killed, murdered, sawn in two, reduced to living torches and massacred by Roman Emperors. These are some pillars of the Church: James who was stoned to death in year 62 A.D. upon orders of high priest; Peter was martyred in Rome in year 64 A.D. then proclaimed as first Pope of Rome; Paul was killed in Rome in year 67A.D. and Apostle John the author of Book of Revelation died a natural death at an old age in Patmos in year 95 A.D. With no one to oppose them, they were successful in changing Sabbath to Sunday which is until now practised by Catholics. For this, Catholics are on the idea that God rested first before He began His creation. That is precisely a distorted belief. That is clearly a false doctrine inculcated by Catholicism to docile people who never consult the Holy Bible. The convenors of Laodicea Council, who were learned cardinals, deliberately structured Sabbath on Sunday knowing fully well that that is maliciously incorrect.God has not changed Sabbath to any day of the week and will never change it through all eternity. It is in Sabbath that people must deny themselves and take a rest. This God's commandment is permanently established forever. In Leviticus 16:31, it says: "It is a Sabbath of solemn rest when you must deny yourselves. It is a lasting ordinance."

In Decalogue, God had emphasized observance of Sabbath. Exodus 20:8-11 says: "Remember the Sabbath day and keep it holy. For six days you will labour and do all your work, but the seventh day is a Sabbath for Yahweh your God. Do not work that day, neither you, nor your son, nor your daughter nor your servants men or women, nor your animals, nor the stranger who is staying with you. For in six days Yahweh made the heavens and the earth and the sea and all that is in them, but on the seventh day he rested; that is why Yahweh has blessed the Sabbath day and made it holy."

In Exodus 23:10-12, it says: "For six years you will sow your fields and reap their produce, but in the seventh you will let the land rest and lie fallow. The poor may eat what it produces and what they leave the wild animals will eat. It will be the same for your vineyard and your olive grove. For six days you shall work but on the seventh you shall rest, so that your ox and your donkey may also rest and the son of your slave girl and the stranger as well may have a breathing space."

What penalties are attached to breaking Sabbath Day? In Old Testament, the penalty for violating Sabbath is death. We are informed about penalty of violating Sabbath in Numbers 15:32-36, which says: "While the people of Israel were in the wilderness, a man was caught gathering wood on the Sabbath day. Those who caught him gathering wood brought him before Moses, Aaron and the whole community. He was kept under guard because the penalty he should undergo had not yet been decided. Yahweh said to Moses, 'This man must be put to death; the whole community shall stone him outside the camp.' The whole community took him outside the camp and stoned him till he was dead, as Yahweh had commanded Moses." The lesson behind why he was put to death is because he had done an activity which is personal in nature which he can also perform before Sabbath day or after Sabbath day. Any activity not related to worship of God during Sabbath day should be penalized by death. In the case of our Lord Jesus Christ healing the sick on Sabbath (Luke 13:10-13) is not a violation of Sabbath as what he did was a proclamation of God's kingdom. Our Lord Jesus Christ performed healing not for his own but for God's glory. What our Lord Jesus did was not a violation of Sabbath but a perfection of Sabbath as it was done for greater glory of God. Whereas, gathering wood during Sabbath is not intended for God's glory. The act of our Lord Jesus Christ in healing the sick on Sabbath is to perfect Sabbath day. In Isaiah 58:13-14, it says: "If you stop profaning the Sabbath and doing as you please on the holy day, if you call the Sabbath a day of delight and keep sacred Yahweh's holy day, if you honour it by not going your own way, not doing as you please and not speaking with malice, then you will find happiness in Yahweh, over the heights you will ride triumphantly, on the inheritance of your father Jacob you will feast joyfully. The mouth of Yahweh has spoken."

To all workers, office employees, manual labourers and blue-collar workers you are hereby commanded by God to join hand in hand in observing Sabbath day strictly on Saturday and not Sunday or any other day. Do not report to your work on this day. Devote this day to worship God in truth and spirit and be saved when time comes as it is very near already. To all employers who will require their workers to report on Saturday for work, you will be condemned together with your family. If you will do that it means that your god is "money" and you do not fit to inherit God's kingdom. This is a stern warning to you by God. It says in Ephesians 5:5 "Know this: no depraved, impure, or covetous person who serves the god 'Money' shall have part in the kingdom of Christ and of God." "Indeed, the love of money is the root of every evil." (1st Timothy 6:10).

To all people who will be observing Sabbath day, you should devote this time to prayer and not to indulge in worldly vices. There will be no drunkenness, no gambling, no smoking, no drugs, no sinful sexual activity, no hatred, no jealousy, no deceit of any kind. Express your love and concern to your family and neighbours. This is what God has to say for all people who observe Sabbath rightly in Isaiah 56:1-8, which says: "This is what Yahweh says: Maintain what is right and do what is just, for my salvation is close at hand, my justice is soon to come. Blessed is the man who does this, and puts his trust in it, who does not defile the Sabbath and who refrains from evil. Let no foreigner say, 'Surely Yahweh will exclude me from his people'. Neither let the castrated man say, 'I have become a mere dry tree.' For this is what Yahweh says: To the castrated men who keep my Sabbaths, who desire to do what pleases me and remain faithful to my covenant: I will give them in my house and within its walls, a memorial and a name that are worth more than sons and daughters; I will give them a name that will never die away or be forgotten. Yahweh says to the foreigners who join him, serving and loving his name, keeping his Sabbath unprofaned and remaining faithful to his covenant: I will bring them to my holy mountain and give them joy in my house of prayer. I will accept on my altar their burnt offerings and sacrifices, for my house will be called a house of prayer for all the nations. Thus says the Lord God, Yahweh, who gathers the exiles of Israel: There are others I will gather besides those already gathered." All you have to do is strengthen your family and be ready for Second Coming of our Lord Jesus Christ. For, God says that He loves you truly. The love that God gives you is a true love, says the Lord."

CHAPTER VI
CHURCHES

Blinded by ignorance and shrouded with ignominy, early Filipinos (Indios) led by Rajah Humabon, weakened by their paltry hospitality, were easily enticed by European colonizers to embrace Catholicism. They thought that Catholicism was better than their "Anito" worship. But they never knew that Catholicism is by far worse than their previous "Anito" worship. Such worship which began centuries before Spanish arrival involved prayer to spirit which has a similarity of worshipping God of truth in spirit. Whereas Catholicism pushes Filipino Indios to embrace pure idolatry which God abhors. Because of Catholicism, Rajah Hamabon's wife received from Ferdinand Magellan on April 14, 1521 a gift of statue of child Jesus which is until now venerated in Cebu city and in the whole province of Cebu. Neighbouring provinces also join the celebration by having similar image worshipped in their provinces- thus spreading widely abhorrent idolatry. People's ignorance made them unaware that God is so furious in this kind of worship. They invite God to destroy them by having this kind of worship. Many Filipinos falsely believed that the Spaniards had brought salvation to Filipinos by receiving from them statue of Black Nazarene, statue of child Jesus and other statues of saints of Roman Catholics. Unknown to them, these statues would become a justification for God to totally destroy them in the last days.

God is very angry for these people who worship graven statues and images. In Baruch 6:38, it says : "These pieces of wood plated with gold and silver are no more worthy than rocks hewn out of a mountain and their worshipers shall be humiliated." Also in Jeremiah 10:5, it says: "Their idols are like scarecrows in a cucumber patch; they cannot speak. They have to be carried because they cannot walk. Have no fear of them, they can do no evil nor are they able to do any good." A stiff-necked priest announced to his parishioners that the statue of child Jesus can save them. It is very wrong. Let all the priests of Roman Catholic Church throughout the world point just one verse from the Bible that a graven image or statue can save man from eternal damnation . They cannot do that. It means that the Roman Catholic Church is a fake Church. Originally, Roman Catholicism was established in Rome, a place where thousands of early true Christians were martyred, killed, crucified, sawn in two, murdered, chopped into pieces and fed to hungry lions. The real motive why it is established is to maintain worship of emperors, and Roman gods and goddesses. That is the reason that they cannot do away with the worship of idols. They were the ones who killed our Lord Jesus Christ on the cross and later used the name of Jesus to spread their idolatry on earth. They never venerated God the Father in any of their worship. Instead of true God, the Infinite God, they divert their worship to dead people they proclaimed as saints. They focused worship on Blessed Virgin Mary but never on our Almighty God. It goes to show that they are not really Church of God. In fact Roman emperors were all cruel and brutish in treating early Christians. Nero who lived from 37 A.D. to 68 A.D., after succeeding Claudius in 54 A.D killed thousands of early Christians by reducing them into living torches. He was infamous as so depraved of over-indulgence, corruption, profligacy, and debauchery. He even opened with a sharp knife his mother's stomach to see for himself where he came from. Tiberius, who lived from 42 B.C. to 37 A.D. who was increasingly despotic, ruled as Roman emperor from 26 A.D. He was indirectly responsible for the crucifixion of our Lord Jesus Christ who died **at 3:00 P.M of April 7, 30 A.D.** Tiberius was also responsible for the deaths of thousands of early Christians. Emperor Claudius who lived from 10 B.C. to 54 A.D., the one who extended Roman Empire to Britain, also killed many early Christians by nailing them alive on trees to die. Augustus or Gaius Octavianus who lived from 63 B.C. to 14 A.D. ruled as first emperor of Rome acquiring a title of Augustus Caesar after defeating Mark Anthony. He ruled from 27 B.C. to 14 A.D. He was emperor of Rome at the time when our Lord Jesus Christ was born on April 14, 12 B.C. He decreed for a census of the whole empire. Luke 2:1-3, tells us: "At that time the emperor issued a decree for a census of the whole empire to be taken. This first census was taken while Quirinus was governor of Syria. Everyone had to be registered in his own town." This fact contradicts Catholics' claim that Jesus was born on December 25. In the last days, however, it would be known to the world that our Lord Jesus Christ was not born on December 25. Roman Catholic Church being an alter ego of Roman Empire after its fall in 476 A.D and later on as alter ego of Holy Roman empire founded by Charlemagne in 800 A.D. continued Roman despotic rule and forced people to celebrate Christ's birth on December 25 during the feast day of Roman highest pagan god, Jupiter. Unknowingly, people who celebrate Christ's birth on December 25 are pagans. Hence, being a pagan religion, with pagan rites, the Roman Catholic Church is not a true church of God. It is rather a church of Roman emperors. Depart from her before the end of time to avoid being destroyed and be saved through our Lord Jesus Christ. People on earth, you have to worship only The Almighty

Father through our Lord Jesus Christ. Do not rely your salvation to Roman Catholic Church. It cannot save you. It will only thrust you into the lake of fire. The only one who can save you is our Lord Jesus Christ and none else.

As pinpointed by Almighty God, the great harlot described in Revelation 19:1-2 is no other than the Roman Catholic Church. It corrupted the world by her harlotry through her false teachings and wanton idolatry scattered throughout human history. In Romans 1:18, it says: "God is now ready to condemn the wickedness and any kind of injustice of those who silenced the truth by their wicked ways." In earnest, we have to analyse the wordings of these verses: "…Alleluia! Salvation, glory and might belong to our God, for his judgments are true and just. He has condemned the great harlot who corrupted the world with her adultery. He has avenged his servants' blood shed by her hand in harlotry." As specified here, God's judgments are true and just. Daniel's revelations states that such judgments proceed after the temple is restored then counting 2300 mornings and evenings. One day in prophecy being considered as one year, it follows then that after 2300 years beginning 457 B.C. when King Artaxerxes of Persia gave his order to Nehemiah to rebuild the Temple of Jerusalem. It means that the 2300 years beginning 457 B.C. has already ended in year 1847 of which judgment has already started in that year. Many Bible scholars believed that judgment has already started in year 1844. They failed to realize that there is no such thing as 3B.C. 2B.C and 1B.C. in world history. And judgment falls upon the great harlot which is the idolatrous Roman Catholic Church where God condemned the great harlot of her harlotry and brazen idolatry. Despite the fact that Roman Catholic Church is already condemned by God Almighty, still many people rely their salvation through this religion of idolatry. How can they be saved? In

Nahum 3:4-5, it says: "The harlot is paying for her harlotries, her deadly charms, her sorceries. She traded nations with her prostitutions and caught people by her spells. 'I am against you,' Yahweh Sabaoth says. 'I will lift your skirts over your face. I will show the nations your nakedness and the kingdoms your disgrace." Being a condemned church before God's eyes, the great harlot Roman Catholic Church enticed more people to be condemned by compelling them to worship pronounced saints carved in wood and adorned in silver and gold. God Almighty becomes furious with these people as they venerate carved statues and images. Yet they are assured by priests of this idolatrous church that they will be saved in the last judgment as long as they will only rely their salvation on the replicas of Santo Nino and the Black Nazarene. Catholics please ask your priest of any verse in the Bible where there is an assurance of salvation in venerating images and statues. If he cannot give you even just one verse from the Bible, it means that salvation of your soul is a big question mark. Depart from that religion. The true religion is in James 1:27. In totality, the majority of Catholicism's teachings are based on lies. They thwarted truth to waylay people toward perdition and eternal fire. All the teachings of Roman Catholic Church come from the Vatican, Rome. Here is a reliable indicator: if the teachings of any religion comes from the Vatican, Rome or any other place, if means that that religion is a fake religion. A genuine and true religion must derive its teachings from Zion alone and none else. In Isaiah 2:3, it says: "All the nations shall stream to it, saying, 'Come let us go to the mountain of the Lord, to the house of the God of Jacob, that he may teach us his ways and we may walk in his paths. **For the teaching comes from Zion, and from Jerusalem the word of Yahweh.**" Roman Catholic's hierarchy being learned and educated people know very well that idolatry worship is condemnable, yet they required people to have such kind of worship with ill-motive to add more people to be condemned in the last days. Is this church a cohort of Satan? Please tell me your answer, Catholics. In fact, among the forty cities on earth to be destroyed in the last days, the primary reason for their destruction is idolatry. You people who engage in idolatry worship be assured that you will be condemned in the last day.

Roman Catholic's harlotry is further described in last sentence of the verse which states: "He has avenged his servants' blood shed by her hand in harlotry." It means that God will avenge his servants' death. God says: Vengeance is mine." Who were killed by this great harlot, Roman Catholic Church? In past history, Roman Catholic Church created an eradication machinery called inquisition. People who were pronounced heretics by reason of their beliefs as opposed to church's doctrines or by political reason were executed in public by hanging or by beheading. The church formed a tribunal to suppress heresy or for political reprisal and the killing was carried out by the state. Many innocent people were martyred using such death machine. Who among those who were killed by this church's murdering machine? In the Philippines, it killed three martyr priests: Gomez, Jose Burgos and Jacinto Zamora. These three innocent priests were accused of calumny to have instigated the Revolt in Cavite City, Philippines. They were put on mock trial, found guilty by inquisition, later executed at Bagumbayan field (presently Rizal Park). Nicolas Copernicus, a Polish astronomer who lived between1473-1543, wrote his great work entitled "DeRevolutionibus" which theorizes that planets orbit around the sun. This theory was opposed to church's teachings that the earth is the centre of solar system and that all planets including the sun revolves around the earth. Being opposed to church's beliefs, Copernicus was convicted by inquisition and beheaded in 1543 at age 70. Other people killed by inquisition were: John Knox, John Wycliffe, and John Calvin. Jan Hus, a theologian and rector of Charles University in Prague, Czech Republic. In 1402, inspired by John Wycliff, he began giving sermons in Bethlehem Chapel. These sermons focused on what were seen as radical reforms of a corrupt Roman Catholic Church. Having become too dangerous for political and religious establishment, Hus was summoned to the Council of Constance put on mock trial for heresy and pronounced heretic by inquisition. He was burned at stake in Konstanz in 1415. Inscribed in his tomb the word in Czech: *"Pan Buh Pomoc Nase"* which is translated in English (The Lord is our Relief/Help). Martin Luther, German Christian Reformer, who lived between1483-1546 was hunted by state and Inquisition because he proclaimed justification by faith and separated from Roman Catholic Church. But he saved his life when Frederic II or Frederic the Great hid him for four years in Frederic's castle. Inside the castle, Martin Luther spent his time translating the Holy Bible from Latin to German language. Separating from the fake Roman Catholic Church, Martin Luther formed the Lutheran Reformation Church with the help of Philipp Melanchthon.

You, devotees of Catholicism, what are you waiting for? Depart from that fake religion. Throw away the filth of your faith by removing idols in your midst. Do not mix idolatry in expressing your faith to God Almighty. Worship alone our Almighty Father in spirit and truth as He is Spirit. Do not worship any other God. Only God Yahweh must you serve; must you praise; must you love with all your heart; with all your mind; with all your soul; and with all your strength. He alone must you adore and none else. Say to Him: "Father God Almighty, I do love you with all my heart, with all my soul, with all my mind and with all my strength, forever and ever through our

Lord Jesus Christ."

The Almighty Father told me also to enumerate the positive beliefs and doctrines of Catholicism which are in accord with divine plan. Here are the following teachings of Catholicism which the Almighty Father agrees: 1. Its belief and teaching of Monotheism; 2. Its belief and teaching of Divine Trinity; 3. Its teaching and belief in our Lord Jesus Christ; 4. Its belief and teaching in Resurrection; 5. Its belief and teaching in eternal life; 6. Its belief and teaching in the final judgment; 7. Its belief and teaching in Baptism; 8. Its belief and teaching in the Second Coming of our Lord Jesus Christ; These beliefs and teachings of Catholicism are all recognized by God. However, God Almighty dislikes the following beliefs and practices of Catholicism such as: 1. Its worship of printed and graven images (idolatry); 2. Its worship of saints who are also human beings instead of worshipping God; 3. Its devotion to holy rosary which is to divert worship from God to the Blessed Virgin Mary; 4.Its prayer in public as the true prayer to God is through spirit and in private. 5. Its declaration and belief of the infallibility of the pope; 6. Its belief and practice of forgiving sins of people as the only ones who can forgive sins are those from heaven: Our Lord Jesus Christ and the Almighty Father. 7. Its celebration of Christ's birth on the feast day of highest pagan god, Jupiter on December 25. The real birthday of our Lord Jesus Christ being on April 14, 12 B.C.; 8. Its practice of vow of chastity and celibacy while its priests scandalously maintain concubines making their church immoral; 9) its practice of vow of poverty but its priests, bishops, cardinals and popes live in luxury keeping billions of assets while its followers suffer extreme poverty; 10. Its practice of church service with corresponding exorbitant fee reducing the church into commercial entity. Most people in hierarchy of Roman Catholic Church seem to be voracious when it comes to money. Many priests would never bless the dead without the bereaved family paying the required fee. Thus, reducing some priests into voracious priests. No priest in this world would ever celebrate any wedding ceremony without the bride and groom paying the required payment based on church's tariffs. In summary, this religion Roman Catholic Church is reduced into Ro-money Catholic Church. In Ephesians 5:5, it says: "Know this: no depraved, impure or covetous person who served the god "Money" shall have part in the kingdom of Christ and of God." Many catholic priests are morally inconsistent as they teach people morality and good behaviour but they themselves practice in actual life the opposite. In Malachi 2: 7-8, it says: "The lips of the priest speak of knowledge, and the Law must be found in his mouth, since he is the messenger of Yahweh of hosts. But you, says Yahweh of hosts, have strayed from my way and moreover caused many to stumble because of your teaching."

Jesus Was Not Born on December 25

It has been more than two thousand years now that Catholicism became victorious in effectively fooling people on earth. Being docile to catholic teachings, people were easily convinced of its falsehood that our Lord Jesus Christ was born on December 25. Analytical mind would investigate primary background of Rome, a place where Catholicism was conceived. Romans have identical culture as that of Greece i.e. worshippers of images and carved statues. Their innate worship of images and statues refers to appreciation of beauty of a figure. They believe in gods and goddesses. They offer festivities to their gods. The most supreme of their gods is Jupiter, the highest pagan god. Pagan Rome celebrates feast of Jupiter every December 25 where people happily exchange gifts, exactly the same fashion the people do during Christmas. The early Christians also celebrated the feast of Jesus on December 25 although they knew that it is not the birth of our Lord Jesus Christ., coinciding with the celebration of highest pagan god. They do this in order to hide from Roman authorities because teachings about Jesus Christ in Roman Empire at that time was strictly prohibited. Anybody caught violating such prohibition is summarily punished by death either by nailing on tree, reducing to living torch, sawing in two, chopping into several pieces, feeding to hungry lions or beheading. As time goes on, Christians follow December 25 as Christ's birth. It becomes a tradition which is wrong. God reveals that in the last days, people would come into full knowledge about the exact birth of Christ.

In order to verify further truth of Christ's birth, let us first examine what the Bible says when Christ was conceived. In Annunciation of Blessed Virgin Mary, in Luke 1:26-33, it says: "In the sixth month, the angel Gabriel was sent by God to a town of Galilee called Nazareth. He was sent to a young virgin who was betrothed to a man named Joseph, of the family of David; and the virgin's name was Mary." The angel came to her and said, 'Rejoice, full of grace, the Lord is with you.' Mary was troubled at these words, wondering what the greeting could mean. But the angel said, 'Do not fear, Mary, for God has looked kindly on you. You shall conceive and bear a son and you shall call him Jesus. He will be great and shall rightly be called Son of the Most High. The Lord God will give him the kingdom of David, his ancestor, he will rule over the people of Jacob forever and his reign shall have no end." It was the sixth month that angel Gabriel announced to Mary about Jesus' birth. If Jesus was born in December, it means that Jesus stayed only in Mary's womb for six months. That is impossible. A child stays in the womb for nine months or if premature delivery seven months.

Catholicism talks about impossibility to twist the truth. They also know that in the month of December the place of nativity is cold and chilly. Shepherds cannot tend their flocks in the cold night. But in Christ's birth there were shepherds camping to watch their flocks. In Luke 2:8-18, it says: "There were shepherds camping in the countryside, taking turns to watch over their flocks by night. Suddenly an angel of the Lord appeared to them, with the Glory of the Lord shining around them."

"As they were terrified, the angel said to them, 'Don't be afraid; I am here to give you good news, great joy for all the people. Today a Saviour has been born to you in David's town; he is the Messiah and the Lord. Let this be a sign to you: you will find a baby wrapped in swaddling clothes and lying in a manger. "Suddenly the angel was surrounded by many more angels, praising God and saying, 'Glory to God in the highest; peace on earth for God is blessing humankind.'"

"When the angels had left them and gone back to heaven, the shepherds said to one another. 'Let us go as far as Bethlehem and see what the Lord has made known to us.' So they came hurriedly and found Mary and Joseph with the baby lying in the manger. On seeing this they related what they had been told about the child, all were astonished on hearing the shepherds."

Based on the facts presented and collaborated by Biblical support, we can deduce a verifiable conclusion that our Lord Jesus Christ was not born on December 25. As revealed by divine intervention, the real birth of our Lord Jesus Christ was **April 14, 12 B.C., a Sunday at 9:41 P.M.** While His death, as officially recorded, was on **April 7, 30 A.D., a Friday at 3:00 P.M.** Relative hereto, Christ will not ask any gift from you. Instead, he wants you to observe his birthday by obeying his commandments which says: "You shall love the Lord your

God, with all your heart, with all your soul, with all your mind and with all your strength. Then, you shall love your neighbour as yourself." In observing his second commandment which pertains to your neighbour, you must accomplish what is written in Ephesians 4:29-32, which says: "Do not let even one word come from your mouth, but only good words that will encourage when necessary and be helpful to those who hear. Do not sadden the Holy Spirit of God which you were marked with. It will be your distinctive mark on the day of salvation. Do away with all quarrelling, rage, anger, insults and every kind of malice: be good and understanding, mutually forgiving one another as God forgave you in Christ." If you can do this, it means that there is a quality in you to be a true son or daughter of God. And you will be a victor of God's Glory of which you deserve a divine reward. In Revelation 2:17, it says: "If anyone has ears, let him listen to what the Spirit says to the Churches: To the victor I will give the hidden manna. I will also give him a white stone with a new name written on it which no one knows except the one who receives it."

Catholics celebrate Christmas every December 25 which in effect, they venerate the highest pagan god Jupiter as this is not Christ's birthday but a feast day of Jupiter. In so doing they become pagans as they worship the highest pagan god, Jupiter. For this, they are not worthy to be called followers of Christ but rather followers of pagan god Jupiter. They ought to be called not as Christians but Jupiterians. They have no place in God's kingdom.

Despite this truth, many Catholics would still continue celebrating Christmas making such justification that it is already a cultural tradition. So they will just continue insulting God and our Lord Jesus Christ. Roman Catholic Church will still encourage people, as it is an idolatrous church, to continue celebrating

December 25. All Catholics who aspire for true salvation, you have to depart from that fake and corrupt religion, Roman Catholic Church.

Idolatry in Roman Catholic Church

Idolatry began in the country when Ferdinand Magellan, a Portuguese Navigator commissioned by Spain in search of spices, endow as a gift to Rajah Humabon's wife the replica of the child Jesus. This replica is still venerated in Cebu City every third Sunday of January. This was given to Humabon's wife on April 14, 1521. This replica has been venerated by people not only in Cebu but the entire archipelago for 502 years already. It means also that God's anger on this place has been lingering for 502 years already. It needs only a blasting cap that God's anger will burst into a deadly destruction. God's heart is fatally wounded by this idolatry. The true worship to Almighty Father is stained by Rome's culture of idolatry worship. Such worship only distanced away people's relationship from God. Thus instead of obtaining salvation through prayer people only pull the rope of condemnation and disgrace.

Rome is indeed the mastermind of idolatry as their original culture of which a portion was derived from Greeks was radically mixed into Catholicism. It further worsened when Emperor Constantine embraced Christianity as official religion of the empire and integrated idolatry into the vein of Christianity. When Christianity came into the countries colonized by Europeans, such Christianity was already immensely diluted by idol worship. That is an apparent reason why most cities sighted by God Almighty for total destruction in the last days are those whose idolatry is widespread. And most of these cities are religiously influenced by Roman Catholicism whose kind of worship is idolatry centred.

In fact Catholicism was founded in Rome to perpetuate worshiping Roman emperors as gods. Those who refused to worship the emperors were summarily executed by torturing and beheading. The cruellest of these emperors/gods were Domitian, Diocletian, Nero and Titus. After the fall of Roman Empire in 476 A.D., as there was no more emperors to be worshipped as gods, Roman citizens adopted nominally our Lord Jesus Christ to be venerated to entice recruitment membership in the world. They radically claimed that their Religion is true and genuine since they were the ones who crucified our Lord. They continue killing true followers of Christianity leaving remnants of half-baked Christians who fatally engaged in disgraceful idolatry.

The idolatry of Roman Catholic Church worsens during Dark Ages when people took refuge in monasteries and formed religious groups such as Benedictine, Franciscan, Augustinian and Dominican orders. It was during that time when idolatry became widespread. They worshipped images consisting of graven images of venerable saints made of hard wood and adorned with silver and gold. They purposely use hard wood so that they can have a very strong god in their midst to protect them from invaders and brigands. In Micah 1:7, it says: "All her carved images will be dashed to pieces and her filthy idols burnt by fire. I will make a waste heap of all her idols for they were made with harlot's wages, and to harlot's wages they will return." Hence, their worship is useless as it is focused on statues of people proclaimed by their church as martyrs and saints. Yet their church assures them that these statues can effectively mediate them to God. True worship to God in spirit and truth had never been introduced in Catholicism. Their worship is pure idolatry. In Psalm 135:15-18, it says: "The nations' idols of gold and silver are the work of human hands. They have mouths that cannot speak, eyes that cannot see; ears that cannot hear; neither is their breath in their mouths. Their makers will be like them, so will all who trust in them".

True worship to God Almighty should be in spirit and truth. In John 4:23-24, it says: "But the hour is coming and is even now here, when the true worshipers will worship the Father in spirit and truth; for that is the kind of worship the Father wants. God is spirit and those who worship God must worship in spirit and truth."

Worship of idols: Santo Nino, Black Nazarene and the Traslacion

Filipinos are absolutely misguided in their expression of faith to God. They very well believe that God would be pleased if they worship replicas and images. They never knew that God becomes angry with them having continued idol worship without Biblical consultation especially those related to forbidden worship. In the same manner Catholic priests, who presumably always read the Bible, intentionally fail to remind people that worship of any graven images either replicas from heaven or earth is strictly prohibited. In effect, European colonizers who introduced Catholicism in pure form of idolatry did not introduce salvation of soul but rather condemnation of soul. In Wisdom 15:6, it says: "Really, idol-makers and those who serve and worship them are looking for disgrace and deserve to have false hope." God says that those who worship graven images and statues also worship the beast, Satan. In the last days, they will be marked with the sign of beast which is 666. At this point in time, we have already a clue of who will be the followers of beast, Satan. Those who presently worship idols such as: Sto. Nino, Black Nazarene and other wooden saints of Catholics are possible members of 666. They will be marked with sign of 666. They cannot experience hardship during Beast's reign as they have easy access to buying and selling of goods. They can buy any goods they want. They will enjoy life with ease during Beast's reign but when our Lord Jesus Christ commenced His Second Coming, they will be condemned. They cannot enjoy the First Resurrection. While those who do not worship idols during their lifetime will find utmost persecution as they will not be members of 666. When Jesus Christ comes, they will be saved and have everlasting life.

People of God, if you really want to be saved, you have to stop worshipping graven images and statues. Do not make any justification of your idolatry. Throw away your idols, replicas of Santo Nino and Black Nazarene the same way the menstrual clothe is thrown. Turn to God Almighty through our Lord Jesus Christ and be saved. Do not pay attention to Catholic priests for their advices lead only to eternal damnation as the religion they lean on is a fake and corrupt religion. In Isaiah 42:8, it says: "I am Yahweh that is my name, I will not give my glory to another; or my praise to graven images." God clearly clarifies that His Glory is never transferred or attached to any graven images. It is a very wrong notion on worshippers' part that God's glory is transferred to graven image. And they falsely believe that a praise to a graven image is also a praise to God. That is purely a crooked belief. God's commandments clearly state that He alone should be prayed, praised and loved and none else. Perverted people make twisted reasoning to justify their being rebellious to God. They continue worshipping idols made of wood despite being warned that it is prohibited. They put complete trust on their idols. In Isaiah 42:17, it says: "But those who trust in graven images and say to idols, 'You are our gods' will be turned back in utter shame."

"Traslacion" Of Quiapo Church

"Traslacion" is a Spanish word whose root is "trasladar" which means to move, to relocate or to transfer. What is to be moved, relocated or transferred? The thing to be moved, relocated or transferred is a wood chiselled into an image which blind devotees called "The Black Nazarene". These blind devotees, proud of their wooden god, are thankful to Spanish friars for bringing to our country wooden god to be venerated by millions of people. These blind devotees take pride to themselves that each year their number increase by leap and bounds such that those in provinces also venerate this wooden god. Some of them also buy wood to be chiselled into replica of black Nazarene to be venerated in their provinces. In this way, idolatry in Philippines becomes already a cancer. These blind devotees have a wooden god while the stiff-necked Israelites had a golden god formed into a calf. They have one thing in common- and that is destruction of their souls in eternal fire.

In Jeremiah 10:8, it says: "They are all brutish and stupid; their idols are proof of their foolishness." This kind of stupidity is widely participated by millions of stiff-necked people with different purposes in attending such "translacion". Most fanatics joined in order that they will be saved by their wooden god in Final Judgment. They might have lost their sense of practical reasoning. How can a wooden god save them in final judgment of God of Truth and Spirit? God Almighty has already informed them that His Glory is never transferred to any graven images or statues. For sure, they and their wooden god will be consumed in the lake of fire. Businessmen also participate in the hope that they can improve their business. Perhaps only Chinese businessmen do not believe on it yet they prosper by far in business. Some celebrities also join so they can be more popular someday. Gamblers also join hoping that they win in cockfight and other kinds of games of chance. Politicians also join so they can win in elections. Spiritualists and quack doctors also join so they can cure their patients. Sorcerers also join so they can be more adept in witchcraft. The Roman Catholic Church, through their "Padre Damasos" in Quiapo Church successfully fooled all credulous people. It means that the trick used by Spanish friars in fooling the "Indios" still effectively work in modern times. With priestly stupidity, the "Padre Damasos" of Quiapo Church proudly announced to their parishioners that they will be abundantly blessed once they participate and pray along the streets they pass by.

The Roman Catholic Church strongly defended this kind of activity since there are millions of people who attend this rite. This is a clear deflection of Catholicism designed primarily to increase the coffers of Quiapo Church and continuously fool the people. It says in Hosea 4:7 "All without exception offended me; they have exchanged me, their Glory, for idols, their shame." These shameless devotees of wooden god insolently justify their sinful act, arguing that the number of devotees increase to millions and still growing. What is sinful before God's eyes is sinful, per se; and can never be justified. Idolatry can never be justified even if billions of people will attend to it. God's Warning says: Those who believe on it only endanger their souls as they will be adversely judged in the last days. Isaiah 44:9-10 says: "Good –for-nothings are all idol makers, and useless are the works they prize so much. Their witnesses, blind and ignorant, will be put to shame. Whoever fashioned a god or cast an idol without hope of gain? See how its devotees will be ridiculed, for its craftsmen are but men. Let them assemble, let them come to court, they will be both terrified and scorned." As this graven image is venerated nationwide, those who reside in distant places duplicated such image to be venerated by provincial folks.

For those people who do this, God has this to say in Wisdom 14:

16-17, "Time will consolidate this unholy practice and eventually it will be observed by law. It has also happened that sculptured images were venerated by order of sovereigns. Those who lived far away and were unable to honour them personally had copies made, that they might honour them as if present by means of their image." Those who venerate the image of Black Nazarene and the child Jesus in Cebu, Cagayan de Oro City and Tagum City: God sternly warn you to stop your stupid worthless kind of worship. If you will insist in continuing such false worship God will fix a date for your total destruction, says the Lord. In Jeremiah 44:4-5, it says: "I sent them my servants the prophets time and time again to tell them: "Do not do this abominable thing that I detest! But they did not listen or pay attention; they did not turn away from their evil ways or give up worshipping strange gods."

People of God, if you aspire for eternal life depart from that useless activity. It is pure idolatry. Its wages is eternal death. In Isaiah 45:20, it says: "Come, gather together, fugitives from among the nations. In ignorance, you have erected idols of wood and prayed to gods that cannot move." This is one reason why God will totally destroy the whole of Metropolitan Manila in the coming days. You have to venerate only the Living God not the wooden god which cannot talk, which cannot walk, which cannot hear, which cannot see and which cannot feel.

Here are God's Words to Catholics who are devotees of wooden god, it says in Micah 5:12-13, "I will abolish your carved images, the sacred stones from your midst, so that you no longer worship the work of your hands. I will pull down your sacred poles and destroy your idols." God says also in Jeremiah 10:14-15: "At this all men feel stupid and without knowledge. Every goldsmith is ashamed of his idol which is a fraud without breath. They are worthless, ridiculous objects, destined to disappear when the time comes for punishment." God wants you to worship Him in spirit and truth as He is Spirit and Truth. Worship God through our Lord Jesus Christ so that you will have life and have it more abundantly. Have faith in God through our Lord Jesus Christ and your salvation is already complete. Do not believe in Catholicism's teachings which leads to perdition. It is not a church founded by our Lord Jesus Christ through Simon Peter, who was himself tortured and later killed by Roman emperor. Join those churches which do not worship images and strictly observe Sabbath Day which is Saturday. God has not changed and will never change His Sabbath Day from Saturday to any day of the week. Do it now for your salvation as Christ's Second Coming is fast approaching. True religion is to follow God's command and walk in His way.

In Jeremiah 7:23, it says: "One thing I did command them: Listen to my voice and I will be your God and you will be my people. Walk in the way I command you and all will be well with you." In Isaiah 45:22-24, God says this to you: "Turn to me and be saved, all you from the ends of the earth, for I am God and there is no other. By my own self I swear it, and what comes from my mouth is truth, a word that will not be revoked. Before me every knee will bend, by me every tongue will swear, saying, 'In Yahweh alone are righteousness and strength." Amen.

Free Masonry

This is not a religion. Rather, this is an organization of prominent men in society who profess to be most worshipful but they do not recognize our Lord Jesus Christ much less Father God. Who are they worshipping then? Possibly, they worship their master, Satan. Members of this organization are loyal advocates of Satan who continue Satan's cause against God. The mission and vision of this organization is to rebel against God as they obey their lord and master Satan. Many of them are professionals who because of their intelligence, believe that they are more intelligent than God. The truth is their intelligence is only foolishness to God. In 1st Corinthians 3:19-20, it says: "For the wisdom of this world is foolishness in God's eyes. To this, Scripture says: God catches the wise in his own wisdom. It also says: The Lord knows the reasoning of the wise, that it is useless." They are called free thinkers who deliberately mock our Lord Jesus Christ. They are the descendants of Roman soldiers who stabbed Christ's side with a spear and the Roman soldiers who nailed our Lord Jesus Christ on the cross. Usually, they put the crucifix of our Lord Jesus Christ under the sole of their left shoe as a sign that they do not respect Christ. They feel that they are smarter than our Lord Jesus Christ. They are Satan's disciples. While they are still alive their one foot that trampled on Christ's crucifix is already placed in hell. To them, the cross of our Lord Jesus Christ has no meaning at all. In 1st Corinthians 2:18-20, it states: "The language of the cross remains nonsense for those who are lost. Yet for us who are saved, it is the power of God, as Scripture says: 'I will destroy the wisdom of the wise and make fail the foresight of the foresighted. Masters of human wisdom, men of letters, Philosophers there is no place for you! And the wisdom of this world? God let it fail." They are people who mention Christ name in a tone of curse. They have no respect to God as they do not show respect to themselves. God warns them in Isaiah 29:14 which states: "Now therefore, I will perform marvels in them once more: I will make the wisdom of their wise men perish; I will make the understanding of their prudent men vanish." Most of them, as they grow old, suffer severe Alzheimer's disease, a degenerative disease of cerebral cortex symptomatic of progress loss of memory and speech and paralysis. They stop believing God as they regard themselves more knowledgeable than God. In 2nd Corinthians 10:4-5, it states: "We destroy arguments and haughty thoughts which oppose the knowledge of God. We compel all understanding to obey Christ…" In Hebrews 6:6, it says: "If in spite of this they have ceased to believe and have fallen away, it is impossible to move them a second time to repentance when they are crucifying, on their own account, the Son of God, and spurning him publicly." Many of them are also members and officers of Catholic organizations such as Cursillo Movement, Knights of Columbus, Samaria and Catholic Women's League. They believe that the more religious organizations they join in, the greater their chances to go to heaven. That is clearly a false reasoning. They cannot clearly go to heaven because it is the place of our Lord Jesus Christ and of God Almighty whom they constantly attack. Their place is where their master lives that is Hell.

Other Churches

Church of Latter-Day Saints

This church was founded in 1827 by Joseph Smith, who wrote the Book of Mormon which contains all their teachings and doctrine. According to God, Joseph Smith was a good person. But his teachings as written in his book are fictitious, farcical and unrealistic. The places mentioned in his book are not real which cannot be located in this world. Seemingly, it is a fairy tale. Hence, people who follow his teachings will only be led astray into unreal world.

To entice people to join in their organization, Joseph Smith's followers later included in their teachings the Holy Bible. But their interpretations of Holy Bible are diluted with contents of Book of Mormon which has a fairy tale aspect.

Again, in order to convert people to their fold, they offer financial help to needy people. For this, their organization can never be called a religion in strictest sense but rather, a foundation.

Religion of Jehovah's Witnesses

This religion teaches truth about God the Father and about Our Lord Jesus Christ; it spreads the Gospel through printed materials; person to person personal conversation about Holy Bible and through website; it teaches against crime, drunkenness, substance abuse; it teaches against abortion, killing, homosexuality; it teaches against greed, against magic sorcery; it teaches against worship of graven or printed images; it teaches about good behaviour and all its teachings are based on Holy Bible. For this, it is strongly recommended that people of God may choose to affiliate with this religion if they want to have a religion. If they want to depart from Roman Catholicism or any other religion, they can transfer to Jehovah's Witnesses religion.

Protestantism

This is a religion that adheres to principles of Reformation which was first started by Martin Luther who lived from 1483-1546. He proclaimed justification by faith which was contrary to Catholic doctrine and thereby broke away from Vatican. Martin Luther, in his 99 theses, exposed evils of Catholic Church in Rome and was later pronounced guilty by inquisition. To save his life, he hid in the castle of Frederic the Great for four years and spent his life there translating Holy Bible from Latin to German language. After leaving the Castle of Frederic The Great, Martin Luther established Protestantism and with the help of Philipp Melanchthon, the religion spread throughout the world branching into numerous denominations. One denomination of Protestantism is Baptist church which strictly adheres to Baptism by immersion. God says that there is no difference between Baptism by sprinkling or by pouring or by immersion as these are only symbolic rites of admitting a person to a Christian church. What is important here is a person being baptized is ready to embrace Christian life. For, baptism is not an assurance of salvation. It is only the starting point for a person to follow the way of our Lord Jesus Christ. If that person accepts our Lord Jesus Christ as his personal saviour and obey God's will and have faith in him, that person can attain salvation and everlasting life. People who are debating between baptism by immersion and baptism by sprinkling or by pouring are only wasting their time, says the Lord. In Titus 3:9, it says: "Avoid stupid arguments, discussion about genealogies and quarrels about the Law, for they are useless and unimportant." Also in 2nd Timothy 2:23, it says: "Avoid stupid and senseless discussions, since such are the cause of misunderstanding."

Baptism is not only performed by immersion or by pouring or by sprinkling, it can also be performed in the cloud. The Israelites, for forty years in the desert, were baptized in the cloud. In 1st Corinthians 10:2-4, it states: "They were in a way baptized in the cloud and in the sea to be the people of Moses, and all of them ate from the same spiritual manna and all of them drank from the same spiritual drink. For you know that they drank from a spiritual rock following them, and the rock was Christ."

Since this religion does not venerate any printed or graven image and does not worship any idols, and believe in God through our Lord Jesus Christ, I fully recommend that God's people may affiliate with this religion if they choose to have a religion. But religion is not essential for salvation of soul. It is just more than enough to venerate God in truth and spirit through our Lord Jesus Christ.

God's people may also affiliate with Seventh Day Adventist Church as they believe in Second Coming of our Lord Jesus Christ and they observe strictly Sabbath Day.

Christian Orthodox Church

This church was an offshoot of a divided church. It separated ways from Roman Catholic Church because it does not like the worship of idols which is inherent in Rome. It is a church that adheres that worshipping God must be in spirit and truth and not through printed or graven image. God's people may also join this religion as it does not venerate idols and statues.

The only true religion found in the Bible is in James 1:27: "In the sight of God, our Father, pure and blameless religion lies in helping the orphans and widows in their need and keeping oneself from the world's corruption." As revealed by God, here is your guide in choosing a religion:

It worships only One God (Monotheism) and it is the Almighty God, the Living God of Spirit and Truth; and strictly and religiously observe Sabbath Day, the Holy Day of Almighty Father on the Seventh Day which is Saturday and not Sunday as erroneously practised in Catholicism which began during Emperor Constantine's reign;

It does not worship any image printed or graven and it prohibits idolatry. Any justification of such worship is unacceptable;

It recognizes our Lord Jesus Christ's divinity without any doubt;

By faith, it believes in Divine Trinity;

Its teachings are directed toward salvation of humanity;

It believes and practices Baptism of any form be it by sprinkling, by pouring, by immersion, by the cloud, or by the sea,

Its teachings are mainly based on Holy Bible;

It believes, hopes, and waits for the Second Coming of our Lord Jesus Christ;

It believes in Final Judgment to come;

It believes in Resurrection of the Dead and Eternal Life.

CHAPTER VII
OTHER ISSUES

666

Sometime in year 90 AD, John the Apostle wrote the Book of Revelation as inspired by our Lord Jesus Christ inscribing therein the Devil with 666 sign. The Book of Revelation was only published by followers of John after his death in 95 AD in the Island of Patmos, a rocky portion of Greek archipelago adjacent to coast of Asia Minor, presently known as Turkey. There was no iota of hint of 666 when John wrote the book. As revealed to me by God's Grace, this 666 is already in this world, appearing abruptly at the turn of Third Millennium. The first 666 is WWM (World Wide Monopsonist). What is WWM doing now in this world? It existed in this world out of nowhere. It began its on-line selling business of any product from simplest product to complicated product in prompt delivery to customers throughout the world. Then it offered promotions of numerous consumer goods starting from cup noodles and other food items. As time goes on, it will control other basic products like coffee, tea, sugar, milk, beans, bread, biscuits, flour, chocolates, beverages, water, soaps, detergents, toothpaste, toiletries, medicines, clothes, apparels, fabrics, machineries, household appliances, construction materials and equipment, computers, electricity, cell phones and cell phone loads in a form of monopsony and monopoly. It will control activity of buying and selling of all goods from smallest to biggest products; from cheapest to most expensive products, from inferior to superior products and from imported to local products. It will be the only one to buy and sell all products and none else. And that those without mark of beast on their forehead and on their right hand cannot buy or sell any kind of products. As revealed to me by God's Grace, the mark that will be used is laser that it cannot be seen by naked eye. Whenever you buy or sell, you will be first verified if you have mark of beast thru automated scanning by laser. A buyer will not use money. Instead, the total amount of purchased goods will be debited from buyer's account deposits from the bank as all banks and banking transactions will be controlled also by the beast. The salaries, wages and other payments of personal services in government and private sectors will be credited to bank accounts of employees, and individuals using automated procedure which will reflect in his account in less than a second. If you do not have the mark of beast you cannot buy or sell any product and you cannot be gainfully employed with any company or enterprise. Instead you will be tagged as enemy of devil and that you will become a target of execution. In the words of Isaiah, if you are destined to prison, you will go to prison as you will be accused in calumny or with fabricated evidences as Satan knows that his time is running low (Revelation12;12). If you are destined to the sword, to the sword you will die. In Revelation 12:17, it says: "Then the dragon was furious with the woman and went off to wage war on the rest of her children, those who keep God's commandments and bear witness to Jesus." God's people will rather prefer to die than to be branded with beast's sign. In doing so, they will be raised to life when Jesus comes. Those who are branded with the beast's mark, can enjoy abundance of life during the reign of the Beast. But when Jesus comes, they will be cast in the lake of fire after the second resurrection. There will be two resurrections. The first resurrection belongs to God's people who will enjoy life for the next millennium in Heaven. They will no longer experience death in second resurrection. Those who will be raised in second resurrection will be judged accordingly. Those sheep or worthy of life will be at the right hand of the Lamb and those goats or unworthy of life will be at the left hand of the Lamb. The goats will be cast together with Satan into the lake of fire. In John 5: 28-29, it says: "Do not be surprised at this: the hour is coming when all those lying in tombs will hear my voice and come out, those who have done good shall rise to live, and those who have done evil will rise to be condemned.

The second "666" is WWC (Whole World Carrier) This is a delivery company that sends any product to any part of the world. It has millions of offices and branches throughout the world. It will monopolize all deliveries of goods in the future. It will control sea vessels, sea voyages, land transportation and air transportation so that all people who want their products transported cannot do it if they have no mark of the beast. Likewise, all passengers without mark of beast cannot board an airplane or sea vessel. As God's people cannot easily travel from one place to another, they have to stay only in one place and be vigilant. They should have their best initiative to procure their foods in order to survive and wait for the second coming of Jesus and His angels. Their thirst can be quenched by one grain of salt, if there is no water available. They have to bring salt in their pockets so that the fallen angels under Satan's rule cannot come near them and cannot hurt them. Death at that time will be hard to find though one would wish for it. In Revelation 9:6, it says: "In those days, people will look for death but will not find it; they will long to die, but death will elude them."

The third "666" is World Wide Web. It is written as w.w.w. on computer "W" is also written as *VI. So that w.w.w. is also written as VI VI VI or in Roman numerals VI VI VI is 666.* This worldwide web has control on yahoo. Googles, X (twitter), you tube, face book, instagram and other internet apps. In the near future any person, entity, company, country, business venture and enterprise cannot make an account with any of these networks of which w.w.w. controls if they have no mark of beast. There will be billions of people who will be marked with 666 as they prefer to stay with their pleasure in face book, you tube, X (twitter), yahoo, google, instagram, and other apps and networks. Besides, they cannot buy computer and cell phone loads if they do not have mark of beast. The beast is described in Revelation 13:1-2, "Then I saw a beast rising out of the sea, with ten horns and seven heads, with ten crowns on its horns. On each head was a blasphemous title challenging God. The beast I saw looked like a leopard, with paws like a bear and a mouth like a lion. The dragon passed on his power, his throne and his great authority to the beast." Only very few will be saved. Those saved people will devote most of their time to serve God through our Lord Jesus Christ. They will completely stop engaging in cell phones. They will stop using face book, yahoo, X (twitter), google, instagram and you tube. They would be willing to sacrifice their lives for God's sake as they will be raised to life when Christ comes. In 2nd Timothy 3:12-13, it says: "All who want to serve God in Christ Jesus will be persecuted, while evil persons and impostors will go from bad to worse, deceiving and being deceived." This 666 comprising of WWM, WWC, and WWW may change from time to time their original names to hide their true identity to waylay people. Truly, they will carry other names to hide their identity but they can be easily detected by their natural activities as partner of beast. For those who cannot endure to the last due to hunger will be tempted to worship the beast to satisfy their basic needs and thereafter become its slave. In Revelation 13: 7-8, it says: "It was allowed to make war on the saints and to conquer them. It was given authority over people of every tribe, language and nation; this is why all the inhabitants of the earth will worship before it, those whose names have not been written in the book of life of the slain Lamb, since the foundation of the world." As a consequence, God will punish them for being unfaithful. As they already belong to the beast, they will lose their share of heavenly inheritance. Revelation 14: 9-11 says: "A third angel then followed, shouting aloud, 'If anyone worships the beast or its image or has his forehead or hand branded, he will also drink the wine of God's anger which has been prepared, undiluted, in the cup of his fury; he will be tortured by fire and brimstone, in the presence of the holy angels and the Lamb.' The smoke of their torment goes up forever and ever; there will be no rest, day or night, for those who worshiped the beast and its image, and for those who were branded with the mark of its name." God's people will be put into a dilemma such that if they will not worship the beast they will be killed and if they will worship the beast they will be punished by God for their unfaithfulness. For this, the best thing that they should do is to prefer to be killed so that when our Lord Jesus Christ comes, they will be raised to life and live forever. In Philippians 1:28-29, it says: "Do not be afraid of your opponents. This will be a sign that they are defeated and you are saved, that is saved by God. For through Christ you have been granted not only to believe in Christ but also to suffer for him." But there will be thousands of God's people who will be taken by God's angels to heaven to escape this suffering. This is rapture. In the song of Moses and the Israelites to Yahweh, Exodus 15:13, it says: "In unfailing love you guided the people you redeemed, in strength you led them to your holy house." They will be carried away by God's holy angels to heaven for them to experience God's love. People will suddenly disappear and be carried away to heaven. Individually or in group, people will be taken by angels. Even people in one town will just disappear altogether. In Isaiah 6:11-12, it says: "…Until towns have been laid waste and left without inhabitant; until the houses are deserted and the fields ruined and ravaged. For Yahweh will send away the men and the fields will be left deserted. Jesus has revealed to us that rapture will take place before the second coming. In Luke 17:34-35, it says: "I tell you, though two men sharing the same bed, it may be that one will be taken and the other left." It would be lucky for anyone who will be taken as he or she is already saved and free from experiencing difficulties in the last days.

God's people will experience suffering for a period of 42 months or 1260 days. But they have to bear in mind that God loves them very much. The love that God gives them is a true love, says the Lord. The start of great suffering of people on Earth before the Second Coming will be on December 1, 2119, a Friday and will end on Friday May 14, 2123. In 1st Peter 1:6, it states: There is cause for joy, then, even though you may, for a time, have to suffer many trials." When will that be? No one knows that. Not even the holy angels in heaven nor Jesus Christ. It is only God who has exclusive knowledge of it. But God has disclosed to me that that event will happen barely 60 years after my death. This is now the last hour. For this, people will experience frequently many strong earthquakes, tsunamis, volcanic eruptions, dreadful calamities, pandemics and other events that will claim millions of lives.

Lgbt (Lesbian, Gay, Bi-Sexual, Transgender)

It says in Deuteronomy 23:18: "There shall not be among the daughters of Israel a consecrated prostitute. Or a consecrated homosexual among the sons of Israel." They have no place in God's kingdom. For, if they are truly with God they will be transformed into real man and woman. Originally, God did not create this kind of gender. Satan adulterated the creation. That is why there are lesbians, gays, bi-sexual and transgender in this world. This is Satan's work. But if these LGBT members will return to God, they will be transformed into real man and real woman and they will be saved. But if they will not return to God, they will be condemned in the Last Judgment. Prayer is number one key in order to return to God Almighty and have a personal relationship with Him. Have faith in Almighty through our Lord Jesus Christ and be saved. Now is the time for you to change because the hour is about to come. In Deuteronomy 22:5, it says: "A woman must not wear a man's clothing, nor a man the clothing of a woman, because whoever does such thing deserves the reprobation of Yahweh." Those who do not follow God's command will have their place in the lake of fire.

Death, Resurrection and Eternal Life

There is nothing to be afraid of death. In Ecclesiastes 7:1, it says: "...Better the day of death than the day of birth." It is only temporary, says God. For, death in this world is not yet a final death. Death is bitter for those who have many possessions as they want still to enjoy more of their wealth. But for needy, old, downtrodden, sick, and destitute people, death is very much welcome. In Tobit 41:1-4, it says: "Death! What a bitter thought for someone who lives happily among his possessions, a prosperous and successful man who is still able to enjoy his food! Your sentence, Death, is welcome to a needy person whose strength is failing, who is old, worn out, and full of worries; to one who is angry and without hope! Do not be afraid of Death sentence; think of those who have gone before you and those who will follow. The Lord has decreed it for every living creature." Death in this world is not yet a final death. It is only a simple separation of body from human soul. Where will the body go and where will the soul go? Genesis 2:7, says: "Then Yahweh formed Man, dust drawn from the clay, and breathed into his nostrils a breath of life and Man became alive with breath." Man's body comes from clay, from the earth, from the dust. Hence, if there is a separation of body and soul, man's body will return to clay, to the earth, to the dust. Remember man that you are dust and to dust you shall return. Genesis 3:19 says: "With sweat on your face you will eat your bread, until you return to clay, since it was from clay that you were taken, for you are dust and to dust you shall return." Catholicism over-emphasizes this verse by having ritual on Ash Wednesday which can never be found in Holy Bible. They are good in ceremonies as they are equally good in worshipping graven images. God says that the words in Holy Bible which state: "...for you are dust and to dust you shall return" are already strong reminder to man that he is dust compared to a showy ritual of placing dust on forehead. They do the placing of dust on their forehead to pretentiously display to many their religiosity as when they proudly pray in public. They have been paid in full, says the Lord. Rituals and ceremonies fade away but God's words will remain forever. That is why God's words in Genesis 3:19 are far greater than the rituals and ceremonies. While man's soul goes back to where it comes from i.e. to God. In Ecclesiastes 12:7, it says: "...The dust returns to the earth from which it came and the spirit returns to God who gave it." In Job 34:14, it says: "For the destiny of man and animal is identical; death for one as for the other. Both have the same spirit; man has no superiority over animals for all pass away like wind. Both go to the same place, both came from dust and return to dust." The original purpose why God created man is for him to be immortal and be with Him throughout eternity, never to die at all. Owing, however, to devil's jealousy that man's privilege to live an immortal life was deceitfully snatched from him. In Wisdom 2:23-24, it says: "Indeed God created man to be immortal in the likeness of his own nature, but the envy of the devil brought death to the world, and those who take his side shall experience death." Those who take devil's side by doing evil will die. However, those who despise devil's work and obey God's will through our Lord Jesus Christ will find life to the fullest after death. In Samuel 2:6, it says: "Yahweh is Lord of life and death; he brings down to the grave and raises up." In Wisdom 1:6, it says: "It is godless that consider death as a friend and call for it in every way. They have made a pact with it and they shall justly belong to it." In John 8:51, it says: "Truly, I say to you, if anyone keeps my word, he will never experience death." Amen.

Many people do not know God's purpose why they were created. If we have to consult the Holy Bible on real purpose why man was created, it is found in Sirach 17:1-14, which says: "The Lord created man from the earth and let him return to earth. He settled a fixed time for them and a set number of days, giving them power over everything on earth. He endowed them with a strength like his own, making them in his own image. He put the fear of men in all living things, thus they had mastery over the animals and birds. He endowed them with knowledge; he gave them tongue and eyes, ears and a mind to think with. He filled them wisdom and knowledge; he taught them good and evil. He put his own eye in their hearts so they would understand the greatness of his works. They will praise his holy Name and relate the magnificence of his creation. He gave them revealed knowledge as well and handed over to them the Law of life. He established an everlasting covenant with them and let them know his judgments. Human eyes saw the splendour of the Glory of God; their ears heard the grandeur of his voice. He said to them, "keep yourselves from all wrongdoing'..." So this is the main purpose on why God created man i.e. to rule over lower animal kingdom and to praise God forever and ever and keep from doing evil.

The days of man in this world is just fleeting. In Psalm 90:12, it says: "So make us know the shortness of our life, that we may gain wisdom of heart." In Job 14:1, it states: "Man born of woman has a short life full of sorrow." It is short that you cannot be sure when will you expire because death does not choose whether you are young or old. In Psalm 144:4, it says: "Man is a mere puff of breath, his days pass like a shadow on earth." You will die any time when God commands you, "Mortals return!" In Psalm 90:3, it says: "You turn humans back to dust, saying, 'Return, O mortals'. If you desire long life in this world, you have to be truthful always, do not practice deceit, reject evil, do good, and always seek peace." In Psalm 34:12-15, it says: "Come, listen to me, my sons; I will show you how to fear the Lord. If you desire long life, if you want to enjoy prosperity, keep your tongue from falsehood, keep your lips from deceit; turn away from evil and do good; seek peace and pursue it." Many people die at a very ripe age. These people had unconsciously followed the advice of Psalm 34:12-15, and lived a long life in prosperity and abundance. Adam lived 930 years; Seth lived 912 years; Enosh lived 905 years; Kenan lived 910 years; Mahalalel lived 895 years; Jared lived 962 years; Enoch lived 365 years and was taken by God to heaven; Methuselah lived 969 years, the longest to live on earth; Lamech lived 777 years; Noah lived 950 years on earth. After the flood, God reduced the span of life to 120 years. In Genesis 6:3, it states:

"Yahweh then said, 'My spirit will not remain in man forever, for he is flesh. His span of life will be one hundred and twenty years," After that the chosen servants of God lived not exceeding 120 years old except for Abraham who lived 175 years (Genesis 25:7); Isaac who lived 180 years (Genesis 35:28); Jacob who lived 147 years (Genesis 47:28); Job who lived 140 years (Job 42:16); Levi who lived 137 years (Exodus 6:16); Amram, the father of Moses and Aaron who lived 137 years (Exodus 6:20); Kohath, the grandfather of Moses and Aaron who lived 133 years (Exodus 6:18); Johoiada who lived 130 years (2nd Chronicles 24:15); Sarah who lived 127 years (Genesis 23:1); Tobias who lived 127 years (Tobit 14:14); Solomon who lived 125 years; Moses who lived 120 years (Deut. 34:7); Aaron who lived 123 years (Numbers 33:39); David who lived 115 years; Tobit who lived 112 years (Tobit 14:1); Joseph who lived 110 years (Genesis 50:26); Joshua who lived 110 years (Joshua 24:29) and (Judges 2:8) and Judith who lived 105 years (Judith 16:23). In Psalm 39:5, it says: "Lord let me know when my end will come, let me know the number of my days; show me how frail and fleeting is my life." If you want to prolong your stay in this world, the secret of which is to honour your parents. In Sirach 3:6, it states: "Whoever glorifies his father will have a long life…" Likewise in Sirach 3:8, it states: "Honour your father in word and deed so that his blessing may come on you…" Also in Sirach 3:3-5, it says: "Whoever honours his father atones for his sins; he who gives glory to his mother prepares a treasure for himself. Whoever honours his father will receive joy from his own children and will be heard when he prays." "Honour your parents to live long." (Deuteronomy 5:16). In Sirach 1:20, it states: "The fear of the Lord is the root of wisdom, its branches are long life." In John 11:26, it says:""Whoever is alive by believing in me will never die…"

Death where is your victory? Death, where is your sting? Our

Lord Jesus Christ indeed is the way, the truth and the life. Death cannot resist our Lord Jesus Christ. He has conquered death on the cross. Romans 6:5 says: "It was an image of his death when we were grafted in him, and so we will also share in his resurrection." We will live with our Lord Jesus Christ after we depart from this world when we have died with him. For, in 2nd Timothy 2:11-13 says: "If we have died with him, we shall also live with him; if we endure with him, we shall reign with him; If we deny him, he will also deny us; If we are unfaithful, he remains faithful for he cannot deny himself." He changed death into life and gives life freely as a gift to all people who believe in Him and the Father. In 2nd Corinthians 5:14-15, it says: "Indeed the love of Christ holds us and we realize that if he died for all, all have died. He died for all so that those who live may live no longer for themselves, but for Him who died and rose again for them." All we have to do is to abide by our Lord Jesus Christ in order to have eternal life. He is the vine and we are the branches; we abide in him to have life but if we detach from him we will die. That is simple logic and clear to be understood. Jesus himself has clearly shown us that he rose from the dead. In Romans 6:6-10, it says: "We know that our old self was crucified with Christ, so as to destroy what of us was sin, so that we may no longer serve sin-if we are dead, we no longer in debt to him. But if we have died with Christ, we believe we will also live with him. We know that Christ, once risen from the dead, will not die again and death has no more dominion over him. There has been death: a death to sin once for all; there is life: a life in God." He defeated death by dying and then rising on the third day. In Hebrews 2:14, it says: "This is why his death destroyed the one holding the power of death, that is the devil, and freed those who remained in bondage all their lifetime because of the fear of death." Why then shall you detach from him? We have to be attached to where there is life and be detached from where there is death. There is death in Satan because Satan himself is death. So we have to detach from Satan by despising his works and focus on virtues and wisdom of God through our Lord Jesus Christ. In John 5:24, it says: "Truly, I say to you, he who hears my word and believes him who sent me, has eternal life; and there is no judgment for him because he has passed from death to life." Have an unwavering faith in God through our Lord Jesus Christ and attain for yourself assured salvation and everlasting life. God did not create man to suffer and then die. The ultimate purpose of God in creating man is for him to have eternal life and happiness. Eternal life is intrinsically in God. Hence, to know God is to know eternal life. For, in John 17:3, it says: "For this is eternal life, to know you, the only true God, and the One you sent, Jesus Christ." It was only distracted by Satan who introduced sin in humanity. Do you think God created gay, lesbian, transgender, bisexual, lame, blind, dumb, deaf, and the people with any physical defect? No! God created us very perfectly but Satan mocks the creation by injecting different defects in man. Do you think God gives us ailments like tuberculosis, asthma, cancer, diabetes, meningitis, arthritis, hepatitis, and other terminal illnesses? No! Do you think God sends us viruses such as SARS (*Severe Acute Respiratory Syndrome), MERS (Middle East Respiratory Syndrome), Bubonic Plague or Black Death, Spanish Flu, H1N1 virus, HIV (Human Immunodeficiency virus), 2019 nCoV (2019 Novel Corona virus) or Covid 19? No! It is Satan that mocks God and humanity by introducing these illnesses. Satan gives ailments and defects on humanity but God cures them through our Lord Jesus Christ. In 1st John 3:9, it says: "…This is why the Son of God was shown to us, he was to undo the works of the devil." Remember when our Lord Jesus Christ came into the world. He healed the sick: lame, blind, lepers, diabetic people, cancer patients, and all other illnesses inflicted by Satan upon humanity and raised the dead because Christ wants to tell the world that He himself is life and that he had already conquered death. "God, who has known Christ before the world began, revealed him to you in the last days. Through him, you have faith in God who raised him from the dead and glorified him in order that you might put all your faith and hope in God." (1ˢᵗ Peter 1:20-21).

Even to this day, Satan pollutes the mind of God's people. He injects untruthful belief that human soul, after death, will transfer to other people or to lower animal kingdom or metempsychosis. Satan also teaches people to communicate with their dead relatives in séance as souls of their dead relatives are just around. This is Satan's deception and trick. Once a man dies he will no longer return to his household and never again be communicated. In Job 7:9-10, it says: "As a cloud dissolves and vanishes, so he who goes to the grave never returns. He will never come back to his house; or be seen by his household." So that if you see your dead relative anywhere that is already devil's work. That is the work of Satan. If you encounter this kind of experience you have to rebuke immediately the devil through our Lord Jesus Christ. You have to be brave. Do not be afraid for God is with you through our Lord Jesus Christ. God is with you, then who will be against you? No one.

Do not ever attempt to consult your dead relative by means of séance. The spirit that you may encounter can be possibly a spirit of fallen angels under Satan's rule. All you have to do is just to pray because the spirit of your dead relatives are already in deep sleep waiting for the day of resurrection. In Job 14:12, it states: "…but once man lies down he does not rise again, the heavens will vanish before he wakes, before he rises from his sleep."

People should never worry if they suffer infirmities like terminal cancer, diabetes, hypertension, tuberculosis, hepatitis, arthritis or any other incurable illnesses. When you suffer such illnesses, it means that you are fortunate enough because God constantly reminds you that your home is not in this world but in heaven. All you have to do is to entrust wholeheartedly to God your ailments and He will be the One to cure you if you pray fervently. God is the ultimate Doctor of all illnesses in universe. In Exodus 15:25-26, it says: "There Yahweh gave the people statutes and laws. There he tested them and said, 'If you listen carefully to the voice of Yahweh, your God, and if you do what is right in his eyes, if you obey his commands and statutes, I will not inflict on you any of the diseases I brought on the Egyptians, for I am Yahweh, the One who heals you." He knows very well when will a person departs from this world. Do not aspire too much for the recovery of your physical health and do not put complete trust and hope on medical interventions alone even if such interventions are scientifically advanced. The One who cures you is God not your doctor specialist or the advanced medical technology. Doctors, medicines, and advanced medical technology are only instruments for your recovery. But the One who cures you is God. What you should aspire to achieve is eternal life by strengthening your personal relationship with God through constant and fervent prayer in Christ Jesus. You should pray to God in truth and spirit as He is Spirit without aid of any printed or graven image and establish a strong foundation of faith with him through our Lord Jesus Christ to have an assurance of everlasting life.

If God wants you to stay longer after you have recovered from your ailments, the maximum length of years of your extended stay is fifteen years as what he had given to his servant Hezekiah. In 2ⁿᵈ Corinthians 7:10, it says: "Sadness from God brings firm repentance that leads to salvation and brings no regret, but worldly grief produces death." In 2ⁿᵈ Kings 20:1-7, it says: "In those days Hezekiah fell mortally ill and the prophet Isaiah, son of Amoz, went to him with a message from Yahweh, 'Put your house in order for you shall die; you shall not live.' Hezekiah turned his face to the wall and prayed to Yahweh, 'Ah Yahweh! Remember how I have walked before you in truth and wholeheartedly, and have done what is good in your sight'. And Hezekiah wept bitterly."

"Isaiah had still not reached the central courtyard when the word of Yahweh came to him, 'Go back and tell Hezekiah the ruler of my people, what Yahweh, the God of his father David, says: 'I have heard your prayer and I have seen your tears. And now I will cure you. On the third day you will go up to the house of Yahweh. See! I am adding fifteen years to your life and will save you and this city from the power of the King of Assyria. I will defend it for my sake and for the sake of David my servant." For those who are mortally sick, try this formula if you wish to live longer. Earnestly and fervently pray to God with all sincerity and ask for another fifteen years extension of your life. If your prayer is sincere as it will be accompanied by tears of faith you will be heard by God and he will truly extend your stay in this world for another fifteen years. Anyway, there is nothing wrong in trying. Do not boast of your money that you can afford to buy medicines and hire best medical specialist. The One who heals the sick is God. You should boast of his power and glory. Amen. In 1ˢᵗ Corinthians 1:31, it says: "Scripture says: Let the one who boasts boast of the Lord."

So do not worry. Stay cheerful with God all your life as death in this world is not permanent, says the Lord. Whenever you can recover from your ailments, you have to give thanks to Him through our Lord Jesus Christ. Angel Raphael in Tobit 12:6-8, says: "Bless God, return thanks to him, proclaim his glory and render him thanks before all the living for all he has done for you. It is good to praise God and to exalt his Name, by making known in a worthy manner the story of God's deeds. Do not be slow in giving him thanks. It is good to hide the secrets of kings but to make known publicly the works of God. Do the works of God. Do good, and evil will not harm you. It is good to accompany prayer with fasting, almsgiving and justice. It is better to do a little with honour than much with injustice. It is better to give alms than to treasure gold."

God will surely cure you. In Psalm 13:4-5, it says: "Look upon me and answer, O Lord my God! Give light to my eyes, lest I sleep the sleep of death; lest my enemy say, 'I have routed him' lest my foes rejoice in seeing me brought to naught." For this, you have to ask Him in fervent prayer for your recovery. This is the prayer. Remember this by heart that you can be healthy again:

"**Yahweh my God, the One who heals, in your loving kindness and mercy uproot this** (Mention here mentally your ailments that you want God to cure you) **from my body and make me well through our Lord Ieshua Mosha, my personal Saviour. Amen, Amen, Amen Rak to the Rabbah to the Abba. (Ieshua Mosha** is the Hebrew Name of our Lord Jesus Christ.) Mentally say this prayer for seven times while gently touching and massaging the affected area with your bare hand. After saying it for seven times mentally, give immediately thanks to God, saying this prayer for three times: "**I love you Almighty Father and I thank you for healing me in your loving kindness and mercy through Ieshua Mosha,** my personal Saviour. **Amen Amen Amen Rak to the Rabbah to the Abba.**" Do this secretly at night time. You have to close your eyes and feel that your hand is guided by God. Do this for six days starting Sunday and ending on Friday. By the seventh day, a Saturday, take a rest. Repeat session for seven weeks and see for yourself the result. You may or may not continue taking your medicines depending on your doctor's advice. Your cancer, diabetes or other terminal ailments will just fade away like wind. God will extend your stay in this world. Psalm 21:5 says: "When he asked, you gave him life-length of days forever and ever." If your ailment is so severe that you wish to have an immediate restoration of your health, you may say this prayer three times a day, one in the morning after waking up, one in the afternoon at around 3:00 O'clock and one in the evening for your speedy recovery. In Psalm 6:5-6, it says: "Come back to me, O Lord, save my life; rescue me for the sake of your love. For no one remembers you in the grave, no one can give you praise in the world of the dead.

Those who wish to stay long in this world for another fifteen years despite mortally ill due to terminal ailment, you may ask God for His mercy by fervently saying this prayer, as follows: "**Heavenly Father, in your loving kindness and mercy, I fervently and humbly ask for your forgiveness of the sins I have committed against you. Endow me an extended stay in this world for another fifteen years as what you have done to your servant Hezekiah that I can continue serving you and loving you with all my heart, with all my mind, with all my soul, with all my spirit, and with all my strength. With my contrite heart and meekness of my being and my unwavering faith in you, I ardently beg for your benevolence through our Lord Jesus Christ, my personal Saviour. Amen.**" (Repeat this prayer for three times.)

This is a strict rule: Only those people who are upright, righteous, and with pure and contrite heart may say this prayer. Wicked people may not say this prayer as they will not be heard by God. Those rebellious people who do not obey God's will and do things by their own desire without consulting God, are considered wicked people. These wicked people can say this prayer only if they honestly and truthfully return to God by having a contrite heart and obey His will.

D) Resurrection

Resurrection time is at hand. In Acts of the Apostles 24:15, it says: "I have the same hope in God that they have, that there will be a resurrection of the dead, both the good and the sinners." We will be raised to life on the day of Resurrection. In 2nd Corinthians 4:14, it says: "We know that He who raised the Lord Jesus will also raise us with Jesus and bring us with you, into his presence." The fall of first man on earth causes our downfall but because of our Lord Jesus Christ, we are reconciled with God, hence we are saved and have everlasting life. In Romans 5:10-11, it says: "Once enemies, we have been reconciled with God through the death of his Son; with much more reason now we may be saved through his life. Not only that, we feel secure in God because of Christ Jesus, our Lord, through whom we have been reconciled." While the sanctuary of heaven has just been restored for 2300 years starting from year 457 BC and closed in year 1847, judgment has already began where the book of life is being prepared and finalized. Those whose names are written in it will be redeemed. In Ezekiel 37:12-14, it says: "So prophesy! Say to them: this is what Yahweh says: I am going to open your tombs, my people, and lead you back to the land of Israel. You will know that I am Yahweh, O my people! When I open your graves, when I put my spirit in you and you live. I shall settle you in your land and you will know that I Yahweh have done what I said I would do." When our Lord Jesus Christ returns to this world, He and His angels will take with Him the redeemed to heaven and that will be the First Resurrection. Those who are risen in the first resurrection will have no more fear of death in the second resurrection. Eternal life is assured them. In Revelation 20:4-6, it says: "There were thrones and seated on them were those with the power to judge. I then saw the spirits of those who have been beheaded for having held the teachings of Jesus and on account of the word of God. I saw all those who had refused to worship the beast or its image, or receive its mark on the forehead or on the hand. They returned to life and reigned with the Messiah for a thousand years. This is the first resurrection. The rest of the dead will not return to life before the end of the thousand years. Happy and holy is the one who shares in the first resurrection, for the second death has no power over them; they will be priests of God and of his Messiah and reign with him a thousand years." Who is the resurrection? Our Lord Jesus is the guaranteed resurrection. If we believe and have faith in Him and to God we will have resurrection and have everlasting life. In John 11:24-27, it says: "Martha replied, 'I know that he will rise in the resurrection, at the last day. But Jesus said to her, 'I am the resurrection; whoever believes in me, though he die, shall live. Whoever is alive by believing in me will never die. Do you believe this? Martha then answered, 'Yes, Lord, I have come to believe that you are Christ, the Son of God, he who is coming into the world." On the appointed time of resurrection, the dead will live, corpses will rise. In Ephesians 5:14. It says: "And what has become clear becomes light. Therefore it is said: 'Awake, you who sleep, arise from the dead that the light of Christ may shine on you." Those who lie in the dust will wake up and rejoice. The earth will throw out the dead even covered by cement or soil. In Isaiah 26:19, it says: "Your dead will live! Their corpses will rise! Awake and sing, you who lie in the dust! Let your dew fall, O Lord, like a dew of light, and the earth will throw out her dead." The sequence of resurrection is that those who are still alive will not be the first ones to go. When the divine trumpet will sound all those who died in the Lord will rise first. Then for us who are still alive we will be carried by holy angels along with the risen dead in the clouds to meet with the Lord. As that is the first resurrection, those carried by angels to heaven will have everlasting life. Death in second resurrection has no more power on those raised in first resurrection. . In 1st Thessalonians 4:13-17, it says: "Brothers, we want you not to be mistaken about those who are already asleep, lest you grieve as do those who have no hope. We believe that Jesus died and rose; it will be the same for those who have died in Jesus. God will bring them together with Jesus and for his sake. By the same word of the Lord we assert this: those of us who are to be alive at the Lord's coming will not go ahead of those who are already asleep. When the command by the archangel's voice is given, the Lord himself will come down from Heaven, while the divine trumpet call is sounding. Then those who have died in the Lord will rise first: as for us who are still alive, we will be brought along with them in the clouds to meet the Lord in the celestial world. And we will be with the Lord forever." In resurrection the human body is transformed from earthly body to spiritual body which cannot decompose anymore. It will live for all eternity. In 1st Corinthians 15:42-44, it says: "It is the same with the resurrection of the dead. The body is sown in decomposition; it will be raised never more to die. It is sown in humiliation, and it will be raised for Glory. It is buried in weakness, but the resurrection shall be with power. When buried it is a natural body, but it will be raised as a spiritual body. For there shall be a spiritual body as there is at present a living body." Those alive and risen in the Lord Jesus Christ will be gathered by our Lord himself with the aid of angels. In Mark 13:24-27, it says: "Later on, in those days after the disastrous time, the sun will grow dark, the moon will not give its light, the stars will fall out of the sky and the whole universe will be shaken. Then people will see the Son of Man coming in the clouds with great power and glory. And he will send the angels to gather his chosen people from the four winds, from the ends of the earth to the ends of the sky." In the coming of the Son of Man, all people will hear and witness this even the dead will hear the voice of the Son of Man and upon hearing His voice they will live. In John 5:25, it says: "Truly, the hour is coming and has indeed come, when the dead will hear the voice of the Son of Man and, on hearing it, will live. After this there will be no more death; no more sadness and God's people will have eternal happiness. In Revelation 21:3-4, it says: "A loud voice came from the throne, 'Here is the dwelling of God among men. He will pitch his tent among them and they will be his people. God will be with them and wipe every tear from their eyes. There shall be no more death or mourning, crying out or pain, for the world that was has passed away."

Even the scattered bones of the dead or their cremated dust wherever they are, upon hearing the voice of our Lord Jesus Christ, will be transformed into eternal being and live forever. In Ezekiel 37:4-10, it says "....Dry bones, hear the word of Yahweh! Yahweh says: I am going to put spirit in you and make you live. I shall put sinews on you and make flesh grow on you; I shall cover you with skin and give you my spirit that you may live. And you will know that I am Yahweh. I prophesied as I had been commanded and then there was a noise and commotion; the bones joined together. I looked and saw that they had sinews, that flesh was growing on them and that he was covering them with skin. But there was no spirit in them.

So Yahweh said to me, 'Speak on my behalf and call the Spirit, son of man! Say to the Spirit: This is the word of Yahweh: Spirit, come from the four winds. Breathe into these dead bones and let them live! I prophesied as he had commanded me and breath entered them; they came alive, standing on their feet..."

In Colossians 1: 13-14, it says: "He rescued us from the power of darkness and transferred us to the kingdom of his beloved son. In him we are redeemed and forgiven." How do you know that you are saved, redeemed and qualified to be raised to life everlasting? In Romans 10: 9-10, it says: "You are saved if you confess with lips that Jesus is Lord and in your heart you believe that God raised him from the dead. By believing from the heart, you obtain true righteousness; by confessing the faith with your lips you are saved." In John 3:18, it says: "Whoever believes in him will not be condemned. He who does not believe is already condemned, because he has not believed in the Name of the only Son of God." Here are the indicators of being saved and redeemed:

If you have Faith in God Almighty through our Lord Jesus Christ, then you are saved and redeemed. In Galatians 3:8-9, it says: "The Scriptures foresaw that by the way of faith, God would give true righteousness to the non-Jewish nations. For God's promise to Abraham was this: "In you shall all the nations be blessed. So now those who take the way of faith receive the same blessing as Abraham who believed..." Compliance of commandments, precepts and commands of Almighty God is inadequate and incomplete without Faith. For, faith is the basic requirement of salvation and eternal life. In Hebrews 11:1-3 Faith is defined: "Faith is the way of holding onto what we hope for, being certain of what we cannot see. Because of their faith our ancestors were approved. By faith we understand that the stages of creation were disposed by God's word, and what is visible came from what cannot be seen." It is through the unwavering faith of Noah that he built the ark 100 years before the coming of great flood that saved him and his family and preserved humanity on earth. "By faith Noah was instructed of events which could not yet be seen and, heeding what he heard, he built boat in which to save his family. The faith of Noah condemned the world and he reached holiness born of faith." (Hebrews 11:7). It is through faith that Abraham had a son despite the advanced age of his wife, Sarah. "By faith Sarah herself received power to become a mother, in spite of her advanced age; since she believed that he who had made the promise would be faithful. Therefore, from an almost impotent man were born descendants as numerous as the stars of heavens, as many as the grains of sand on the seashore." (Hebrews 11:11-12). It is through faith that Moses was able to accomplish successfully the task given him by God in delivering the Israelites from the bondage in Egypt. In Hebrews 11: 26-27, it says:"Moses considered humiliation for the sake of Christ greater riches than the wealth of Egypt, and he looked ahead to his reward. By faith he left Egypt without fearing the king's anger, and he persevered as if he could see another invisible wrath." It is through faith that Joshua was able to conquer the enemies of Israelites who were mightier than they. In Hebrews 11:30, it says: "By faith the walls of Jericho crumbled and fell, after Israel had marched round them for seven days." It is through faith that King David was able to defeat the strong enemies of Israelites. In Colossians 1:23, it says: "Only stand firm, upon the foundation of your faith, and be steadfast in hope. Keep in mind the Gospel you have heard, which has been preached to every creature under heaven..." But faith alone without good works is useless. Do you profess to have faith in God if you deny food to the hungry; if you deny water to the thirsty; if you deny clothes to the naked of which you are capable of giving? Faith without good works is dead. In James 2:14-17, it says: "Brothers, what good is it to profess faith without showing works? Such faith has no power to save you. If a brother or sister is in need of clothes or food and one of you says, 'May things go well for you; be warm and satisfied; without attending to their material needs, what good is that? So it is for faith without deeds: it is totally dead." Also in James 1:22-25, it says: "Be doers of the Word and not just hearers, lest you deceive yourselves. The hearer who does not become a doer is like a man who looks at himself in the mirror. He looks and then promptly forgets what he looks like. But he who fixes his gaze on the perfect law of freedom and hold onto it, not listening and then forgetting, but acting on it, will find blessing on his deeds." Proverbs 3:27-28 says: "Do not hold back from those who ask your help, when it is in your power to do it. Do not say to your neighbour, 'Go away! Come another time; tomorrow I will give it to you!' when you can help him now." Also in Proverbs 21:13, it says: "He who is deaf to the poor man's cry will not be heard when he himself calls out." In Isaiah 58:10, it says: "...if you share your food with the hungry and give relief to the oppressed, then your light will rise in the dark, your night will be like noon."

You are saved and redeemed if you detach yourself from Roman Catholic Church, which is the great harlot described in Book of Revelation 9:1-2 and free yourself from its idolatry and false teachings. Roman Catholicism has been pushing billions of people in the world to the ultimate destiny of eternal condemnation by requiring them to worship graven and printed images. As a cohort of Satan, Roman Catholicism knows very well that God Almighty is fiercely angry on idol worship and there is no pardon to it. Their popes, cardinals, bishops and priests openly tolerate people to worship graven images in compliance with Satan's will to usher them into eternal destruction. What Catholicism gives to the people is not salvation but only eternal death in hell. So, people of God, if you are truly part and parcel of people of God detach yourself from Roman Catholic Church. It will only usher you toward eternal spiritual suicide. The best thing for you to do is to worship the Almighty Father in spirit and truth through our Lord Jesus Christ for your assured salvation and everlasting life. God commands you to do it now. In John 6:40, it says: "This is the will of the Father, that whoever sees the Son and believes in him shall live with eternal life, and I will raise him up on the last day."

You are saved and redeemed if you stop worshipping Satan by despising all his works. Satan entices people to love the world by letting them become materialistic; acquiring worldly things and wealth by whatever means. Inspired by Satan, people employ deceit, trick, dishonesty and all forms of crime to acquire material gains. That is the reason that most people in today's world love money more than anything else. This is Satan's design to drive away people from worshipping the God of Truth as most people devote most of their time looking for material wealth without any more time to serve God. This is one of Satan's strategy to let people divert their attention away from God Almighty. God's people who truly worship the Lord God Almighty do not look for too much money or aspire to become extremely wealthy. God's people normally and modestly work for their basic needs. They do not overwork their body trying to be rich but devote some of their time to God's service. They seek first the kingdom of God and the rest are added unto them. They take the advice in Psalm 62:11, which states: "...Even if wealth accumulates, keep your heart detached." It would be known in the last days that those who love money have no money to satisfy their needs but those who do not love money are abundantly blessed with plenty of money more than what they need. In Psalm 127:2, it says: "It is in vain that you rise early and stay up late, putting off your rest, toiling for your hard-earned bread; for he provides for his loved ones even when they are asleep."

The Principle of Salvation

Man has sinned against God. It is by the sin of one man that the whole humanity suffers and become sinful. In Romans 5:12, it says: "Now, sin entered the world through one man and through sin, death, and later on death spread to all humankind, because all sinned." And because of this sin, man cannot attain eternal life without a redemption. From the fall of humanity, men in history have been making animal offerings to God in hope of being forgiven to qualify for eternal life. But such offering has been proven to be inadequate for man's total redemption. The ultimate solution for this inadequacy is the offering of precious blood of our Lord Jesus Christ on the cross. Only the Lamb of God can take away the sin of the world and redeem humanity. In Ephesians 2:4-6, it says: "But God, who is rich in mercy, revealed his immense love and gave us life with Christ after being dead through sins. By grace you have been saved! And he raised us to life with Christ, giving us a place with him in heaven." Hence, the basic principle of salvation states: That the fall of humanity was caused by one man, Adam that made all people sinners, and the redemption of the whole humanity is made by one man also in Jesus Christ, the Son of God, our Lord and Saviour.

In Acts of the Apostles 15:11, it says: "We believe, indeed, that we are saved through the grace of the Lord Jesus, just as they are." In Romans 5:18-19, it states: "Just as one transgression brought sentence of death to all, so, too, one rehabilitation brought pardon and life to all; and as the disobedience of only one made many sinners, so the obedience of one person allowed a multitude to be made just and holy." Our Lord Jesus Christ has changed death to life in the same way that He raised the dead to life when He was here in this world. Only those who believe and have faith in God through our Lord Jesus Christ will have life. Those who will not recognize our Lord Jesus Christ as their personal saviour will not find life after their earthly death. Those who believe in our Lord Jesus Christ will find life to the fullest even if they are already dead. Those who believe in our Lord Jesus Christ will avoid sin as the consequence of sin is death. But if they commit sin, our Lord Jesus Christ will intercede for their forgiveness. In 1st John 2:1-2, it states: "...But if anyone sins, we have an intercessor with the Father, Jesus Christ, the Just One. He is the sacrificial victim for our sins and the sins of the whole world." If we remain with our Lord Jesus Christ we will not sin. Only those who have not known our Lord Jesus Christ remain in sin. In 1st John 3:5-6, it states: "You know that he came to take away our sins, and that there is no sin in him." Whoever remains in him has no sin, whoever sins has not seen or known him." What should be done in order not to sin and be acceptable to God? You should not love the world. Even if your riches increase, do not be attached to it. (Psalm 62:11). In 1st John 2:15-17, it states: "Do not love the world or what is in it. If anyone loves the world, the love of the Father is not in him. For everything in the world-the craving of the flesh, the greed of eyes and people boasting of their superiority- all this belongs to the world, not to the Father. The world passes away with all its craving but those who do the will of God remain forever." In Psalm 119:166, it says: "O Lord, I wait for your salvation and I keep your commands in faith.

Judgement

The judgment of universe and of mankind began after the restoration of the temple which took place for 2,300 years starting when King Artaxerxes of Persia gave permission for Nehemiah to rebuild the walls of Jerusalem. When did it happen? King Artaxerxes ruled Persia from 464-424 B.C. In his seventh year of his rule in year 457 B.C., he gave permission to Nehemiah to restore the Temple. In Daniel 8:14, it says: "...Until two thousand three hundred evenings and mornings have gone by, then the Temple shall be restored." One day for a prophecy is equivalent to one year while one day for God is equivalent to 1000 years. The 2,300 years which started in year 457 B.C has ended in year 1847. Other Bible scholars wrongfully interpreted this ending as in year 1844. They failed to realize that there is no such thing as 3 B.C.' 2B.C.and 1 B.C. as the reckoning of ancient history ended in the middle of 4B.C. This divine knowledge is hard to be understood by mere human understanding alone without being enlightened by Holy Spirit. For, even the Prophet Daniel himself found difficulty in understanding it. In Daniel 8:27, he confessed this: "I, Daniel, fainted and was sick for several days." But he was helped by Michael, the Archangel to understand this heavenly knowledge. After the restoration of the Temple in 1847, Judgment of mankind had started already. In John 3:19-21, it says: "This is how Judgment is made: Light has come into the world and people loved darkness rather than light because their deeds were evil. For whoever does wrong hates the light and doesn't come to the light for fear that his deeds will be shown as evil. But whoever lives according to the truth comes into the light so that it can be clearly seen that his works have been done in God." Starting from that year onwards, Satan has been in a hurry to deceive mankind by all means. Satan knows that his time is short. In Revelation 12:12, it says:

"Rejoice, therefore, O you heavens and you who dwell in them; but woe to you, earth and sea, for the devil has come to you in anger knowing that he has but a little time." The devil knows that he has just a little time. So, he caused his evil disciples to establish false religions so that people of God would be led astray and will not be redeemed. He caused the inventions of many modern gadgets and appliances, digital instruments to divert the attention of God's people that they will not worship the God of Truth and Spirit. In 2nd Timothy 4:3, it says: "For the time is coming when people will no longer endure sound doctrine but will be so eager to hear what is new, that they will never have enough teachers after their own liking."

Satan distorted God's creation by introducing lesbian, gay, bisexual, transgender and many more so that they will not be saved because he knows that God has created only man and woman. In Psalm 1:5, it says: "The wicked will not stand when judgment comes, nor the sinners when the righteous assemble." But those gays, lesbians, bisexual and transgender people will be saved when they fervently ask God's help and mercy. They have to detest Satan's work and return to God for salvation. Now is the time for them to do this. They should not wait for the Second Coming of our Lord Jesus Christ because when that time comes, judgment is already through. In order to be saved, they should have unwavering faith in God through our Lord Jesus Christ. In John 3:35, it says: "The Father loves the Son and has entrusted everything into his hands. Whoever believes in the Son lives with eternal life, but he who will not believe in the Son will never know life and always faces the justice of God." They have to act swiftly because when the Lord Jesus comes He will only bring with Him the redeemed and that would constitute as part of First Resurrection described in the book of Revelation. In John 12:46, it says: "I have come into the world as light, so that whoever believes in me may not remain in darkness." Only God's people will be brought by our Lord Jesus Christ to heaven in First Resurrection and will enjoy life in Heaven for 1,000 years. Those who will be raised in First Resurrection will have no more fear of death in Second Resurrection. The death in Second Resurrection is already final where their souls will be cast into the lake of fire together with Satan for all eternity. In Revelation 20:11-15, the Apostle John described the last judgment in his vision as this: "After that I saw a great and splendid throne and the one seated upon it. At once heaven and earth disappeared, leaving no trace. I saw the dead, both great and small standing before the throne while books were opened. Another book, the Book of Life, was also opened. Then the dead were judged according to the records of these books, that is, each one according to his works. The sea gave up the dead it had kept, as did death and the netherworld so that everyone might be judged according to his works. Then death and the netherworld were thrown into the lake of fire. This lake of fire is the second death. All who were not recorded in the Book of Life were thrown into the lake of fire." In Tobit 13:1-2, it says: "Blessed be God, living and reigning for all ages. It is he who punishes and he who has mercy; who makes people go down to hell and rise up again..."

After final judgment, God's people will be with Him in heaven enjoying happiness forever. In Isaiah 35:8-10, it says: "There will be a highway which will be called The Way of Holiness; no one unclean will pass over it nor any wicked fool stray there. No lion will be found there nor any beast of prey. Only the redeemed will walk there. For the ransomed of Yahweh will return: with everlasting joy upon their heads, they will come to Zion singing, gladness and joy marching with them, while sorrow and sighing flee away." In Revelation 21:1-8, Apostle John described what will happen after the final judgment in this: "Then I saw a new heaven and a new earth. The first heaven and the first earth had passed away and no longer was there any sea. I saw the New Jerusalem, the holy city coming down from God, out of heaven, adorned as a bride prepared for her husband. A loud voice came from the throne, "Here is the dwelling of God among men: He will pitch his tent among them and wipe every tear from their eyes. There shall be no more death or mourning, crying out or pain, for the world that was has passed away."

"The One seated on the throne said, "See, I make all things new." And then he said to me. "Write these words because they are sure and true. It is already done! I am the Alpha and the Omega, the Beginning and the End. I myself will give the thirsty to drink without cost from the fountain of living water. Thus the winner will be rewarded: For him I shall be God and he will be my son. As for cowards, traitors, depraved, murderers, adulterers and sorcerers, idolaters and liars, their place is the lake of burning sulphur. This is the second death." The judgment of the Lord are true, just and right. For, in Psalm 19:8-10, it says:

"The law of the Lord is perfect:
it gives life to the soul.
The word of the Lord is trustworthy:
it gives wisdom to the simple.
The precepts of the Lord are right:
they give joy to the heart.
The commandments of the Lord are clear:
they enlighten the eyes.
The fear of the Lord is pure,
it endures forever;
the judgments of the Lord are true,
all of them just and right."

People may say that I am the reincarnation of Nostradamus or Michel de Notredame, a French astrologer and physician who lived from 1503-1566. His two books entitled *Centuries* consists of cryptic prophecies .which are very hard to be interpreted. That is the reason why it took another six years before his books were published after his death. Basically, the prophecies of Nostradamus were patterned on astrology which cannot be true most of the time. God does not want astrology and He condemns it (Leviticus 19:26). While my prophecies are directly given by God to me with the instruction to clearly write them for people to know directly. In Isaiah 49:1, it says: "Yahweh called me from my mother's womb; he pronounced my name before I was born." These prophecies are not written in cryptic signs nor in parables as what our Lord Jesus had done while here on earth. In Psalm 78:2-3, it says: "I will speak in parables, I will talk of old mysteries which we have heard and known, which our fathers have told us." Matthew 13:34-35 also affirms this. But in the last days, Jesus said that everything, every prophecy will be said clearly not in parables nor in signs. In John 16:25, it says: "I taught you all this in veiled language, but the time is coming when I shall no longer speak in veiled language, but will tell you plainly of the Father."

What makes me different from Nostradamus? First, the prophecies of Nostradamus were based on human understanding and knowledge which is Astrology, the study of planetary arrangements and movements that may influence human affairs as in horoscope; while my prophecies come from the infinite Wisdom of God through our Lord Jesus Christ. Second, Nostradamus was an astrologer and physician while I am a Religious Philosopher inspired by God of Truth and Spirit to write events in the last days. Third, Nostradamus was a physician by profession but cannot heal terminal illnesses while I, ordained and blessed in truth and spirit by God Almighty through our Lord Jesus Christ, can heal ailments upon laying hands (Mark 16:18). Fourth, Nostradamus was a Frenchman while I am a true-bloodied Filipino from Philippines. Fifth, Nostradamus as a prophet having prophesied so many things but had not prophesied the date when he will die while I, a prophet of God through our Lord Jesus Christ in the last days, know when will I leave earth as I am being told in advance by God about the date and time of my departure from this world. In Isaiah 65:20, it says: "...He who reaches a hundred years will have died a mere youth, but he who fails to reach a hundred will be considered accursed." In Daniel 3:40, it says: "...for I know that those who trust in you shall never be disappointed." In Psalm 16:11, it says: "You will show me the path of life, in your presence the fullness of joy at your right hand happiness forever." Sixth, Nostradamus prophesied for the individual persons only as his prophecy is like a horoscope; while I prophesy through the infinite Wisdom of God of Truth and Spirit about the end of time not of individual person but about the destruction of nations and big cities of the world. Seventh, Nostradamus was not a man of God while I am a man of God, an adopted son of God Almighty who talks to God intimately, as a friend talks to a friend.

I am not an instrument of God, I am a man of God. By the grace of God, I am an adopted son of God. I am the son of God. In Romans 9:24-25, it says: "And he called us, not only from among the Jews, but from among the pagans, too, as he said through the prophet Hosea: *I will call 'my people' those that were not my people and 'my beloved' the one who was not beloved. And in the same place where they were told: 'You are not my people', they will be called children of the living God.*" While I am still in this world, I am not for this world as I detach myself from material things that the world has. "I do not seek my own interest, but that of many, for I want them to be saved" (1st Corinthians 10:33). In John 15:18-19, it says: "If the world hates you, remember that the world hated me before you. But you are not of the world since I have chosen you from the world; because of this the world hates you." Before I was born I was already appointed by God as His prophet as what He revealed to me. In Jeremiah 1:5, the Lord God Almighty has said to me: Before you were born, I appointed you a prophet. "Before I formed you in the womb I knew you; before you were born I set you apart, and appointed you a prophet to the nations!" Stricken by a great lightning when I was seven years old, I saw a very big bright light that engulfed me. That happened in 1962. But I was not hurt, not even a scratch in my body. Only the seven big coconut trees fell around me. I had no idea of such event's message. I only realized the message when Almighty God called me to write the events in the last days in 2019. The message of such lightning event came clear to me after 57 years only. The Almighty Father showed me His immense love and care that I was not hurt even a bit. He really preserved me as prophet in the last days. The Almighty Father has appointed many prophets in Israel of exceptional quality like Elijah, Isaiah, Hosea, Jeremiah and many more to tell people of Israel in advance of his plan. In the last days, He appointed me who is not from the country of Israel as the message to be delivered is not for Israel alone but to all cities and nations of the world. He chooses me as a prophet from the Philippines since my country is a younger sister to Israel. When Israel was persecuted by Nazi Germany during Second World War, it was her younger sister Philippines that helped her by allowing her to sojourn in the Philippines to escape Adolf Schicklegrubber's extermination machine /gas chambers. Out of more than eight billion people in the world today, He appointed me to tell the whole world on impending destruction of places before the Second Coming. He has chosen me although I am a scum of the world. I am just nothing—a worthless person. In Corinthian 1:27-29, it says: "Yet God has chosen what the world considers foolish, to shame the wise; he has chosen what the world considers weak to shame the strong. God has chosen common and unimportant people, making use of what is nothing to nullify the things that are, so that no mortal may boast before God."

Why did God not choose any person from Israel to relay the message in the end of time? We have to remember that when our Lord Jesus Christ came into the world, he was not accepted by the people in Israel. Because they had not accepted our Lord Jesus Christ, it means that they had not accepted God Almighty although they remain the descendants of Abraham, Isaac and Jacob. In John 1:10-13, it says: "He was already in the world and through him the world was made, the very world that did not know him. He came to his own, yet his own people did not receive him; but all who have received him he empowers to become children of God for they believe in His name. These are born, but without seed or carnal desire or will of man; they are born of God.

The Second Coming

God's people have been eagerly expecting the Second Coming of our Lord Jesus Christ since his ascension to heaven. He will return in the same way when he departs the world. In Acts of the Apostles 1:18, it says: "While they were still looking up to heaven where he went, suddenly, two men dressed in white stood beside them and said, 'Men of Galilee, why do you stand here looking up at the sky? This Jesus who has been taken from you into heaven, will return in the same way as you have seen him go there." As there is no definite day of the second coming, the Holy Bible tells us of the signs that will take place before this event comes. In Matthew 24: 29-31, it says: "For later, after that distress, the sun will grow dark, the moon will not give its light, the stars will fall from the skies, and the whole universe will be shaken. Then the Son of Man will appear in the heaven: as all the nations of the earth beat their breasts, they will see the Son of Man coming in the clouds of heaven with divine power and the fullness of Glory. He will send his angels to sound the trumpet and gather the chosen ones from the four winds, from one end of the earth to the other." Also in Matthew 24:7-8, it says: "Nations will fight one another, and kingdom oppose kingdom. There will be famines and earthquakes in several places, but all these are only the beginning; the pains of childbirth." This prophecy is also echoed by Prophet Joel which can be read in Acts of the Apostles 2:20 which states: "The sun will be darkened and the moon will turn red as blood, before the great and glorious Day of the Lord comes.

All these Second Coming signs had already occurred and experienced by man. But the Second Coming has not yet happened. The reason why our Lord Jesus Christ has not yet returned to the world is because the universal restoration, spoken by prophets of long ago, is not yet through and that God's people are still given ample time to repent and be saved. In Acts of the Apostles 3:21, it says: "For he must remain in heaven until the time of the universal restoration which God spoke of long ago through his holy prophets." In 1st Thessalonians 5: 1-3, it says: "You do not need anyone to write to you about the delay and the appointed time for these events. You know that the Day of the Lord will come like a thief in the night. When people feel secure and at peace, the disaster will suddenly come upon them as the birth pangs of a woman in labour, and they will not escape." In 2nd Peter 3:9, it says: "The Lord does not delay in fulfilling his promise, though some speak of delay; rather he gives you time because he does not want anyone to perish, but that all may come to conversion."

The physical signs that will precede the second coming of our Lord Jesus Christ are: a great earthquake, the sun darkens, the moon turns to red as in blood, and the stars fall. All these signs have already occurred and experienced by man.

The strongest earthquake ever experienced by man on earth was the one that occurred in Lisbon, Portugal on November 1, 1755. The other strong earthquakes that the world had experienced were the Alaska Earthquake in 1964 with 8.4 strength on Richter scale, the San Francisco Earthquake in 1906 with 7.8 strength on Richter scale and the Luzon Earthquake in 1990 with 8.2 on Richter scale. But the forthcoming earthquake that will strike the forty primary cities in the world will be far stronger than these earthquakes. That Lisbon earthquake had greatly influenced the thinking of philosophers in Europe which reflected in their philosophical treatises. Immanuel Kant who lived between 1724 and 1804, a German philosopher, published his work in 1781 entitled: "The Critique of Pure Reason" was greatly influenced by Lisbon Earthquake. Jean Jacques Rousseau who lived between 1712 and 1778, a Swiss- born French philosopher had written 12 volumes of his autobiography entitled "Confessions" was also influenced by Lisbon Earthquake. Voltaire whose real name was Francois Marie Arouet who lived between 1694 and 1778 was also influenced by Lisbon Earthquake. Relative to this earthquake, these three philosophers philosophized that we should merely be concerned with our own welfare if God is not interested in us. This kind of reasoning indicates that these three philosophers have no faith in God. They are self-conceited. They think that their minds are greater than God's wisdom. Very wrong. They are fools. In Psalm 14:1, it says: "The fool says in his heart, 'God does not exist." All have strayed, all are perverted, there is no one who does good."

The sun darkened in the morning of May 19, 1780 in the North Eastern part of the United States of America followed by the appearance of the moon as red as blood on the same day. Thousands of meteorites fell in the East Coast of the United States of America on November 13, 1833. All of these are recorded documentaries of the world.

No one knows when will be the second coming of our Lord Jesus Christ. The only One who knows this is the Almighty Father. In Mark 13:32, it says: "But regarding that Day and that Hour, no one knows when it will come, not even the angels or the Son, but only the Father." But before any event happens in universe that affect humankind, God always informs people in advance through his messenger or prophet. In Amos 3:7, it says: "Yet Yahweh does nothing without revealing his plan to his servants, the prophets." For this, God reveals to me this: **IN A CLEAR BLUE SKY OF MAY 15, 2123 A SATURDAY, THE LORD'S DAY THE MOUTH OF HEAVEN WILL OPEN AND PEOPLE WILL WITNESS A SPECTACULAR EVENT, SAYS THE ALMIGHTY FATHER. MILLIONS AND MILLIONS OF ANGELS WILL VISIT THE EARTH, ADDED THE LORD. THEY WILL BE HERE FOR THE HARVEST.** In Revelation 14:15-20, it says: "An angel came out of the sanctuary, calling loudly to the one sitting on the cloud, 'Put in your sickle and reap, for the harvest time has come and the harvest of the earth is ripe. He who was sitting on the cloud swung his sickle at the earth and reaped the harvest. Then another angel, who also had a sharp sickle, came out of the heavenly sanctuary. Still another angel, the one who has charge of the altar fire, emerged and shouted to the first who held the sharp sickle, 'Swing your sharp sickle and reap the bunches of the vine of the earth for they are fully ripe.' So the angel swung his sickle and gathered in the vintage, throwing all the grapes into the great winepress of the anger of God. The grapes were trodden outside the city and blood flowed from the winepress, to the height of the horses' bridles and over an area of sixteen hundred furlongs." Romans 16:25-26 says: "Now is revealed the mysterious plan kept hidden for long ages in the past. By the will of the eternal God it is brought to light, through the prophetic books, and all nations shall believe the faith proclaimed to them." This messages is echoed in Colossians 1:26. Therefore, God's people should remain holy, steadfast, unblemished, undefiled and pure in heart to be ready for the Second Coming of our Lord Jesus Christ. In 1st Peter 1:12-13, it says: "Thus, in these days, after the Holy Spirit has been sent from heaven, the Gospel's preachers have taught you these mysteries which even the angels long to see. So, then, let your spirit be ready. Be alert, with confident trust in the grace you will receive when Jesus Christ appears." This is also the fulfilment of what is said in John 1:51: "Truly, I say to you, you will see the heavens opened and the angels of God ascending and descending upon the Son of Man." This is also the fulfilment of what the Apostle John had said in Revelation 19:11-16, which says: "Then I saw heaven opened and a white horse appeared. Its rider is the *Faithful and True*; he judges and wages just wars. His eyes are flames of fire; he wears many crowns and written on him is his own name, which no one can understand except himself. He is clothed in a cloak drenched in blood. His name is the Word of God. The armies of heaven clothed in pure white linen follow him on white horses. A sharp sword comes out of his mouth. With it he will strike the nations for he must rule them with an iron rod. He treads the winepress of the burning wrath of God, the Master of the universe. This is why this title is written on his cloak and on his thigh: King of kings and Lord of lords." May 15, 2123 is a summer, the Second Coming of our Lord Jesus Christ. This was indirectly said by our Lord Jesus Christ in Matthew 24:32-33, which says: "Learn a lesson from the fig tree. When its branches grow tender and its leaves begin to sprout, you know that summer is near. In the same way, when you see all that I have told you, know that the time is near, even at the door." "A little, a little longer-says Scripture- and he who is coming will come; he will not delay. My righteous one will live if he believes; but if he distrusts, I will no longer look kindly on him." (Hebrews 10:37-38)

Many people, especially those whose names are not written in the book of life, will say that this prophecy is obscure, incomprehensible, and false. In 2nd Corinthians 4:3-4, it says: "In fact if the Gospel we proclaim remains obscure, it is obscure only for those who go to their own destruction. The God of this world has blinded the minds of these unbelievers lest they see the radiance of the glorious Gospel of Christ, who is God's image."

"We ourselves have seen and declare that the Father sent his Son to save the world. When someone acknowledges that Jesus is the Son of God, God remains in him and he in God." (1st John 4:15).

There is no available calendar yet for the year 2123. You may check this day if it is really Saturday. If it is so, then it is correct. And what the Lord declares is true and correct. For I, myself, am fully and faithfully confident of the infinite wisdom of God through our Lord Jesus Christ.

"And this is the promise he himself gave us: eternal life." (1st John 2:25). In Hebrews 6:17, it says: "So God committed himself with an oath in order to convince those who were to wait for his promise that he would never change his mind."

What will happen after the Second Coming of our Lord Jesus Christ? God's chosen people, who will be risen in the first resurrection, will have one thousand years of vacation in heaven to enjoy heavenly life with the Lord. Satan will be left alone on earth chained and locked for a thousand years that he cannot deceive God's people. In Revelation 20:1-3, it says: "Then an angel came down from heaven, holding in his hand the key to the Abyss and a huge chain. He seized the monster, the ancient serpent, namely Satan or the devil, and chained him for a thousand years. He threw him into the abyss and closed its gate with the key, then secured it with locks, that he might not deceive the nations in the future until the thousand years have passed. Then he will be released for a little while." By then, within the period covering a thousand years, earth will be desolate as there will be no one in this world to be tempted by Satan. In Jeremiah 4:23-28, it says: "I looked at the earth and found it formless and void, and then at the sky but it was without light. I looked at the mountains and they were quaking, and all the hills were swaying. I looked and saw that there were no people and all the birds had fled. I looked and saw that the fruitful land was a desert and that all the towns were in ruins because of Yahweh and his anger. Yes, thus speaks Yahweh, 'The whole land may be desolate but I will not destroy it completely! This is why the earth shall mourn and the skies be darkened; because I have spoken and will not relent; it is my decision and I will not go back on it." At the end of a thousand years, Satan will be released to deceive again God's people. In Revelation 20:7-10, it says: "At the end of these thousand years, Satan will be released from his prison; then he will set out to deceive the nations of the four corners of the world, namely Gog and Magog, and gather them for war. What an army, so numerous like the sand of the seashore! They invaded the land and surrounded the camp of the holy ones, the most beloved city, but fire came down from heaven and devoured them. Then the devil, the seducer, was thrown into the lake of fire and sulphur, where the beast and the false prophet already were. Their torment will last day and night for ever and ever."

The second resurrection will occur after the one thousand years. The dead will be risen in order to face the final judgment. Those who were risen in first resurrection have no more fear of death in second resurrection as they are already redeemed. In Revelation 20:5, it says: "The rest of the dead will not return to life before the end of the thousand years."

In totality, the length of stay of humanity on earth is 7,000 years. To the Almighty God that is only 7 days. God created Adam in the year 4880 B.C. based on infinite Wisdom of God. There being no 3 B.C. no 2 B.C. and no 1 B.C., the length of stay of mankind until May 15, 2123 is 7,000 years which started from creation of first man, Adam (a Hebrew word which means soil or earth). After that there will be a one thousand years vacation in heaven for those who are saved and redeemed and who observed the Sabbath Day of the Lord while they were still on earth. But for those who do not observe Sabbath Day while they were still on earth will not spend vacation in heaven as they will not be risen to life. Those who wrongfully observe Sabbath Day of the Lord on Sunday will not be risen to life as the indicator of resurrection is observance of Sabbath Day of Yahweh on Saturday and none else.

I) Climate Change

As revealed to me by God's Grace , the climate change that occur in today's world is a natural phenomenon similar to the time when there was drought in Cana-an (Genesis 42) and during the time of Elijah (1st Kings Chapter 17) resulting in severe famine. The only difference is that the climate change that occur in olden times was merely God's will, while today's climate change is worsened by man's disregard of environment for material gain and greed inherent in human nature. According to God, this climate change will become worse and unbearable starting ten years after this writing if man himself will totally neglect and continue to neglect the rejuvenation of earth thereby increasing the temperature to at least 1.75 degrees centigrade or as if the earth nears the sun by five kilometres. God says, this is the penalty of people for destroying the environment. The poor will be most affected while the rich have their means to lessen the ill-effects of this climate change such as famine, lack of oxygen to breathe, lack of water and worsening pollution. In Isaiah 24:3, it states: "The land lies polluted, defiled by its inhabitants who have transgressed the laws, violated the ordinances, and broken the covenant." Thousands will die due to climate change as this will cause flooding in some places and landslides. The only solution left for mankind is to stop greed of wealth and start taking care of the environment. The Roman Catholic Church is the worst contributor in worsening climate change as they invest most of their resources, assets and wealth which they collected from the people in coal energy. The Catholic Bishops in the world support the use of coal energy that increase to a great extent carbon emissions and catastrophic pollution for assured double gain of return of their investments. This is greed in the truest sense. The Catholic Bishops of other countries especially Belgium, Ireland and Australia already expressed their desire to divest their capital from coal energy in response to the call of Vatican's encyclical "Laudatu Si" subtitled as: "On care for a common home" which says that global warming is a symptom of the world in pursuit of short-term economic gains at the expense of the planet. Also the Catholic Bishops Conference of the Philippines promised to divest their investment and assets to coal energy. But all of these promises are only lip service since they cannot disregard the huge profits they obtain in destroying the environment. They would prefer to destroy the earth and its inhabitants than to lose their big monetary gains. The earth is owned by God and man is only a steward over it. Therefore, man has no right whatsoever to abuse the earth much less destroy it for monetary gains. Throughout the whole world, the Roman Catholic Church invested billions of dollars in coal energy and make a profit to a tune of billions of dollars. Voracious in money, they are not contented of what they divest from people's purse. Hence, the appropriate response of people in the world is to totally stop giving contributions or tithes to Roman Catholic Church in order that they can help prevent environmental destruction. If people in the world will communally avoid giving money to popes, cardinals, bishops and priests of Roman Catholic Church, they can prevent them from investing in coal energy that ultimately destroys the earth and worsens climate change. So, people of the world you have to join hand in hand in solving climate change by not giving money to Roman Catholic Church so we can save our planet earth from extinction. If you give money to them, it goes to say that you are in favour of environmental destruction and worsening of climate change. In Psalm 24:1-2, it says: "The earth and its fullness belong to the Lord and all that dwell in it. He has founded it upon the ocean and set it firmly upon the waters." This planet earth should be preserved as this will be inherited by the next generation. For in Isaiah 45:18, it says: "Yes, this is what Yahweh says, who created the heavens, who is God himself, who formed it to be inherited; I am Yahweh, and there is no other." People must have an unwavering faith in God

Almighty through our Lord Jesus Christ in order that this climate change will be solved as in the days of Elijah. This is not a sign of the end of the world, says the Lord.

J) Viruses in the World

There are hundreds of viruses in the world. Normally, they are carried by animals which are capable of replicating rapidly within living organism and can create dreadful diseases that are virulent without any known medical remedy. The world has already experienced some of these viruses which claimed thousands of lives. In 14th century, Europe was heavily invaded by bubonic plague or Black Death, a disease transmitted to human beings caused by rat flea from infected rats that killed hundreds of thousands. Spanish Flu claimed 100 million lives from 1918 to 1921. At the turn of Third millennium, the world was afflicted by 2002/2003 SARS (Severe Acute Respiratory Syndrome) which originated in China; MERS (Middle East Respiratory Syndrome) which came from camels, the EBOLA virus which came from Ebola river connecting Rwanda and Uganda; the H1N1 virus; the H2N2 , the HIV (human immunodeficiency virus) which came from monkeys. Lately, we experienced the pandemic 2019-novel coronavirus 2019-nCoV) Acute Respiratory Disease or Covid- 19 (Coronavirus Disease-19) as dubbed by World Health Organization which came from animals such as rodents, bats, snakes, dogs, geckoes, wild boars, wildcats, wild fowls, frogs, insects, cats, birds, eels, worms, turtles, monkeys and crocodiles prepared as exotic food from Wuhan, China. God says that all these viruses will just fade away without any medicine for their prevention. As noticed, these Black Death or Bubonic Plague, Spanish Flu, SARS, MERS,, H1N1, H2N2, Ebola virus and other viruses that invaded the world have just faded away without a medicine that can prevent them from spreading after leaving deaths to thousands. There will be no medicine or vaccine that can contain the virus from spreading and contaminating humans. The only solution for people to prevent spreading of virus is for them to isolate patients, monitor them and observe health protocols. Travel restraint can also prevent virus spreading. Another measure to prevent virus spreading is community quarantine, restriction of movement and preventing people from converging.

Why is there no effective medicine for these viruses? It is because these viruses are inflicted by Satan upon God's people as he knows that his time is running short as inscribed in Revelation 12:12. Satan is angry that he wants to destroy God's people by sending viruses that can cause deadly ailments. These viruses usually originate from countries that do not know God and Christ. As these countries do not have God and Christ, they are vulnerable to Satan's invasion. For this, they become soft targets of Satan's attacks. From these soft targets, illnesses will easily spread throughout the world that can endanger people's lives. Soft target countries are those countries that steadily grow in sinfulness and boastful of their wealth. Those who survive from attacks of these viruses are those people who know God and Christ as they are divinely protected. In Psalm 91:1-7, it says: "You who dwell in the shelter of the Most High, who rest in the shadow of the Almighty, say to the Lord,' My stronghold, my refuge, my God in whom I trust!' He will rescue you from the fowler's snare and from the deadly pestilence. He will cover you with his pinions and give you refuge under his wings; his faithfulness is your shield. You shall not fear the terror of the night nor the arrows that fly by day, nor the pestilence that stalks by night, and the plague that destroys at noonday. A thousand may fall at your side, ten thousand at your right hand, but nothing shall befall you." Those countries and people who take refuge in the Most High who rest in the shadow of the Almighty will not be attacked by these viruses. Satan cannot directly attack God's people as they are divinely protected. But those people who have no divine protection can easily be subdued by Satan. As revealed, there will be more viruses and variants of these viruses that Satan will inflict the world as time comes near. Satan will design viruses which cannot be detected while they invade humans. There will be no apparent symptoms for these viruses. When symptoms come out, a patient will already be very ill and dying. That is how deceitful Satan is. In Genesis 3:1, it says: "Now the serpent was the most crafty of all the wild creatures that Yahweh God had made." Indeed, Satan is full of deceit. The illnesses produced by these viruses have no known cure. No human intelligence on earth can invent an effective medicine for this. Despite the increasing monetary rewards for the one who can produce an effective vaccine, the world is still at a loss for an effective cure. Scientists can invent a palliative vaccine for temporary protection but often with adverse side effects that may lead to death. As the virus continuously mutates, the vaccine earlier invented may no longer be effective so that people who are already vaccinated will still be infected. But they have spiritual cure that can easily remedy the infection. God says that these viruses and the diseases they produce will just fade away as like the wind. It is God through our Lord Jesus Christ who can cure these illnesses and none else. In 2nd Chronicles 7:13-14, it says: "When I close the skies and there is no rain, when I command the locust to devour the land, when I send an epidemic among my people, and my people who bear my name humble themselves, and pray and look for me and turn from their wicked ways then I myself will hear from heaven and forgive their sins and restore their land." In Exodus 15:25-26, it says: "There Yahweh gave the people statutes and laws. There he tested them and said, 'If you listen carefully to the voice of Yahweh, your God, and if you do what is right in his eyes, if you obey his commands and statutes, I will not inflict on you any of the diseases I brought on the Egyptians, for I am Yahweh, the One who heals you." The only effective Doctor who can cure all these illnesses brought by these viruses is no other than God through our Lord Jesus Christ. These are the requirements that infirmed people can be cured completely:

They have to listen carefully to God's voice;

They have to do what is right and just before God's eyes;

They have to obey God's commands and statutes.

But how can a person accomplish these requirements if he has not known God. In knowing God, a person should also know our Lord Jesus Christ and accept Him heartily as his personal Saviour. And through our Lord Jesus Christ, he will be mediated to God who is the ultimate Doctor of all these ailments. In Isaiah 26:20-21, it says: "Come my people, enter your rooms and shut the doors behind you; hide yourselves for a short time until his wrath is over. For look, Yahweh is coming out of his dwelling to punish the inhabitants of the earth for their sins. The earth will reveal the blood shed upon her and will not conceal her slain any longer."

Another secret of an effective cure on Covid-19 pandemic is to believe in our Lord Jesus Christ. In Acts of Apostles 16:30-31, it says: "...Sirs, what must I do to be saved? They answered, 'Believe in the Lord Jesus Christ and you and your household will be saved." In believing our Lord Jesus Christ, it is not you alone who will be saved from this pandemic but your entire household as well. It does not say here that you will believe in Blessed Virgin Mary, or in Muhammad, or in Buddha, or in Zoroaster, or in Confucius, or in Joseph Smith or in your Emperors to be saved. It is very clear here that you believe in our Lord Jesus Christ and be saved, you and your household. And in order that you remain alive and continue on living in this world you have to treasure God's words in your heart. In Proverbs 4:4, it says: "Treasure my words in your heart; listen to my directions and you will live." Those who listen to God's words but forget them after a while do not treasure God's words in their hearts. For this they have no protection from pandemic. For those who live in sinfulness and wickedness in their lives, turn to God and seek Him for His divine mercy and be saved from pandemic and do not just die helplessly. In Baruch 6:28-29, it says: "Thus, as you distanced yourself from God, return to him and seek him ten times more earnestly. For he who caused these evils to fall on you will bring you salvation and eternal joy." Also in Isaiah 55: 6-7, it says: "Seek Yahweh while he may be found; call him while he is near. Let the wicked abandon his way, let him forsake his thoughts, let him turn to Yahweh for he will have mercy, for our God is generous in forgiving."

You may notice that even in the epicentre of Covid-19 which is Wuhan, China those who believe in God and in our Lord Jesus Christ are not infected by the virus and are safe. It is because they have divine protection. But for those people who do not believe in God and in our Lord Jesus Christ, despite their strict sanitation and hygiene, wearing always protective masks and other protective equipment, are easily invaded by the virus. It is because they have no immunization in God and in our Lord Jesus Christ. In order to have an effective immunization, they should have faith in God and in our Lord Jesus Christ. In Psalm 33:18-19, it says: "But the Lord's eyes are upon those who fear him, upon those who trust in his loving kindness to deliver them from death and preserve them from famine."

Also, in Exodus 23:25, it says: "If you serve Yahweh, your God, he will bless your bread and your water-and I will keep sickness away from you." Any kind of sickness whether it be cancer, diabetes, pneumonia, tuberculosis, hepatitis and other terminal illnesses will be completely cured by God if you have faith in Him and serve, love, worship and praise His Name through our Lord Jesus Christ.

What will happen if people will not obey God? In Leviticus 26:14-16, it says: "But if you do not heed me and keep my commandments, if you reject my precepts and ignore my decrees, refusing to obey my commandments and so break my covenant, I, in turn, will do this: I will bring upon you a terror, a tuberculosis and fever, weakening your eyes and draining your life." A fever referred to in this verse is a form of pneumonia such as the one produced by these viruses.

If you will obey God, he will truly love you. For, God tells me to let you know that He loves you very much. The love that God gives you is a true love, says the Lord. For this, you have to respond to Him that you love Him so that you will be protected against Satan who send viruses to people.

Quarantine is best way to put people to safety as they are safeguarded from the virus. But no amount of quarantine can prevent viruses from attacking people if they will not repent. They have to undergo quarantine and return to God that they will be cured. Those who have no knowledge of God have also no knowledge of the correct cure. But those who have knowledge of God can call upon His name through our Lord Jesus Christ and be saved. The longest ever recorded quarantine in the world was experienced by Noah and his household. They stayed in the ark for one year and ten days to be saved. In Genesis 7:11-13, it says: "In the six hundredth year of Noah's life, in the second month and on the seventeenth day of the month, all the fountains of the great deep burst forth and there was a downpour on the earth lasting forty days and forty nights. On that same day Noah went into the ark, as well as Shem, Ham and Japheth, his sons, and his wife and his daughters-in-law." That was the start of quarantine on Noah and his household in order to be saved. And they came out of the ark as recorded in Genesis 8:13-16 which states: "In the year six hundred and one, in the first month, on the first day of the month, the waters dried up from the earth. Noah then removed the covering from the ark and looked out and saw that the surface of the earth was dry. On the twenty-seventh day of the second month, the earth was dry. Then God said to Noah, 'Come out of the ark, you and your wife, your sons and their wives with you."

The modern day quarantine lasts for fourteen days only. People are prevented from going out of their homes. They are also prevented from reporting to their respective work. Their needs are being taken care of by government in subsidy. But how long will government sustain their needs as pestilence continues. The best thing the government, the people and the general public should do is to humble themselves and turn away from their wicked ways and pray to God. God clearly says this in 2nd Chronicles 7:14 "...and my people who bear my name humble themselves, and pray and look for me, and turn from their wicked ways then I myself will hear from heaven and forgive their sins..."

God says that these viruses and the diseases they brought will just fade away as like the wind. The apparent indicator that Covid-19 is already gone is when a very strong wind blows from West to the East, says the Lord. In Exodus 10:18, the fading away of a pestilence is brought by a very strong wind from the West and it says: "Moses left

Pharaoh and interceded with Yahweh who brought a very strong wind from the west that carried off the locusts and swept them into the Red Sea. Not one locust was left within the boundaries of Egypt." The question is: who will intercede with Yahweh? The one who can effectively intercede with Yahweh should be blameless, undefiled and perfect, such as the likes of Moses, Noah, Daniel and Job. We have to pray hard to find one. In Jeremiah 9:11-12, it says: "Who is wise enough to understand these events? And who is the one Yahweh has chosen to reveal them? Why has the land perished and been laid waste like a desert where no one passes? Yahweh answered, 'It is because they have abandoned the Law that I gave them. They have not listened to me..." I asked the Lord: When will it end? The answer is March 2028.

K) First Nuclear World War

On August 29, 2099 a Saturday, there will be wars, says Almighty God. This will be the final war between the forces of evil and the forces of Good. This is dubbed as the Armageddon in Holy Bible. The United States of America, Russia, China and their allies will be involved. Specifically, it will involve Vietnam, Germany, Poland, France, Canada, Australia, North Korea, Japan, Israel, England, Iran and Iraq. The world will witness a great display of sophisticated, advanced and destructive nuclear armaments. The atomic bombs they will be using will be more than 50 times destructive than the atomic bombs that were dropped in Hiroshima on August 6, 1945 which killed instantly 78,000 people and in Nagasaki on August 9, 1945 which killed more than 40,000 people in an instant. For the first time, America will experience being hit by a nuclear bomb; "the evil that their hands have done shall be done to them." (Isaiah 3:11). In Obadiah verse 15, it says: "...As you have done to another, so to you will it be done. Whatever has been your deed will come back upon your head." The ratio will be one is to seven. For every one bomb dropped in America, it will retaliate by dropping seven bombs to its enemies. America, by that time, will have already well improved a shield designed after the Iron Dome of Israel to protect itself from nuclear attacks. This is not the Third World War but rather this will be called as the First Nuclear World War. Millions will die. This will truly happen because people of the world have already rejected the Almighty God. They became rebels before the God of Truth. In Jeremiah 15:6-11, it says: "It was you who rejected me-word of Yahweh-you turned your back on me, and because of that I have stretched out my hand to destroy you. I was weary of showing mercy! I winnowed them with a fork in the cities of the land. I left my people without children; I brought them to ruin, but they will not change their ways. Their widows are more numerous than the sand of the seas. On the mothers of young men I have brought a destroyer who ravages in broad daylight. Suddenly terror and fear grips them. The mother who had seven sons is confused and discouraged as if breathing her last. Although it is still day her sun has set. As for those who remain, I shall let them be slain by the sword in sight of their enemies-it is Yahweh who speaks."

This event will first be preceded by economic embargoes that will adversely affect people's lives resulting in widespread hunger, famines and untold poverty. No amount of diplomatic negotiations by United Nations General Assembly can pacify the conflicts. This war will last for twelve years or until the year 2111. "Yes, thus speaks Yahweh, 'The whole land may be desolate but I will not destroy it completely!" (Jeremiah 4:27-28).

CHRONOLOGY OF EVENTS IN THE LAST DAYS

July 8, 2064. At around 2:30 A.M. a Tuesday, Oslo Norway will be completely destroyed by strong, violent earthquake and heavy rains of consuming fire.

February 14, 2069. An undisclosed populous city in American continent will be destroyed by strong, violent earthquake and heavy rains of consuming fire.

January 8, 2078. An undisclosed populous city in Asia will be destroyed beyond recovery by strong, violent earthquake and heavy rains of consuming fire.

February 9, 2083. An undisclosed populous city in Asia will be completely destroyed by strong, violent earthquake and heavy rains of consuming fire.

April 4, 2087. At 10:30 P.M., a Friday Wellington, New Zealand will be totally destroyed by strong, violent earthquake and heavy rains of consuming fire.

July 5, 2090. AT 7:50 P.M., a Wednesday, Guatemala City, Guatemala will be totally destroyed by strong, violent earthquake and heavy rains of consuming fire.

July 6, 2090. At 8:46 P.M., a Thursday, London, England will be totally destroyed by strong, violent earthquake and heavy rains of consuming fire.

July 7, 2090. At 4:18 A.M. a Friday, Dakar, Senegal will be totally destroyed by violent, strong, violent earthquake and heavy rains of consuming fire.

July 7, 2090. At 9:46 P.M., a Friday, Vadus, Leichtenstein will be completely destroyed by strong earthquake and heavy rains of consuming fire.

July 14, 2090. At 9:08 P.M. a Monday, Monrovia, Liberia will be completely destroyed by strong, violent earthquake, tsunami and heavy rains of consuming fire.

July 17, 2090. At 8:00 P.M. a Monday, Metropolitan Manila, Philippines will be totally destroyed by strong, violent earthquake, tsunami and heavy rains of consuming fire.

September 8, 2090. At 7:42 P.M., a Friday, Dhaka (Dacca), Bangladesh will be completely destroyed by strong, violent earthquake and rain of consuming fire.

September 8, 2090. At 8:30 P.M. a Friday, Moskva (Moscow), Russian Federation will be completely destroyed by strong, violent earthquake, hailstones, and heavy rains of consuming fire.

December 15, 2090. At 9:30 P.M., a Friday, New York City, USA will be completely destroyed by strong, violent earthquake and heavy rains of consuming fire.

January 4, 2091. At 7:50 P.M., a Thursday, Ho C|hi Minh, Vietnam will be totally destroyed by strong, violent earthquake and heavy rains of consuming fire.

January 15, 2091. At 7:49 P.M., a Monday, Rome and Vatican Cities, Italy will be totally destroyed by strong, violent earthquake and heavy rains of consuming fire.

April 6, 2091. At 6:58 P.M. , a Friday, Honolulu, Hawaii, USA will be completely destroyed by strong, violent earthquake, volcanic eruptions, tsunami and heavy rains of consuming fire.

July 4, 2091. At 7:41 P.M., a Wednesday, Valleta, Malta will be totally destroyed by strong, violent earthquake and heavy rains of consuming fire.

July 7, 2091. At 4:30 P.M. , a Saturday, Stockholm, Sweden will be totally destroyed by strong, violent earthquake and heavy rains of consuming fire.

July 17, 2091. At 2:10 A.M. , a Tuesday, Brussels, Belgium will be totally destroyed by strong, violent earthquake and heavy rains of consuming fire.

July 18, 2091. At 8:41 P.M., a Wednesday, Athens (Athinai), Greece will be totally destroyed by strong, violent earthquake and heavy rains of consuming fire.

August 4, 2091. At 3:30 A.M., a Saturday, Jakarta, Indonesia will be totally destroyed by strong, violent earthquake, volcanic eruptions, tsunamis and heavy rains of consuming fire.

August 9, 2091. At 2:00 A.M., a Thursday, Ankara, Turkey will be totally destroyed by strong, violent earthquake, volcanic eruptions and heavy rains of consuming fire.

August 11, 2091. At 11:05 P.M., a Saturday, Budapest, Hungary will be totally destroyed by strong, violent earthquake and heavy rains of consuming fire.

August 14, 2091. AT 6:33 P.M., a Tuesday, Cairo (El Qahira), Egypt will be totally destroyed by strong, violent earthquake and heavy rains of consuming fire.

August 19, 2091. At 11:30 a Sunday, Tashkent, Uzbekistan will be totally destroyed by strong, violent earthquake and heavy rains of consuming fire.

September 4, 2091. At 11:08 P.M., a Tuesday, Phnom Penh, Cambodia will be totally destroyed by strong, violent earthquake and heavy rains of consuming fire.

November 22, 2091. At 7:45 P.M., a Thursday, New Delhi, India will be totally destroyed by strong, violent earthquake and heavy rains of consuming fire.

December 16, 2091. At 7:42 P.M., a Sunday, Reykjavik, Iceland will be totally destroyed by strong, violent earthquake and heavy rains of consuming fire.

January 9, 2092. At 7:18 P.M., a Wednesday, Prague (Praha), Czech Republic will be totally destroyed by strong, violent earthquake and heavy rains of consuming fire.

July 14, 2092. At 9:10 P.M., a Monday, Lima, Peru will be completely destroyed by strong, violent earthquake, tsunami and heavy rains of consuming fire.

August 4, 2092. At 8:17 P.M., a Monday, Minsk, Belarus will be totally destroyed by strong, violent earthquake and heavy rains of consuming fire.

August 9, 2093. Complete destruction of undisclosed populous city in Asia.

September 16, 2093. At 7:14 P.M. , a Wednesday, Sofia (Sofiya), Bulgaria will be totally destroyed by strong, violent earthquake and heavy rains of consuming fire.

October 6, 2093. At 4:25 A.M., a Tuesday, Port Louis, Mauritius will be completely destroyed by strong, violent earthquake, volcanic eruptions and heavy rains of consuming fire.

November 15, 2093. At 7:18 P.M., a Sunday, Tegucigalpa, Honduras will be totally destroyed by strong, violent earthquake and heavy rains of consuming fire.

August 4, 2094. Complete destruction of undisclosed populous city in the continent of Europe.

August 28, 2094. At 7:59 P.M., a Saturday, Czestochowa ((Chentokhov), Poland will be totally destroyed by strong, violent earthquake and heavy rains of consuming fire.

September 14, 2095. At 10:30 P.M., a Wednesday, Vilnius, Lithuania will be totally destroyed by strong, violent earthquake and heavy rains of consuming fire.

September 17, 2098. At 2:03 P.M., a Wednesday, Kathmandu, Nepal will be totally destroyed by strong, violent earthquake and heavy rains of consuming fire.

August 29, 2099. A Saturday. First Nuclear World War. This will last for twelve years or in 2111.

December 1, 2119, a Friday. Start of the bitter trials of God's people.

May 14, 2123. A Friday. End of the bitter trials of God's people.

May 15, 2123. The Second Coming of our Lord Jesus Christ.

SYNOPSES

In the last days, it would be known that there will be forty cities on earth that will be completely destroyed by God of truth and spirit including those cities near them that will refuse and continue to refuse to repent as a prelude to Second Coming of our Lord Jesus Christ. The main reason for their destruction are their sinfulness and wickedness as they worship printed and graven images and statues which God vehemently abhors. They failed to worship the living God of mercy. Most of these cities improve economically and become too proud and totally forget God.

In the last days, it would be known worldwide that Roman Catholic Church is a fake Church. It only usurped authority of early Christians in spreading the Gospel of Christ by first killing them in many ways such as: reducing them into living torches; crucifying them inhumanly; hanging them on trees until they die; sawing them in two from head to foot; feeding them to hungry lions inside Roman amphitheatres as they delightfully watched them torn to pieces. This happened during the time of Roman Emperors Domitian, Diocletian, Nero and Titus.

In the last days, it would be known that Jesus Christ's birthday is not December 25. It is rather the feast of highest pagan god, Jupiter. It is practiced by Catholicism to perpetuate worship of their pagan god. Thus, it follows that those who celebrate Christ's birthday on

December 25 are pure pagans and not Christians as they worship the highest pagan god, Jupiter. It would be known also in the last days that upon divine revelation that those who remain worshiping the highest pagan god, Jupiter will drink the cup of undiluted God's wrath in the Day of Atonement.

In the last days, it would be known that the real birthday of our Lord Jesus Christ is April 14, 12 B.C., a Sunday at 9:41 P.M. based on divine revelation and not December 25.

In the last days, it would be known that those who worship printed images and graven images and statues of any kind will be condemned in the last Judgment.

In the last days, it would be known that those God's people who consistently observe Sabbath Day of the Lord will be given first priority by God's angels to be marked as saved. Saturday is the true Sabbath Day- not Sunday. As Satan's cohort, the Roman Catholic Church changed Sabbath Day from Saturday to Sunday in compliance with Satan's dictates.

In the last days, it would be known that the only acceptable prayer to God is the one taught by our Lord Jesus Christ i.e. *OUR FATHER (PATER NOSTER; PADRE NUESTRO; AMA NAMIN)* The prayer: Hail Mary is not acceptable to God as it is intended only to praise Virgin Mary and not the Almighty God. Likewise, the praying of Rosary only infuriates the Almighty Father as it only praises Virgin Mary but not God Almighty. This prayer is only invented by Roman Catholic Church to divert attention of people to worship anybody or anything other than God Almighty.

In the last days, it would be known that those who frequent the Roman Catholic Church and their priests, bishops, cardinals and popes have no assurance of being saved as thousands of them will be condemned and be destined to hell.

In the last days, it would be known that practically all people would love money more than God. And those who love money will find themselves without money and very poor; but those who do not love money and prefer to seek first God's kingdom will have plenty of money that they can be able to share them to the needy.

In the last days, it would be known that the great harlot described in Chapter 19:1-2 of Book of Revelation is no other than the Roman Catholic Church based on divine revelation. For, it corrupted, for many centuries, the whole world with her idolatry and false teachings.

In the last days, it would be known that the 666 described in Book of Revelation is already in the world. And they are: WWM, WWC and WWW (World Wide Web)

In the last days, people would know fully well God's will, His qualities, His truthfulness, His faithfulness and His love for humanity. And those who have unwavering faith in God through our Lord Jesus Christ will be saved even how sinful or wicked they are.

In the last days, the Divinity of our Lord Jesus Christ would be unquestionably accepted and known to mankind.

In the last days, Satan as his time is running low, will send several fatal viruses to the world that have no cure at all and will result into death of millions to mankind. Symptoms for these viruses cannot be detected in early stage. Symptoms will only come out when a patient is already at the verge of death.

In the last days, the world will experience bitterly the First Nuclear World War starting August 29, 2099 and will last for twelve years. Millions will die.

In the last days, people will personally witness the Second Coming of our Lord Jesus Christ which is May 15, 2123 based on divine revelation.

In the last days, scoffers or those people whose names are not found in the Book of Life will mock at the Second Coming of our Lord Jesus Christ.

In the last days, the just will be separated from the wicked such that the just will be at the right side of the Lamb while the wicked will be at the left side of the Lamb.

And finally, in the last days, the just, the repentant and those who have unwavering faith in God Almighty through our Lord Jesus Christ will be ushered by God's angels to heaven to enjoy life there for one millennium and have no more fear of death in the second resurrection.

N.B.

These revelations should first be made known to other places before these be made known to the country where the author comes from, which is the Philippines. For, a prophet is not accepted in his own country. In Mark 6:4, it says: "...A prophet is despised in his own country, among his relatives and in his own family." This is also affirmed in Matthew 13:57 and in Luke 4:24.

LINCOLN P. MIRAFLOR

BOOK AUTHOR: "IN THE LAST DAYS-APROPHECY"

AUTOBIOGRAPHY OF THE AUTHOR

I, **LINCOLN P. MIRAFLOR**, the author of this book entitled: *"IN THE LAST DAYS - A PROPHECY*, a Filipino citizen of Bacolod City, Philippines, do hereby declare with complete honesty and sincerity that the contents hereof, more specifically the prophecies, are not mine personally but are purely the divine revelations given to me by God Almighty to be shared to all humanity. Those who want to believe, believe it as it is based on truth by God's wisdom. Those who do not want to believe it just don't believe it In Ezekiel 3:27, it conveys to you this message: "But when I speak to you I shall open your lips and you shall say to them: This is the word of the Lord Yahweh! He who listens, let him listen and he who refuses to listen, let him refuse for they are a rebellious people." Also in Habakkuk 2:4, it says: "The proud will never possess my favour, the upright on the other hand, will live by his faithfulness." Also in John 12:44, it says: "...He who believes in me, believes not in me but in him who sent me." In 1st Corinthians 14: 22, it says"" ,,, while prophecy is a sign for those who believe, not for those who refuse to believe." . In Proverbs 1:24-27, it says: "Indeed if I cry out and you refuse to listen, if I offer my hand and no one cares, if you ignore my advice and reject my warning, I, in turn, will laugh at your disaster, I will sneer when terror grips you; when terror comes down on you like a hurricane, and distress and anxiety befall you."

I was born on February 2, 1955 at Villacin Zone 1-B, ILCO (Insular Lumber Company), Fabrica, Sagay City, Negros Occidental, Philippines. I am the fifth of seven broods in the family. My mother was Ester Quirubin-Parreno (deceased) who was a public-school teacher and my father was Primo Lucero-Miraflor (deceased) who formerly worked as executive secretary to general manager of ILCO; editor-in-chief of ILCO Family News and later a notary public.

As a young boy, I woke one morning with a shallow mark on my forehead which amazed me where it came from. I just didn't mind it. It is still existing until today. By God's grace, I know later that that is the mark of Jesus which is echoed in Galatians 6:17 which says: "... for my part, I bear in my body the marks of Jesus.." Also in Jeremiah 1:5 God Almighty has said to me: Before you were born, I appointed you a prophet. "Before I formed you in the womb I knew you; before you were born I set you apart, and appointed you a prophet to the nations!"

As of the moment, I live an ascetic life as a semi-hermit, an outcast, a scum, despised by the world and a garbage of society (1st Corinthians 4:13). Though afflicted, I remain happy; I'm poor but I helped others who are in need; I have nothing but I possess everything. For, in 2nd Corinthians 6:10, it says: "We appear to be afflicted, but we remain happy, we seem to be poor, but we enrich many; apparently we have nothing, but we possess everything!" I am weak but I boast of my weakness. For, in 2nd Corinthians 12:9-10, it says: "Gladly, then, will I boast of my weakness that the strength of Christ may be mine. So I rejoice when I suffer infirmities, humiliations, want, persecutions: all for Christ! For when I am weak, then I am strong." I live away from family, away from relatives, without friends and away from my children so that no one would call me "father" as there is only one Father in heaven who is Father God Almighty. In Matthew 16:24, it says: "Then Jesus says to his disciples, 'If anyone wants to follow me, let him deny himself take up his cross and follow me." I denied myself in order to be considered child of God Almighty through our Lord Jesus Christ. In Matthew 10: 39, it says: "He who cares for his own life will lose it; he who loses his life for my sake will find it." Also in John 12:25, it says: "Whoever loves his life destroys it, and whoever despises his life in this world keeps it for everlasting life." It is in following our Lord Jesus Christ that there is eternal life. Mark 10:29-30 says: "...Truly, whoever has left house or brothers or sisters, or father or mother, or children, or lands for my sake and for the Gospel, will not lose his reward. I say to you; even in the midst of persecution he will receive a hundred times as many houses, brothers, sisters, mothers, children, and lands in the present time and in the world to come he will receive eternal life."

When I was born, the political situation of the world was relatively stable and considerably peaceful. The Philippine President at that time was Ramon Magsaysay whose term was from 1953 to 1957 when it ended in his demise due to plane crash. He was succeeded by President Carlos P. Garcia. The president of the United States at that time was the 34th US President Dwight David Eisenhower whose term covered from 1953 to 1960. In Canada, the Prime Minister was Louis Stephen St. Laurent whose term covered from 1948 to 1957. In United Kingdom, it was Sir Winston Churchill who sat as Prime Minister whose leadership ranges from 1951 to 1955, then he was replaced by Sir Anthony Eden whose leadership covered between 1955 and 1957. In Australia, it was led by Prime Minister Sir Robert Gordon Menzies whose political leadership ranged between 1949 and 1966. And in South Africa, it was led by Prime Minister Jahannes Gerhardus Strijdom whose term ranged from 1954 to 1958.

As a young lad, I studied elementary grades in public school. Then, I continued high school in a private institution managed by Catholic nuns. There I learned about Catholicism. After graduating high school, I joined the seminary aspiring to become a Catholic priest. But I was dismayed of what I observed in seminary which prompted me to decide to go out and pursued my studies in Bachelor of Arts in Philosophy. Then I studied law and jurisprudence while working as personnel clerk, assistant personnel manager/ editor-in – chief of Atkins, Kroll Company/Inchcape Group of Companies, credit investigator, college professor teaching world history, Spanish language and political science.

Equipped with Master's Degree in Education, my last work was teaching World History, Asian History and Economics in public high school where I retired at age 62. Even before I retired from government service, I have already established a personal relationship with God Almighty through our Lord Jesus Christ by constant prayer. Then come this calling to tell the world about God's will so that people would be aware of forthcoming catastrophe and total destruction of forty primary cities in the world before the Second Coming on May 15, 2123, a Saturday, the Lord's Day based on divine revelation. It is expected that those whose names are not written in the Book of Life will surely scoff at this revelation. In 2nd Peter 3:3-4 says: "Remember, first of all, that in the last days scoffers will appear, their mockery serving their evil desires. And they will say, 'What has become of his promised coming? Since our fathers in faith died, everything still goes on as it was from the beginning of the world."

REFERENCES

Book of Jonah 33: 32-4; Jonah 4:11 Christian Community Bible Catholic Pastoral Edition, 11th Edition.

Census of Population (2015) Highlights of the Population 2015 of Population Philippine Statistics Authority. Retrieved 20 June 2016.

"Tashkent shahri, Uzbekistan-Population Statistics Charts, Map and Location..City Population.

"Urban and rural population by district" (PDF) (in Uzbek). Tashkent City department of statistics.

Encyclopedia Britaannica.(2019). United Provinces of Central America. Retrieved June 26, 2022. Archived 12 July 21022 at the Wayback Machine

Quinonez, Edgar (15 August 22023) Assumption Day: Why August 15 is celebrated in Guatemala) Republika. Retrieved 21 November 2023.

Hondutel (14 October 2009). "Honduras Coun try Codes" Calling Codes. Org. Archived from the original on 26 December 2018. Retrieved 29 June 2010.

Anonymous at the Honduras National Library (19 May 2008). "Spanish: Tegucigalpa, a particular story-pg 3" (PDF) Francisco Morazan National Pedagogic University. Archived from the original

(PDF) ON 4 November 2011.

Governm,entr of Honduras (31 January 2001). "1982 Constitution of Honduras- Title 1 Chapter 1, Article 8." Honduras. Netr. Archived from the original on 1 November 2017. Retrieved 29 June 2011.

Japan International Cooperation Agency (13 January 2011). "Spanish: Honduras-Geological faults identified in Tegucigalpa".Tierra America. Archived from the original on 14 July 2011. Retrieved 9 July 2016

Wright, Tom (11 November 2011).."Why Delhi? The Move From Calcutta" The Wall Street Journal.. Archived from the original on 27 July 2020. Retrieved 16 November 2011.

Pritchard, Evan T. (2002). Native New Yorkers: The Legacy of the Algonquin people of New York. Council Oak Books. P27. ISBN 1-57178-107-23.

Jones, Huw (March 24, 2022). "New York widens lead over London in top finance centres index" Reuters., com. Retrieved June 25, 2022.

"Honolulu History". Hellohonolulu.com. Archived from the original on January 4, 2013. Retrieved May 22, 201`21.

Kuykendall, Ralph S. (June 1923). "A Northwest Trader at the Hawaiian Islands.". The Quarterly of the Oregon Historical Society. Oregon Historical Society.24 (2):121.JSTOR 20610240

Zaide, Gregorio. "History of the Philippines" The Discovery of the Philippines

Daws, Gavan (1967). "Honolulu in the 19th Century: Notes on the Emergence of Urban Society in Hawaii." The Journal of Pacific History. Taylor & Francis.2:77-78, 83. Doi: 10.1080/00223346708572103. JSTOR25167896.

"Honolulu History" Honolulu.city.com. December 7, 1941. Archived from the original on March 18, 2016, Retrieved May 22, 2012.

Stearns, Harold T.: Vaksvik, Knute N.(1935). "Geology and ground-water resources of the island of Oahu, Hawaii, Maui Publishing Company, Limited. P.536.

Bennett Murry (February 14, 2015). "Ancient kiln site poised to disappear forever". Retrieved March 14, 2021.

Phon Kaseka. "Choeung Ek archaeological site: The priceless cultural resource for national heritage of Cambodia. (in Khmer)' (PDF). Retrieved March 14, 2021.

Federal State Statistics Service. Archived from the original on 1 September 2022. Retrieved 1 September 2022.

Major Agglomerations of the World. Population Statistics and Maps". Archived from the original on 7 July 2023. Retrieved 2 May 2023.

Akishin, Alexander (17 August 2017). "A 3-Hour Commute: A Close Look At Moscow The Megapolis". Strelka Mag. Archived from the original on 23 May 2020.

"History of Moscow. from village to metropolis". moskau. ru. Archived from the original on 24 May 2012. Retrieved 12 November 2020.

The origins of Moscow: What archaeological finds, chronicles and urban legends tell us". Mos. ru. 5 April 2017. Archived from the original on 30 October 2020. Retrieved 12 November 2020.

1977 Constitution of the Soviet Union- Section VIII, Article 172: "The Capital. of the Union of Soviet Socialist Republics is the city of

Moscow."

(General statistics for Population and households investigation 2019) (in Vietnamese). General Statistics Office of Vietnam. Archived from the original on 13 November 2019. Retrieved 20 March 2020.

Taylor, K.W. (2013). A History of the Vietnamese. Cambridge University Press.p.547.ISBN 978-0-521-87586-8

"Bevolkerungsstatistik : Vorlaufige Ergebnisse 31 Dezember 2019. (PDF). Llv.li., Retrieved 13 August 2020

"Global Statistics". GeoHive. 2009-07-01 Retrieved 2010-07-04.

Roman Adrian Cybriwsky,, Capital Cities around the World. An Encyclopedia of Geography, History, and Culture, ABC-CLIO. USA, 2013, p. 193

Britannica, Monrovia, Britannica.com.USA, accessed on July 7 2019

Zeleza, Tiyambe; Eyoh, Dickson (2003). Encyclopedia of Twentieth-Century African History. . Routledge ISBN 9780415234795. Retrieved 2010-07-04.

"Liberia Celebrates 90 Years of Independence with Champagne." Life. Vol.3, no.11. 1937-09-13. Pp. 87-88 ISSN 00245-3019.

"African women look within for change." CNN.com. 2010-09-23. Retrieved 2019-08-25.

Lord Kinross (1965). Ataturtk:"A Biography of Mustafa Kemal, Father of Modern Turkey. William Morrow and Company. Archived from the original on 29 May 2021. Retrieved 13 January 2021.

"The Results of Address Based Population Registration System. 2022": Turkish Statistical Institute. 31 December 2022. Retrieved 6 February 2023.

"TURKEY; Ankara City". City Population.

"l numeri di Roma Capitale". (PDF). Commune di Roma.31 December 2018. Archived (PDF) from the original on 4May 2020. Retrieved 4 May 2020.

"Popolazione residente al 1 gennaio." Archived from the original on 8 April 2020. Retrieved 10 April 2020.

"Principal Angglomerations of the World." City population. January 2017. Archived from the original on 4 July 2010. Retrieved 6 APRIL 2012. .

"What is the smallest country in the world?" History.com. Archived from the original on 16 September 2018. Retrieved 27 September 2018.

"Why is Rome Called The Eternal City?" 27 September 2021. Archived from the original on 16 September 2021. Retrieved 16 September 2021.

Beretta, Silvio (2017). Understanding China Today: An Exploration of Politics, Economics, Society, and International Relations. Springer. p.320. .ISBN 9783319296258.

B. Bahr, Anne arie (2009). Christianity: Religions of the World. Infobase Publishing. p. 139. ISBN 9781438106397.

R. D'Agostino, Peter (2005). Rome in America:Transnational Catholic Ideology from the Risorgimento to Fascism. Univ of North Carolina Press. ISBN 9780807863411.

Heiken, G., Funiciello, R. and De Rita, D. (2005), The Seven Hills of Rome: A Geological Tour of the Eternal City. Princeton University Press.

"Old Age in Ancient Rome-History Today." Archived from the

original on 12 June 2018.

"Dhaka ranks world's sixth most populous city." Dhaka Tribune. 14 January 2022. Archived from the original on 15 January 2023. Retrieved 15 January 2023.

"Population & Housing Census-2011." (PDF). Bangladesh Bureau of Statistics. Archived from the original (PDF) on 8 December 2015. Retrieved 17n May 2021.

"The World's Most Densely Populated Cities." World Atlas. 4 October 2020. Archived from the original on 19 March 2022. Retrieved 11 March 2022.

Demographia World Urban Areas 17th Annual Edition: 2021 06(PDF). Demographia. Archived (PDF) from the original on 3 May 2018. Retrieved 2 February 2022.

Ferreira, Luana (3 September 2021). "Here's How Many People Live in The Most Densely Populated City on Earth." Grunge.com. Archived from the original on 2 February 2022. Retrieved 2 Feb ruary 2022.

"400 years of Dhaka." The Daily Star (Editorial). 1 December 2008. Archived from the original on 18 December 2022. Retrieved 18 December 2022.

"Bangladesh CA Inaugurates Three-year Gala. Celebrations of 400 Anniversary of Dhaka." VOA Bangla. 28 November 2008. Archived from the original on 18 December 2022. Retrieved from the original on 18 December 2022. Retrieved 18 December 2022.

400 Years of Capital Dhaka and Beyond: Economy and culture. Vol.2. Asiatic Society of Bangladesh. 2011. ISBN 9789845120128. Archived from the original on 11 February 2023. Retrieved 29

January 2023.

National Statistics Agency. "Population Projections 2013-2063" (PDF) Retrieved January 3, 2021.

Report in the 1453 chronicle of Gomes Eanes de Zurara

. B. W. Diffie and G.D. Winius (1977) Foundation of the Portuguese empire, 1415-1580 Minneapolis: University of Minnesota Press, pp.83-85.

. A. Teixeira da Mota (1946). "A descoberta da Guine', Boletim cultural da Guine' Portuguese, Vol.1. No.2 (Apr), p. 273-326.

A. Teixeira da Mota (1968) "ilha de Santiago e Angra de Bezeguiche, escalas da carreira da India'" Do tempo e da historia, Lisbon, v. 3, pp. 141-149.

Trisos, C.H, et al. 2022: Chapter: 9: Africa. In Climate Change 2022: Impacts, Adaptation and Vulnerability. Cambridge University Press Cambridge, United Kingdom and New York, NY, US, pp. 2043-2121

Technical Summary. In: Climate Change 2021: The Physical, Science Basis. Contribution of Working Group to the Sixth Assessment Report of the Intergovernmental Panel on Climate Change (PDF). IPCC. August 2021. p. TS14. Retrieved 12 November 2021.65

"Population and household estimates. England and Wales. Census 2021. ons.gov.uk. Office for National Statistics. Retrieved 15 October 2022.

Number 1Poultry (ONE 94). Museum of London Archaeology, 2013.Archaeology Data Service, The University of York.

Fowler, Joshua (5 July 2013). "London Government: Essex, Kent, Surrey and Middlesex 50 years on". BBC News.

"The baffling map of England's counties". BBC News. 25 April 2014. Retrieved 25 September 2021.

"London Government Act 1963." legislation.gov.uk. Retrieved 26 September 2021.

"Global Power City Index 2020.", Institute for Urban Strategies- The Mori Memorial Foundation. Retrieved 25 March 2021.; Adewunmi,Bim (10 March 2013)., "London:The Everything Capital of the World." The Guardian. London. .,;"What's The Capital of the World?" More Intelligent Life. Archived from the original on 22 September 2013. Retrieved 4 July 2013.

"Leading 200 science cities." Nature. Retrieved 10 June 2022.

"The World's Most Influential Cities 2014". Forbes. 14 August 2014. Retrieved 25 March 2021.; Dearden, Lizzie (8 October 2014). "London is'the most desirable city in the worl;d to work in', study finds. The Independent. London. Retrieved 25 arch 2021.

Denison, Simon (July 1999). "First 'London Bridge' in River Thames at Vauxhall." Britisah Archaeology 46). Archived from the original on 27 April 2011. Retrieved 15 April 2011.

"London's Oldest Prehistoric Structure.". BAJR.3 April 2015. Archived from the original on July 2018. Retrieved 19 August 201.

Milne, Gustav. "London's Oldest Foreshore Structure." Frog Blog. Thames Discovery Programme. Archived from the original on 30 April 2011. Retrieved 15 April 2011.

Brown, Robert W. "London in the Nineteenth Century." University of North Carolina at Pembroke. Archived from the original on 30 December 2011. Retrieved 13 December 2011.

"Suffragettes, violence and militancy". British Library. Retrieved 9

October 2021.

"Bomb-Damage Maps Reveal London's World War II Devastation." Nationalgeographic.com.au. 18 May 2016. Archived from the original on 30 April 2017. Retrieved 18 June 2017.

Godoy, M<aria (7 July 2005). "Timeline: London's Explosive History." NPR. Retrieved 25 March 2021.

Census 2021 GR" (PDF) (Press release). Hellenic Statistical Authority. 19 July 2022. Archived (PDF) from the original on 9 October 2023. Retrieved 12 September 2022.

Vinie Daily, Athens, the city in your pocket, p. 6.

"v4.ethnos.grJuly 2011. Archived from the original on 21 July 2011. Retrieved 26 October 2018

"Contents and Principles of the Programme of Unification of the Archaeological Sites of Athens." Hellenic Ministry of Culture. Yppo.gr. Archived from the original on 21 August 2016. Retrieved 31 December 2009.

CNN & Associated Press (16 January 1997). "Greece uncovers 'holy grail' of Greek Archaeology" CNN Archived from the original on 6 December 2007. Retrievced 28 March 2007.

Encarta Ancient Greece from the Internet Archived- Retrieved on 28 February 2012. Archived 31 October 2009.

"Athens" Archived from the original on 6 January 2009. Retrieved 31 December 2008. Ancient Greek Athenai historic city and capital of Greece. Many of classical civilization's intellectual and artistic ideas originated there, and the city is generally considered to be the birthplace of Western civilization

BBC History on Greek Democracy Archived 19 December 2019 at

the Wayback Machine- accessed on 26 January 2007

"ELSTAT" www.statistics.gr. Retrieved 10 June 2023.

"The World According to GaWC 2020". GaWC- Research Network. Globalization and World Cities. Archived from the original on 24 August 2020. Retrieved 31 August 2020.

"Maritime passenger statistics." Eurostat. Eurostat. 21 November 2022. Retrieved 25 March 2023.

"World Shipping Council-Top 50 Ports." World Shipping Council. Retrieved 7 July 2022.

"Estimated Population by Locality 31st March 2014." Government of Malta. 16 May 2014. Archived from the original on 21 June 2015. Retrieved 21 June 2015.

"Population on 1 January by age groups and sex-functional urban areas." Eurostat.2020. Retrieved 5 March 2022.

"Population on 1 January by broad age group, sex and metropolitan regions 2020." Eurostat. 2020. Retrieved 5 March 2022.

Badan Pusat Statistik. Jakarta 2023.

"Localities 2010, area, population and density in localities 2005 and 2010 and change in area and population". Statistics Sweden. 29 May 2012. Archived from the original on 16 January 2013.

"citypopulation.de". www.citypopulation.de. Archived from the original; on 5 November 2023, Retrieved 5 November 2023.

"Birka-step back into the Viking Age". Visitsweden.com. Archived from the original on 28 October 2023. Retrieved 28 October 2023.

Carlquist, Erik; Hogg, Peter c.; Osterberg, Eva (1 December 2011). The Chronicle of Duke Erik: A Verse Epic from Medieval Sweden.

Nordic Academic Press. ISBN 9789185509577.. Archived from the original on 25 February 2021. Retrieved `19 June 2016.

"Retrieved from" Archived from the original on 16 September 2012.

"Finansiella sektorn bar frukt- Analys av den finansiella, sektorn ur ett svenskt perpertiv" (PDF). Government of Sweden. Archived from the orginal (PDF) on 28 July 2014. Retrieved 19 July 2014.

"Regional GDP per capita in the EU in 2010: eight capital regions in the ten first places." (PDF). Eurostat.2013. Archived from the original (PDF) on 3 April 2013. Retrieved 19 July 2014.

"The World According to GaWC 2020". GaWC- Research Network. Globalization and World Cities. Archived from the original on 24 August 2020. Retrieved 31 August 2020.

Olshov, Anders (2010). The location of Nordic and global headquarters 20101. Malmo:resundsinstituttet. p. 197.OCLC 706436140. Stockholm is the main centre of headquarters in the Nordic region.

"World University Rankings 2011-12:Europe." TSL Education Ltd. Archived from the original on 1 August 2014. Retrieved 19 July 2014.

"De storste byene og tettstedene I Norger" SSB (in Norwegian Bokmal). Retrieved 9 January 2023.

"Osloregionen". (The Osloregion) SNL (in Norwegian). 15 August 2021. Archived from the original on 22 September 2022. Retrieved 2 November 22022.

"Inside Oslo: Inside". Trip Advisor. Archived from the original on 22 February 20101. Retrieved 25 March 2010.

"GaWC-The World According to GaWC 2008". Lboro.ac.uk. 13

April 2010. Archived from the original on 26 August 2011. Retrieved 2 November 2022.

Rachel Craig (13 February 2012). European Cities and Regions of the Future 2012/13".fD,Intelligence.com. Archived from the original on 15 December 2018. Retrieved 12 March 2013.

"Sydney rockets up the list of the world's most expensive cities" ECA International. 8 June 2011. Archived from the original on 3 October 2011. Retrieved 10 July 2011.

"Metropolitan Area Populations". Eurostat.21 October 2019. Retrieved 18 November 2019.

"Functional Urban Areas- Population on 1 January by age groups and sex-2019". Eurostat 2020. Retrieved 18 November 2019.

"Best view in Budapest from the city's highest hilltop". Stay.com-Budapest. 11 September 2014. Archived from the original on 23 June 2010. Retrieved 11 September 2014.

Torok, Andras. "Budapest". Encarta. Archived from the original on 29 October 2009. Retrieved 6 April 2008.

"About Budapest Transport Association". Archived from the original on 14 October 2008. Retrieved 1 June 2016.

"telep lista". (PDF). Archived from the original (PDF) on 25 November 2006. Retrieved 1 June 2016. "telep lista". (PDF). Archived from the original (PDF) on 25 November 2006. Retrieved 1 June 2016.

"Aquincum". Encyclopedia Britannica. 2008.

Sugar, Peter F.; Peter Hanak; Tibor Frank (1990). Hungary before the Hungarian Conquest". A History of Hungary. Indiana University Press.p. 3. ISBN 0-253-20867-X.

"Budapest". Travel Channel. Archived from the original on 9 OPctober 2008. Retrieved 22 May 2008.

Chisholm, Hugh, ed. (1911). "Budapest". Encyclopedia Britannica. Vol.4 (11th ed.). Cambridge University Press..pp. 734-737

Drake, Miriam A. (2003). "Eastern Europe, England and Spain." Encyclopedia of Library and Information Science. CRC Press. P.2498. ISBN 0-8347-2080-6. Retrieved 22 May 2008.

Casmir, Fred L. (1995). "Hungarian culture in Communication". Communication in Eastern Europe: The Role of History, Culture, and media in contemporary conflicts. Lawrence Erlbaum Associates. p122. ISBN 0-8058-1625-9. Retrieved 21 May 2008.

Nagy, Balazs; Rady, Martyn; Szende, Katalin; Vadas, Andras (2016). Medieval Buda in Context. Leiden, Boston: Brill. ISBN 9789004307674. OCLC 1030542604.

Molnar, A Concise History of Hungary, Chronology p.15

Molnar, A Concise History of Hungary, Chronology p.15

Alexander Watson, Ring of Steel: Germany and Austria-Hungary at War, 1914-1918 (2014). Pp. 536-540: In the capital cities of Vienna and Budapest, the leftist and liberal movements and opposition parties strengthened and supported the separatism of ethnic minorities.

U.N. General Assembly Special Committee on the Problem of Hungary (1957) Chapter 11. C. para 58 (p.20)" (PDF). Archived (PDF) from the original on 9 October 12022. (1.47 MB)

John Lukacs (1994). Budapest 1900: A Historical Portrait of a City and Its Culture. Grove Press. p. 222. ISBN 978-0-8021-3250-5.

"Hungary: Emerging Economic Powere in Central and Eastern

Europe." Thomas White International. Archived from the original on 10 October 2017. Retrieved 18 June 2017.

"The World According to GaWC 2020". GaWC- Research Network Globalization and World Cities. Retrieved 31 August 2020.

"EU nations pick Budapest for technology institute." The Sydney Morning Herald. 18 June 2008. Retrieved 43 December 2014.

European Union Document Nos 2013/0812 (COD), ENFOPOL 395 CODEC 2773 PARLNAT 307

"Budapesten nyilik az elso kinai befektetesi tamaszpont kulfildon"(First Chinese investment base abroad opens in Budapest). Heti Vilaggazdasag (in Hungarian). 26 May 2009. Retrieved 26 May 2018.

"Academic Ranking of World Univeresities 2015". Shanghai Ranking Consultancy. Archived from the original on 30 October 2015. Retrieved 27 August 2015.

"CWUR 2015-World University Rankings." Center for World University Rankings. Retrieved 25 July 2015.

The Belgian Constitution (PDF). Brussels, Belgium Belgian House of Representatives. May 2014.p. 63. Archived from the original (PDF) on 10 August 2015. Retrieved 10 September 2015. Article 194:The city of Brussels is the capital of Belgium and the seat of the Federal Government.

Decret instituant Bruxelles capitale de la Communaute francaise. Brussels, Belgium: Parliament of the French Community. 4 April 1984 . Archived from the original on 15 October 2015. Retrieved 11 September 2015.

"The Flemish Community". Belgium.be.24 October 2011. Archived from the original on 1 April 2018. Retrieved 1 April 2018.

Decreet betreffender de keuze van Brussel tot hoofstad van de Vlaamse Gemeenschap (PDF). Brussels, Belgium : Flemish Parliament. 6 March 1984. Archived from the original (PDF) on 7 March 2021. Retrieved 11 September 2015.

"Gross domestic product per resident, at current prices- Ratio in relation to the total of the Kingdom". National Bank of Belgium. Archived from the original on 8 August 2014. Retrieved 20 April 2014.

Average income in Belgium reached 19,105 euros in 2019. Belgian Federal Government 26 October 2021. Archived from the original on 3 October 20223. Retrieved 3 October 2022.

"Structuur van de bevolking/Statbel". Statbel.fgov.be. Archived from the original on 14 February 2021. Retrieved 13 August 2020.

"Statistics Belgium: Population de droit par commune au/ janvier 2008." Archived from the original (excel-file) on 17 September 2008. Retrieved 17 September 2008. Population of all municipalities in Belgium on 1 January 2008. Retrieved on 18 October 2008.

"St atistics Belgium: De Belgische Stadsgewesten 2001". (PDF). Archived from the original (PDF) on 29 October 2008. Retrieved 19 October 2008. Definitions of metropolitan areas in Belgium. The metropolitan area of Brussels is divided into three levels. First, the central agglomeration (geoperationaliseerde agglomeratie) with 1,457,047 inhabitants (2008-01-01, adjusted to municipal borders). Adding the closest surroundings (suburbs, banlieue or buitenwijken) gives a totyal of 1,831,496. And, including the outer commuter zone (forensenwoonzone) the population is 2,676,701.

"Demographia World Urban Areas"./ (PDF). April 2017. Archived

(PDF) from the original on 17 May 2017. Retrieved 29 October 2017.

"Europe l Country profiles l Country profile: Belgium". BBC News. 14 JKune 2010. Archived from the original on 1 July 2010. Retrieved 29 June 2010.

Demey 2007.

"Protocol (No. 6) on the location of the seats of the institutions and of certain bodies, offices, agencies and departments of the European Union Consoilidated version of the Treaty on the Functioning of the European Union. OJC 83.30.3.2010 p. 265-265". EUR Lex. 30 March 22010. Archived from the original on 20 May 2013. Etrieved 3 August 2010.

"Spain to ask Brussels for extra year to meet deficit target". Reuters. 10 April 2016. Archived from the original on July 2020. Retrieved 23 June 2017.

"Secretariat general".A propos du Benelux (in French). Archived from the original on 14 December 2021. Retrieved 22 August 2017.

"Nato Headquarters". NATO. 16 March 2018. Archived from the original on 18 December 2021. Retrieved 22 August 2017.

"About Cairo". Cairo Governorate. Archived from the original on 24 March 2023. Retrieved 22 December 2022.

"Cairo, Egypt Metro Area Population 1950-2023". Macrotrends. Retrieved 25 February 2023.

Gabra et al. 2013. P. 18.

Bloom, Jonathan M.; Blair, Sheila S., eds. (2009). "Cairo". The Grove Encyclopedia of Islamic Art and Architecture. Oxford University Press. ISBN 9780195309911.

Snape, Steven (2014). The complete Cities of Ancient Egypt. Thames & Hudson.pp.170-177. ISBN 9780500051795.

"Al-Ahram Weekly I Features I City of the sun". Weekly. Ahram. Org.eg. 1 June 2005. Archived from the original on 25 March 2013. Retrieved 26 March 2013.

"Memphis (Egypt)". Encarta. Microsoft. 2009. Archived from the original on 6 October 2009. Retrieved 24 July 2009.

Amelineau, Emile (1980). La Geographie de l "Egypte A l' Epoque Copte. Paris. p. 491.

"The World According to GaWC 2016". Globalization and World Research Network. Loughborough University. 24 April 2017. Archived from the original on 10 October 2013. Retrieved 26 May 2017.

"NGDC page on the Cairo earthquake". Archived from the original on 1 September 2013. Retrieved 9 June 2010.

"Resident population by city / town at the middle of the year." Vilnius. Statistics Department of Lithuania. 1 July 2023. Retrieved 24 July 2023.

"Population on 1 January by age groups and sex functional urban areas". Appsso. Eurostat.ec. Europa.eu. Retrieved 14 June 2022.

"Vilniaus teritorine' ligoniu kasa- Prisirasiusiu gyventoju skaicius" (in Lithuanian) Retrieved 21 November 2023.

"Vilniaus teritorine' ligoniu kasa- Prisirasiusiu gyventoju skaicius ligoniukasa. Irev. Lt (in Lithuanian) Retrieved 21 November 2023.

"Vilniaus istorija". vle.lt (in Lithuanian). Retrieved 8 November 2019.

"Pries 100 metu lenkai uzeme Vilniu: kad jis vel bus Lietuvos sostine, galejo tiketi tik don kichotai". (in Lithuanian). 19 April 2019. Retrieved 22 September 2019.

"Archived copy". (PDF).cbs.gov.np. Archived from the original (PDF) on 6 February 2022. Retrieved 22 February 2022.

"Managing Nepal's Urban Transition". World Bank. Archived from the original on 24 July 2011. Retrieved 1 December 2009.

Ekantipur com. 9 June 2010. Archived from the original on 11 September 2010. Retrieved 15 January 2012.

"Local Data Bank". Statistics Poland. Retrieved 21 July 2022. Data for territorial unit 2464000.

"Czech Republic Facts". World Info Zone. Archived from the original on 18 ay 2011. Retrieved 14 April 2011.

"Population on 1 January by five-year age group, sex and metropolitan regions". Eurostat. Archived from the original on 14 March 2020. Retrieved 21 February 2020.

"Praha by mela byt metropole pro dva miliony lidi". Ekonomicky Magazin (in Czech). Archived from the original on 26 September 2018. Retrieved 26 September 2018.

Demetz, Peter (1997). "Chapter One: Libussa or Versions of Origin: Prague in Black and Gold: Scenes from the Life of a European City. New York: Hill and Wang. ISBN 978-0-8090-7843-1. Retrieved 7 April 2016.

Dovid Solomon Ganz, Tzemach Dovid (3rd edition), part 2, Warsaw 1878, pp. 71, 85 (online Archived 21 April 2022 at the Wayback Machine).

Kenety, Brian (29 October 2004). "Unearthing Bohemia's Celtic heritage ahead of Samhain, the "New Year". Czech Radio. Archived 9 August 2016.

Kenety, Brian (19 November 23005). "Atlantis ceske archeologie". (in Czech). Czech Radio. Archived from the original on 13 September 2016. Retrieved 9 August 2016.

"Archaelogical Research- Prague Castle". Hrad.cz. 8 July 2005. Archived from the original; on 1 April 2009. Retrieved 30 May 2011.

Czech Republic". Worldatlas.com. Archived from the original on 1 December 2011. Retrieved 4 December 2011.

"Short History of Bohemia. Moravia and then Czechoslovakia and Czech Republic". Hedgie.eu.2015. Archived from the original on 189 ay 2016. Retrieved 7 April 2016.

"Charles University Official Website". Archived from the original on 29 October 2007. Retrieved 21 April 2022.

"The World According to GaWC 2020". GaWC. Archived from the original on 16 March 2023. Retrieved 8 October 2023.

Quality of Living City Ranking". Mercer : Global Mobility Solutions. Archived from the original on 18 April 2018. Retrieved 30 May 2019.

"The PICSA Index". PICSA. Archived from the original on 8 March 2021. Retrieved 2 July 2021.

"Top 100 City Destinations Revealed :Prague among Most Visited in the World". Expats.cz.8 November 2017. Archived from the original on 29 August 2018. Retrieved 28 August 2018.

belsat.gov.by. Archived from the original on 25 May 2023. Retrieved 19 August 2023.

Greenbaum, Masha (1995). The Jews of Lithuania: A History of a Remarkable Community 1316-1945. Jerusalem. Gefen.p.2. ISBN 9789652291325.

Litopys org.us. Retrieved 5 May 2009.

"The Celebration of the 940 anniversary of Minsk will start with ringing of bells-Minsk City Executive Committee". Minsk.gov.by. .Archived from the original on 15 June 2008. Retrieved 5 May 2009.

CTB (in Russian). Archived from the original on 7 June 2021. Retrieved 30 May 2019.

history-belarus.by (in Russian). Retrieved 30 May 2019.

Hill, Melissa. "Belarus". Worldmark Encyclopedia of Nations. Gale. Retrieved 4 June 2019.

minsk 950.belta.by. Retrieved 31 May 2019.

Lauwerys, Joseph (1970). Education in Cities. Evan's Brothers. ISBN 0-415-39291-8. Archived from the original on 11 July 2020. Retrieved 12 September 2017.

Rogers, Clifford (2010). The Oxford Encyclopedia of Medieval Warfare and Military Technology. Vol.1. Oxford University Press.p.301. ISBN 9780195334036. Archived from the original on 17 July 2020. Retrieved 27 June 2019.

Internet Hostel Sofia, Tourism in Sofia. Archioved 28 December 2011 at the Wayback Machine. Internethostelsofia.hostel.com, Retrieved Jan 2012

"Triangle of Religious Tolerance (1903)-iCultural Diplomacy".www.i-c-d.de. Archived from the original on 27 January 2020. Retrieved 27 December 2019.

"10 Things We Can all Learn from Bulgaria's Square of Religious Tolerance". 15 February 2017. Archived from the original on 29 September 2020. Retrieved 4 September 2020.

"Sofia is one of the top 10 places for start-up businesses in the world. Bulgarian National TV." Bnt.bg. Archived from the original on 22 December 2015. Retrieved 11 April 2018.

Clark, Jayne. "Is Europe's most affordable capital worth the trip? USA TODAY. Archived from the original on 6 April 2016. Retrieved 12 February 2016.

"Museum of Socialist Art-National Gallery". Archived from the original on 21 December 2019. Retrieved 27 December 2019.

www.kmeta.bg. 10 May 2017. Archived from the original on 31 October 2018. Retrieved 31 October 2018.

www.nsi.bg (in Bulgarian). Archived from the original on 12 April 2021. Retrieved 29 May 2021.

"NATIONAL STATISTICAL INSTITUTE –Information for the area of city of Sofia".Nsi.bg. Archived from the original on 7 February 2018. Retrieved 11 April 2018.

"Eurostat-Sofia urban area population". Archived from the original on 3 September 2015. Retrieved 24 June 2017.

"CITIES AND THEIR URBANISED AREAS IN THE REPUBLIC OF BULGARIA" (PDF). National Statistical Institue: 91. Archived (PDF) from the original on 15 July 2018. Retrieved 15 July 2018.

"Metropolitan areas in Europe." (PDF).*Der Markt fur Wohn- und Wirtschatsimmobilien in Deutschland Ergebnisse BBSR- Expertenpanel Immobilienmarkt Nr.* 95 ISSN 1868-0097. Archived from the original (PDF) on 15 July 2018. Retrieved 15 July 2018.

"Eurostat-Data Explorer". Appsso.eurostat.ec. Europa.eu. Archived from the original on 3 December 2018. Retrieve d 21 December 2016.

Statistics Mauritius: Demography Unit (2018) "DIGEST OF DEMOGRAPHIC STATISTICS 2018 (pdf). Dec. Government of Mauritius.p.33. Retrieved 21 May 2020.

Auguste Toussaint, Histoire des iles Mascareignes, p. 24

Britannica, Port Louis, Encyclopedia Britannica, USA. Retrieved 7 July 2019.

Guinness World Records 2009. London United Kingdom. Guiness World Records Ltd. 2008. p.. 277 ISBN 978-1-904994-36-7.

Karl Mathiesen (15 October 2015). "Where is the world's windiest city? Spoiler alert: its not Chicago." The Guardian. Archived from the original on 12 July 2016. Retrieved 13 August 2016.

Waitangi Tribunal. (2003). Te Whanganui a Tara me ona takiwa: report on the Wellington District. Wellington, N.Z : Legislation Direct. P. 17. ISBN 186956264X. OCLC 53261192

"Maori history." Wellington City Council. 30 December 2015. Archived from the original on 10 April 2019. Retrieved 9 July 2019.

Waitangi Tribunal (2003). Te Whanganui a Tara me ona takiwa: report on the Wellington District. Wellington, N.Z.: Legislation Direct.p.13. ISBN 186956264X.OCLC 53261192.

Waitangi Tribunal, Te Whanganui a Tara me ona Takiwa, page 18, https://forms:justice govt. nz/search/Documents

Waitangi Tribunal Te Whanganui s Tara me ona Takiwa, page 18.

Waitangi Tribunal (2003). Te Whanganui a Tara me ona takiwa: report on the Wellington District, Wellington, N..Z. : Legislation Direct. ISBN 186956264X OCLC 53261192.

"Deed of Settlement of Historical Claims signed between Taranaki Whanui ki Te Upoko o Te ika and the Port Nicholson Block Settlement Trust and The Sovereign in Right of New Zesland." (PDF). New Zealand Government 19 August 2008.p.8. Archived from the original (PDF) on 4 February 2018. Retrieved 15 September 2018. The importance of the Harbour to Taranaki Whanui ki Te Upoko o Te Ika increased as trade was entered into early in the 19th century.

Easther, John (1991). The Hutt River = Te-Awa-kai-rangi: a modern history. 1840-1990. Wellington (N.Z.): Wellington Regional Council. pp. 24-29. ISBN 0-909016-09-7.OCLC 34915088.

Taonga, New Zealand Ministry of Culture and Heritage Te Manatu. "Wellington's plan". Teara.govt.nz. Retrieved 15 November 2021.

Schrader, Ben (26 March 2015) [11 March 2010]. "City planning-Early settlement planning." Te Ara: The Encyclopedia of New Zealand. Archived from the original on 23 September 2023. Retrieved 23 September 2023. Wellington's plan was designed by New Zealand Company surveyor William Mein Smith in 1840. It comprised a series of interconnected grids which expanded along the town's valleys and up the lower slopes of hills.

Subnational population estimates (RC.SA2), by age and sex, at 30 June 1996-2023 (2023 boundaries".) Statistics New Zealand. Retrieved 25 October 2023 (regional councils);Subnational population estimates (TA.SA2), by age and sex, at 30 June 1996-2023 (2023 boundaries)." Statistics New Zealand. Retrieved 25 October

2023 (territorial authorities) "Subnational population estimates (urban rural), by age and sex, at 30 June 1996-2023(2023 boundaries)". Statistics New Zealand. Retrieved 25 October 2023. (urban areas)

Levine, Stephen (20 June 2012) " Capital city-Wellington, Capital city." Te Ara: The Encyclopedia of New Zealand. Archived from the original on 5 February 2019. Retrieved 23 May 2019.

Lim, Jason (29 November 2015). "Wellington is Bigger On Tech And Innovation Then You Think." Forbes. Retrieved 15 November 2016.

"Culture and creativity." www.wellingtonnz.com. Retrieved 21 April 2022.

"Arts and culture". 10yearplan.wellington.govt.nz. Retrieved 21 April 2022.

Media, Shermans Travel. "Kiwi Culture in Wellington: New Zealand's Creative Capitall Shermans Travel." www.shermanstravel.com. Retrieved 21 April 2022.

Choudhury, Saheli Roy (9 June 2021)." These are world's most liveable cities in 2021." CNBC. Retrieved 2 June 2022.

"2014 Quality of Living Worldwide City Rankings- Mercer Survey." www.mercer.com. 19 February 2014. Archived from the original on 22 June 2013. Retrieved 11 April 2014.

"Wellington named most liveable city for second year running". Stuff. 25 May 2018. Archived from the original on 223 June 2019. Retrieved 23 June 2019.

"Huffington Post lauds Wellington's 'remarkable' creative resurgence." Stuff 19 September 2016. Archived from the original on 9 July 2019. Retrieved 9 July 2019.

"Wellington: New Zealand's creative capital."TNZ Media. Archived from the original on 9 July 2019. Retrieved 9 July 2019.

"Wellington is a Smart City of the future."iStart leading the way to smarter technology investment. Archived from the original on 90 July 2019. Retrieved 9 July 2019.

"The World According to GaWc 2020.GaWC- Research Network. Globalization and World Cities. Retrieved 31 August 2020.

"The 1848 Marlborough earthquake-Te Ara: The Encyclopedia of New Zealand." Teara govt.nz.30 March 2005. Archived from the original on 14 June 2009. Retrieved 6 February 2009.

The 1855 Wairarapa earthquake- Te Ara: The Encyclopedia of New Zealand."Teara. govt.nz.21 September 2007. Archived from the original on 21 February 2009. Retrieved 6 February 2009.

"Government Buildings". New Zealand Heritage List/Rarangi Korero. Heritage New Zealand. Retrieved 6 February 2009.

Dave Burgess (14 March 2011)."Shuddering in Wellington." Fairfax NZ. Archived from the original on 23 March 2011. Retrieved 28 October 2012.

Hank Schouten (2 June 2012)."How safe are the capital's office buildings?" Dominion Post. Archived from the original on 4 June 2012. Retrieved 28 October 2012.

Kate Chapman (16 October 2012)" Councilors question quake costs." Dominion Post. Archived from the original on 19 October 2012. Retrieved 28 October 2012.

Dave Burgess and Hank Schouten (1 October 2011). "Quake shakes capital insurance market" The Dominion Post. Archived from the original on 24 October 2012. Retrieved 28 October 2012.

"Silent quake gently rocks Wellington." 3 News NZ. 28 May 2013. Archived from the original on 23 August 2014. Retrieved 28 May 2013.

"M7 slow release earthquake under Wellington." GeoNet NZ. 27 May 2013. Archived from the original; 7 June 2013. Retrieved 28 May 2013.

New Zealand's capital shaken by a magnitude 6.5 earthquake.". ABC News. 21 July 2013. Archived from the original on 223 July 2013. Retrieved 21 July 2013.

Strong 6.6. earthquake hits Wellington, aftershocks. Archived 13 October 2013 at the Wayback Machine. Stuff.co.nz. Retrieved on 7 September 2013.

"6.2 earthquake cuts power, phones, stops trains." One News. 20 January 2014. Archived from the original on 16 May 2015. Retrieved 21 June 2015.

"Quake:'Hobbit' sculpture crashes down at N.Z. airport." USA Today. 20 January 2014. Archived from the original on 27 December 2017. Retrieved 21 November 2016.

"Defence House in Wellington to be demolished after investigations show repairs to earthquake damage uneconomic." The New Zealand Herald. 3 March 2017. Archived from the original on 28 September 2018. Retrieved 16 May 2018.

"Freyberg House to be demolished." Stuff (Fairfax). 3 March 2017. Archived from the original on 9 January 2018. Retrieve d 16 May 2018.

"Unacceptable performance of building says Minister." Stuff (Fairfax). 26 July 2017. Archived from the original on 10 January

2018. Retrieved 16 May 2018.

"Maersk to return to Wellington when CentrePort's cranes are repaired." Stuff.co.nz. 31 July 2017. Archived from the original on 28 September 2018. Retrieved 28 September 2018.

Ibuafjoldi eftir sveitarfelogum September 2022. Skra.is.september 8th 2022.

Yunlong, Sun (23 December 2007). "Reykjavik rated cleanest city in Nordic and Baltic countries." Xinhua News Agency. Archived from the original on 4 March 2016. Retrieved 29 September 2013.

"15 Green Cities." Grist. 20 July 2007. Archived from the original on 23 September 2013. Retrieved 29 September 2013.

"Iceland among Top 10 safest countries and Reykjavik is the winner of Tripadvisor Awards." TRAVEL10net 20 May 2010. Archived from the original on 21 February 2014. Retrieved 29 September 2013.

Jon Gunnar Jorgensen. "Ingolfr Amarson Bjornolfsson Ingolv Ornss." (inb Norwegian) Norsk biografisk leksikon. Retrieved 20 April 2022.

https://www.marines.mil/Portals/1/ Publications/ The%20United% 20 States% 20 Marines% 20in% 20icel and.% 201941-1942% 20% 20PCN%2019000412300.pdf.

"About KEF Airport." www.isavia.is. Retrieved 30 November 2023.

ABOUT THE AUTHOR

Inspired by divine revelations, the author endeavours to impart the events at the end of times so that people may repent and be faultless, blameless and perfect before God's eyes in preparation for the Second Coming of our Lord Jesus Christ. Such repentance is aimed at achieving salvation, everlasting life, and eternal happiness.

www.ingramcontent.com/pod-product-compliance
Lightning Source LLC
Chambersburg PA
CBHW070854120626
46546CB00001B/8